# American Inside Out Evolution

Student's Book

Upper Intermediate

SUE KAY
VAUGHAN JONES

macmillan education

# Contents

# Walkthrough

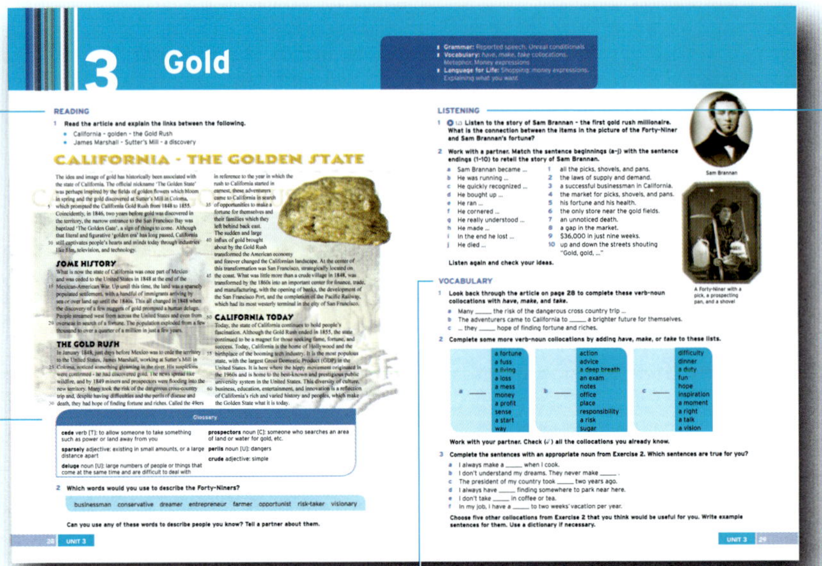

**READING**
Contemporary reading texts have been adapted and graded to suit the level. They have been selected not only for their language content but also for their interest and appropriacy. The texts are supported by recordings.

Glossaries give simple definitions for more challenging words. This minimizes interruptions and help you read more fluently.

**LISTENING**
The listenings include texts specially written for language learning – dialogues, conversations and monologues. They were carefully designed to develop real-life listening skills.

**VOCABULARY**
- Vocabulary is presented in context.
- Practice acitivities will help expand your knowledge of selective lexical items and will give you the opportunity to use vocabulary in meaningful exchanges.

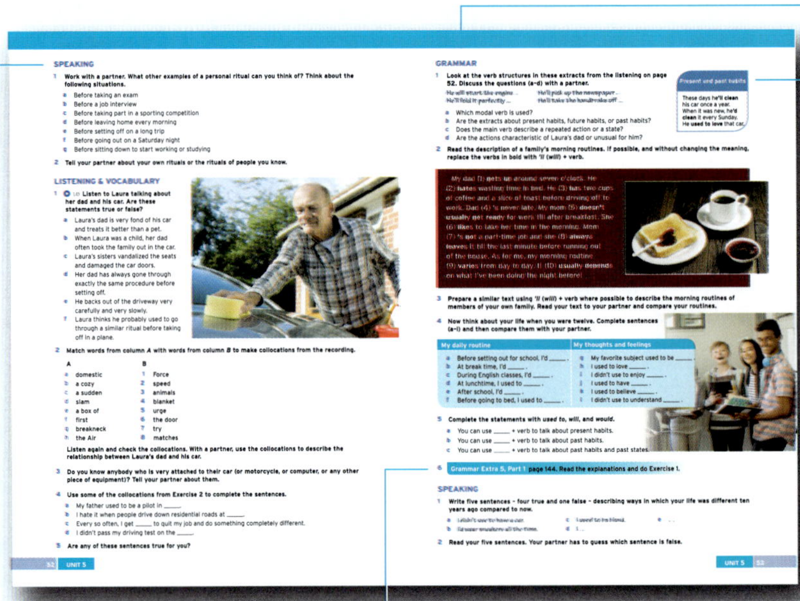

**SPEAKING**
You are encouraged to relate the topics to your own life, views, and feelings.

**GRAMMAR**
- Here you will explore new grammatical structures that have been contextualized in the reading / listening sections. You will focus on the way language works.
- A brief summary of the grammar point is provided in the box.
- Language is explored in realistic and meaningful practice exercises.
- You will use target language in controlled and personalized practice.

The Grammar Extra pages at the back of the Student's Book extend explanations and provide further practice.

## LANGUAGE FOR LIFE

The Language for Life section gives you a portable toolkit of functional language. Here, you notice how language is more than just form. You will see language in fun, engaging social situations.

## VOCABULARY EXTRA

The Vocabulary Extra pages at the end of every unit recycle the key vocabulary items taught in the unit. This provides an activated wordlist and a useful bank of vocabulary.

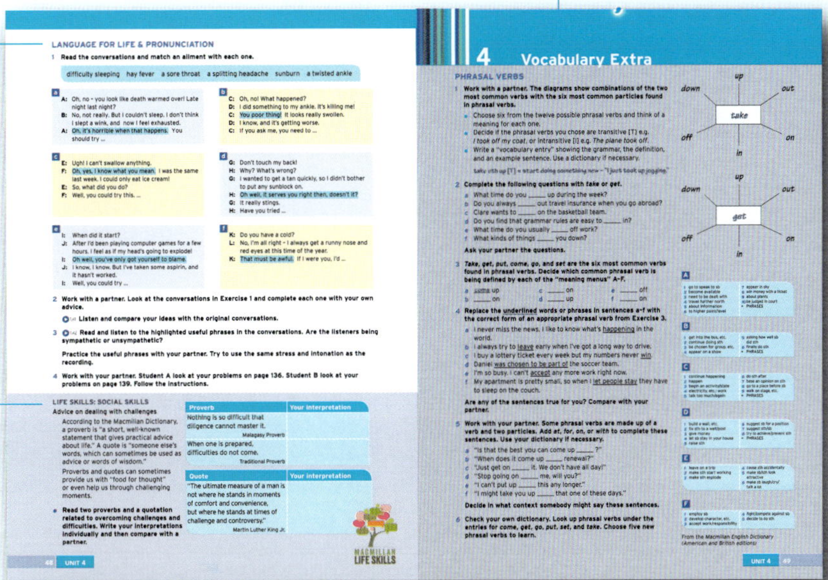


## LIFE SKILLS

Developing life skills alongside language skills is an essential requirement to meet the demands of the contemporary world.

*American Inside Out Evolution* has a Life Skills section in every unit. Life Skills presents activities that require you to reflect on and discuss the skills for you for social and work situations in today's world.

## REVIEW

There are Review units in the Student's Book. They review the new structures and vocabulary taught in the previous teaching units.

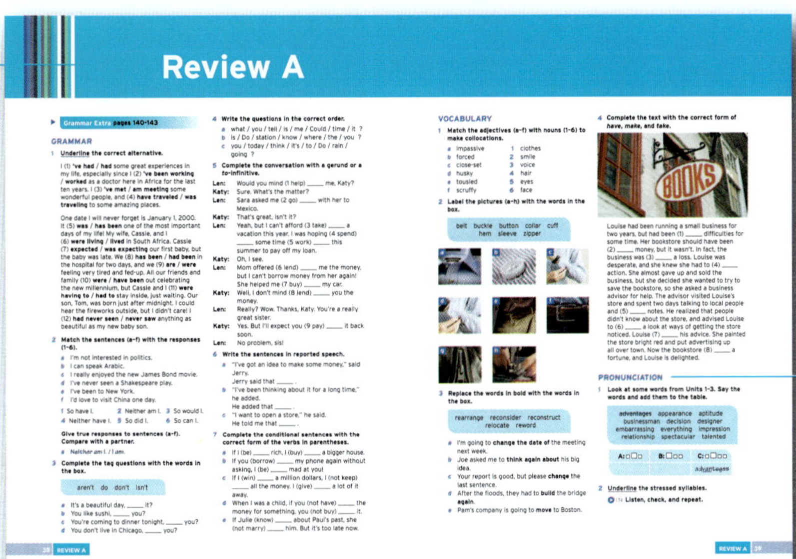


## PRONUNCIATION

Pronunciation work on particular areas of sound, stress, and intonation is integrated into every unit.

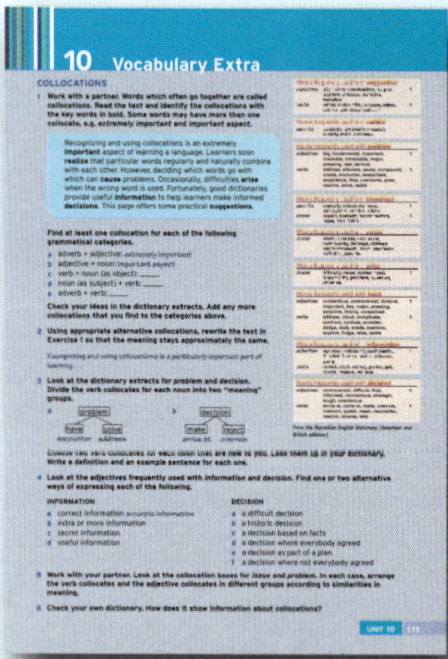
10 Vocabulary Extra

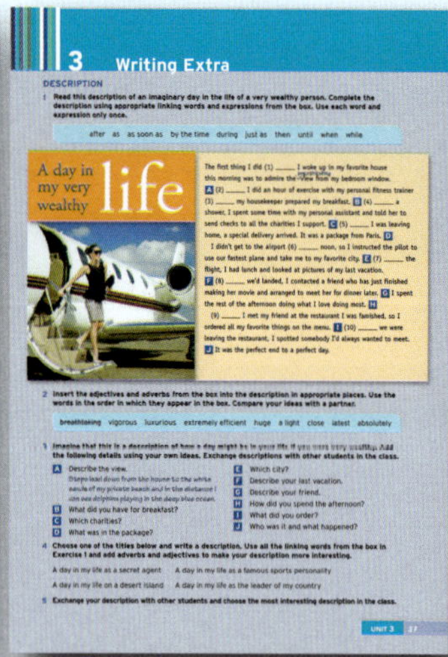
3 Writing Extra

The Vocabulary Extra pages alternate with the Writing Extra pages at the end of each unit. The Writing Extra pages develop important writing skills in a variety of genres.
The Vocabulary Extra pages explore key lexical areas such as collocations, metaphor, phrasal verbs, etc. They provide detailed practice activities and help promote useful dictionary skills.

## GRAMMAR EXTRA

The Grammar Extra pages at the back of the Student's Book provide extended explanations and further practice.

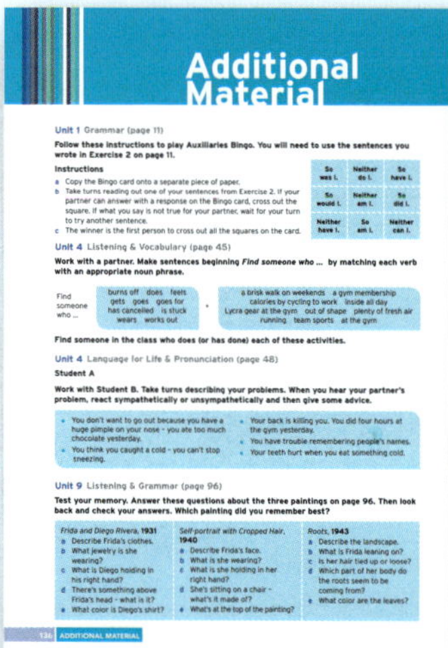
Additional Material

The section Additional Material includes pairwork activities as well as answers to quizzes and activities from the units.

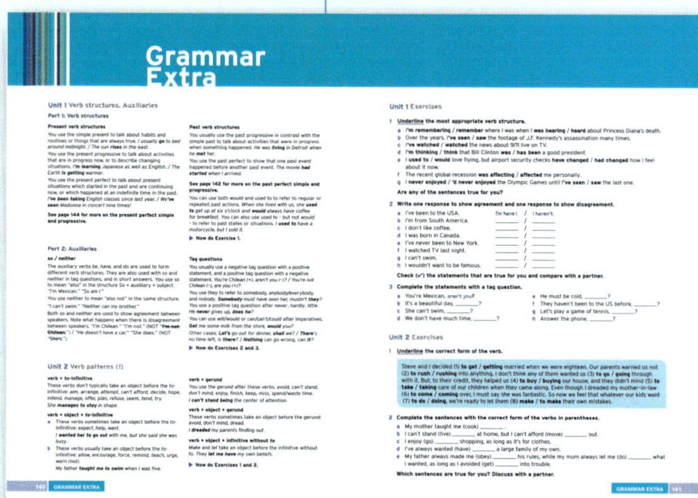
Grammar Extra

8 Attraction

The Workbook provides a review of all the main points in the Student's Book, plus extra listening practice, pronunciation work, and a writing program.

# Student's Components

Student's Book with access code to Digital Student's Book

Workbook with access code to Digital Workbook

# 1 Impressions

## SPEAKING

1 **Work with a partner. Look at the pictures (a-d) and match them with the events in the box.**

"The Great American Eclipse" Invention of the iPhone Rio de Janeiro Olympics Climbing Mount Everest

a

b

c

d

**Put the events in the order in which they happened.**

2 **Work with your partner. Write down as much additional information as you can about the events in the pictures.**

**Discuss your information with other people in the class. Did any of these events make an impression on you?**

- **Grammar:** Verb structures. Auxiliaries. Tag questions. Indirect questions
- **Vocabulary:** Collocation. Word formation. Clothing idioms
- **Language for Life:** Talking about appearance

## LISTENING & READING

1 1.02-1.05 **Listen and match the journalists, Chris, Margot, Ritu, and Rafael, with the pictures (a-d).**

2 **Read and complete what each journalist said with an appropriate verb structure.**

**a**

Unlike some other stories, we knew in advance when it (1 go) was going to happen, so we were really prepared that day. I remember people were going crazy, trying to find special glasses and a good place to see it, and everyone was happy to talk to us. As a journalist, I'm always reporting on negative events, and I (2 do) ______ this for a long time, so this was a nice change for me. When it actually happened, it was truly spectacular and there was no need to say anything - we just watched and filmed, amazed like everyone else.

**b**

I had come all the way from Europe to San Francisco just to go to this event, so I definitely (3 have) ______ a feeling that something important was going to be revealed. I (4 already come) ______ to these kinds of things for a few years now, but when Steve Jobs gave us his presentation, we were all blown away - the camera, the internet, we had never seen anything quite like it! Even so, I would never have guessed just how much that little handheld device would change all of our lives! Nowadays, we (5 take) ______ them for granted, but back then, it was way ahead of its time.

**c**

This was a long time ago, and I'd only been reporting the news for a couple of months at that point. But already, I (6 see) ______ a lot of people come to try to do the impossible. So, even though I knew it could happen, I was still shocked when they actually made it to the peak. I knew everyone would want all the details, so I made sure to ask everyone involved as many questions as I could, especially our new local national hero! Many people (7 reach) ______ the summit since, but it (8 be) ______ more difficult back then, and plus, it's always more special the first time.

**d**

As a television reporter, this was maybe the most exciting time of my career. The whole country was filled with visitors and the international media, and there was just so much going on every single day for those two weeks. I (9 get) ______ up at dawn and stayed out until late at night - I think I (10 still recover) ______ from it! The highlight for me was reporting live from the beach volleyball tournament where our men's team took home the gold. Interviewing Alison and Bruno afterwards, I knew the whole country was cheering them on.

**Listen again and check.**

3 **Write down three memorable events that have been important ...**

- in your own life.
- in the history of your country.

**Tell a partner about the events you chose. Find out about the events your partner chose.**

## GRAMMAR

1 **Underline the most appropriate verb structure.**

a **I've been knowing / I've known / I know** Alice since I was a child.
b **I had / I've had / I used to have** breakfast with Ben this morning.
c **I'm talking / I've been talking / I was talking** to Cathy just before the class started.
d **I like / I'm liking / I'd like** Dan a lot - he's one of my best friends.
e **I've learned / I've been learning / I'm learning** English for about the same number of years as Erica.
f **I've gone / I was going / I've been going** out to dinner with Frank lots of times.
g **I've already met / I'm already meeting / I'd already met** Gina before I joined this class.
h **I was having / I used to have / I'd have** a friend named Harry, but we lost touch with each other.

2 **Choose five sentences from Exercise 1 and change the names to make the sentences true for you.**

3 **Grammar Extra 1, Part 1** page 140. Read the explanations and do Exercise 1.

**Verb structures**

Simple present / past
I **work** / I **worked**

Present / Past progressive
I**'m working** / I **was working**

Present / Past perfect simple
I**'ve worked** / I**'d worked**

Present / Past perfect progressive
I**'ve been working** / I**'d been working**

*used to / would*
I **used to work** / I**'d work**

## VOCABULARY

**1 What do you notice most about a person when you meet them for the first time? Look at the ideas in the box below and discuss with a partner.**

> clothes  eyes  face  hair  handshake
> manner  smile  voice

**2 "Collocation" refers to the way that words form predictable relationships with other words. Look at the alternative adjectives (a–h) and ~~cross out~~ the adjective which does not form a strong collocation with the noun. Use your dictionary if necessary.**

a **designer** / ~~**brand**~~ clothes
b **shiny** / **bright** eyes
c **round** / **circular** face
d **spiky** / **pointy** hair
e **strong** / **firm** handshake
f **charming** / **fair** manner
g **heated** / **warm** smile
h **profound** / **deep** voice

"You never get a second chance to make a first impression."

**3 Match the nouns from Exercise 1 with the adjectives below to make additional strong collocations.**

a hearty / limp handshake
b expressive / impassive ___________
c fake / forced ___________
d close-set / staring ___________
e sleek / tousled ___________
f husky / shrill ___________
g old-fashioned / scruffy ___________
h abrasive / mild ___________

**Which of the characteristics described above or in Exercise 2 would you find appealing / unappealing? Tell your partner.**

## LISTENING

**1** 1.06 **Listen to a man and a woman who meet in a coffee shop in Mexico City. Answer the questions.**

a Where are they from?
b What are they doing in Mexico City?
c Why does the conversation stop?

**2 Complete the table with a ✓ or a ✗. Then listen again and check your answers.**

| | The man | The woman | |
|---|---|---|---|
| a | ✓ | ✓ | is American. |
| b | ✗ | ✗ | is on vacation. |
| c | | | is working in Mexico City. |
| d | | | works for a bank. |
| e | | | likes Mexico City. |
| f | | | has been in Mexico City a long time. |
| g | | | is an artist. |
| h | | | is from New York. |
| i | | | was a good student. |
| j | | | graduated from high school in 2006. |

**3 Have you ever "put your foot in your mouth" – accidentally said something that was embarrassing or that annoyed someone? Or have you been with someone when they "put their foot in their mouth"? Tell your partner.**

## GRAMMAR

1 **Work with a partner. Make ten sentences based on the information in the table on page 10. Use *and so* ... , or *and neither* ... , or *but* ... as appropriate.**

a The man is American and so is the woman.

2 **Use the sentence beginnings to write some sentences which are true for you and which you *believe* are also true for your partner. (Do *not* check with your partner yet.)**

a I was born ...
b I'm not used to ...
c I'm interested in ...
d I used to ...
e I have ...
f I can't ...
g I've never been to ...
h I'd like to ...
i I hardly ever go ...

***I was born in the 1980s. / I was born in a hospital. / I was born in this city. / I was born ..., etc.***

3 **Work with your partner. Go to the Additional material on page 136.**

**Auxiliaries (1): *so / neither***

"I went out last night."
✔ **"So did I."**
✗ "I didn't."

"I haven't done my homework yet."
✔ **"Neither have I."**
✗ "I have."

## GRAMMAR & PRONUNCIATION

1 **Work with your partner. Look at the examples from the conversation on page 10 and match the information in columns A and B to explain the form and use of tag questions.**

1 Sorry, but you're American, aren't you?

2 It isn't very busy here today, is it?

| A | B |
|---|---|
| positive statement | asking a real question |
| negative statement | negative tag question |
| rising intonation | asking for agreement |
| falling intonation | positive tag question |

**Auxiliaries (2): Tag questions**

We haven't finished yet, **have we**?

You're not listening, **are you**?

2 **Underline the correct tag question for each statement. Is each tag question more likely to be said with a rising or falling intonation?**

a It's a little cold today, **isn't it?** / **is it?**
b I'm late again, **isn't it?** / **aren't I?**
c The traffic was awful, **isn't it?** / **wasn't it?**
d You haven't been waiting long, **isn't it?** / **have you?**
e Nobody's missing today, **isn't it?** / **are they?**
f You don't have Mike Smith's phone number, **isn't it** / **do you?**

1.07 **Listen, check, and repeat.**

3 **Grammar Extra 1, Part 2** page 140. Read the explanations and do Exercises 2 and 3.

## SPEAKING: ANECDOTE

**You are going to tell your partner about a person who made a big impression on you.**

- Ask yourself the questions below.
- Think about *what* to say and *how* to say it.
- Tell your partner about the person.

a Who was this person? A teacher? A boss? A member of your family? ...
b What was his/her name?
c When and how did you meet him/her?
d How old were you? How old was he/she?
e What were you doing at this time? What was he/she doing?
f How did you get to know him/her?
g Why did he/she make such a big impression?
h What did you learn from him/her?
i What is he/she doing now?
j When was the last time you saw him/her?

## READING

1 **Work with a partner. Look at the adjacent picture and the pictures on the next page. What do you know about this person? Why is he famous? What first impression does his image give you?**

2 **Read the article on page 13. Complete the summary with the words in the box.**

| himself | honesty | ~~remain~~ | success | aware | popular | family |
|---|---|---|---|---|---|---|

These days celebrities often don't *remain* famous for very long, but Adam Levine is different. Since 2002, he has been a very (1) _______ performer as a musician and TV personality. His continued (2) _______ is possibly due to two features of his personality: his ability to adapt, and his ability to be (3) _______. These days, he is more of a (4) _______ man, but continues to work hard and to value (5) _______ - he isn't afraid to say what he believes, and he is very (6) _______ of his image and also how lucky he is.

3 **Read the article again and write the questions for the answers.**

- **a** When did Maroon 5 release their first album? 2002
- **b** _______ Kara's Flowers
- **c** _______ 'groove-based' dance music
- **d** _______ Sharky
- **e** _______ yoga
- **f** _______ Men's fragrance, clothing collection, record label
- **g** _______ coach
- **h** _______ People magazine

4 **Decide if the statements are true or false. Correct the false statements.**

- **a** In recent years, Adam's popularity has been declining.
- **b** Adam's bands did well commercially, right from the start of his career.
- **c** His record label was not responsible for the look or sound of his band.
- **d** Adam is excited to release an 'Adam Levine' album in the future.
- **e** These days, health and his relationships are high priorities for Adam.
- **f** Adam doesn't really know what the public thinks about him.

5 **Work with a partner. What advice would you give to someone who wants to be famous?**

## VOCABULARY

1 **The article on Adam Levine talks about *redefining stardom* and *refocusing priorities*. ~~Cross out~~ the word in each line which does not form a new verb with *re*, according to the Word formation panel.**

- **a** change / do / define / focus
- **b** arrange / organize / prepare / schedule
- **c** build / construct / erect / make
- **d** consider / contemplate / examine / think
- **e** copy / draft / word / write
- **f** discover / find / locate / unite

2 **Look up words with the prefix *re* (meaning *again*) in your dictionary. Check (✓) the words you know or can understand easily. Choose three more to learn. Write your own example sentences.**

**Word formation**

**re** prefix meaning *again*: used with many verbs, nouns, and adjectives: *rearrange, rebuild, reconsider, reconstruct, rediscover, redo, redraft, re-examine, redefine, relocate, remake, reorganize, refocus, reschedule, rethink, reunite, reword, rewrite*

# STAYING ON TOP

a

b

c

In today's world of instant celebrities and short attention spans, it's rare for anybody to stay in the limelight year after year. But when we look at Adam Levine, that's exactly what we see. A superstar singer and TV show personality, Adam has been in the public eye since his band, Maroon 5, released their first album in 2002. So just how does he do it? Finding a balance between staying true to himself and adapting to the times, Adam has never been better as he redefines what it means to be a star.

Born in 1979, in Los Angeles, California, Adam has always been near the center of American celebrity. And yet, his fame was not instant, and unlike many other popular young musicians, his image was not manufactured by a record label. Instead, in 1994 he formed a rock group with his high school friends called *Kara's Flowers*. After signing a record deal, they experienced early failure, selling only 5000 albums, and eventually split up.

At this point, Adam's ability to adapt became apparent. Moving away from the style of his original band, Adam formed a new group, Maroon 5, with some of the same members, and they began experimenting with different genres. After testing out alternative rock, country, and folk music, the band finally settled on the 'groove-based' dance music that we associate with the band today, putting out their first album in 2002. Just don't ask Adam what genre it is now - he refuses to say and tries to avoid being trapped by labels. Always looking to grow, the band has continued to collaborate with many different artists in different genres including Alicia Keys (R&B), Slash (Rock and Roll), and Eminem (Hip hop).

On the flip side, there has been great consistency in Adam's musical career. Despite opportunities and pressure to become a solo artist, Adam has stuck with his band and has no desire to go solo. Now with 6 albums, 3 Grammy awards, and 12.9 million albums sold in the US, who can blame him! Even Adam's name has remained the same (although he used to have the nickname 'Sharky'), and he does not have a stage name like so many other performers.

His personal life also reflects these two aspects of his personality: adaptability and consistency. In terms of change, his past and present are drastically different. Known earlier in his life as a "ladies' man", Adam has refocused his priorities and is now a family man with a wife, daughter, and another child expected soon. And though the band, his tattoos, and his good looks might cause some people to believe he leads a traditional bad boy rock 'n' roll lifestyle, in reality, Adam considers himself a spiritual person, he is a vegan, and he practices yoga daily.

Since 2002, the public spotlight has continued to shine brighter and brighter on Adam, and even if you don't know his music, you might know him as a coach on the popular TV series, *The Voice*, which he has been doing since 2011. Or perhaps you have seen ads for one of his many business ventures including his own men's fragrance, his clothing collection, his record label, and the list goes on. He even started acting too, so now you can see him on even more screens! Adam is clearly very self-aware of this celebrity image and isn't ashamed of it. He knows how lucky he is and doesn't pretend otherwise. He even named his band's 2012 album *Overexposed*, describing how his image could be seen everywhere.

So why isn't the public sick of him? The answer may be his honesty. More than anything, Adam values his independence – he once tried taking media training, but says it was stupid. Now, he just says what he means, and doesn't worry if everyone agrees or not. In fact, in an interview with *USA Today* Adam said, "I get myself in trouble all the time – and I prefer that. I can always talk and defend myself."

## Glossary

**attention span** noun [C]: length of time that you can pay attention to one thing

**limelight/spotlight** noun [U]: when you get a lot of attention from the media

**public eye** noun [U]: well known to people in general

**split up** verb [T/I]: end a relationship

**genre** noun [C]: a particular style used in movies, writing, or art

**on the flip side** phrase: on the other hand

**stage name** noun [C]: name used by a performer instead of their real name

**ladies' man** noun [C]: a man who enjoys spending time with women

**vegan** noun [C]: someone who doesn't eat anything made from animals

## LISTENING

**1 Look at the pictures and answer the questions.**

- **a** How would you describe the image each man is trying to achieve: cool, professional, trendy, casual, sporty, etc.?
- **b** What kind of image do you find most/least appealing?
- **c** Do you think men are more image-conscious these days than in the past?

Charles Rick Adam Matt

**2** 1.08-1.11 **Listen to the way each man describes his personal style to a journalist. In what order does the journalist speak to the men?**

Charles ☐ Adam ☐

Rick ☐ Matt ☐

**Check (✓) the words in the box that best describe the journalist's attitude towards the four men.**

angry apprehensive friendly frustrated nervous polite respectful rude

**3 Work with a partner. Answer the questions about the four men.**

- **a** Who never dresses up to go out?
- **b** Who couldn't live without his sneakers?
- **c** Who wants people to notice his clothes?
- **d** Who bought something pink recently?
- **e** Who just wears clothes he feels comfortable in?
- **f** Who hasn't changed his style for years?
- **g** Who thinks it's important to make a good impression?
- **h** Who likes his jeans and T-shirts to be neat and clean?

**Listen again and check your answers.**

**Try to answer the same questions with the names of men you know. Tell your partner about the men you have noted down.**

## GRAMMAR & SPEAKING

**1** **The journalist on page 14 used indirect questions to interview the four men. Complete the table by writing some of the questions she asked. Check the Audioscript on page 152 if necessary.**

| Direct questions | | Indirect questions |
|---|---|---|
| **a** What image are you trying to achieve? | → | Could you tell me what *image you're trying to achieve?* |
| **b** Are you aware of fashion? | → | Do you think that _____ ? |
| **c** What do you wear to go out at night? | → | Do you mind telling me what _____ ? |
| **d** What do your clothes say about you? | → | I'd like to know what _____ . |
| **e** Do you care about your image? | → | Would you say that _____ ? |
| **f** Does your appearance affect your life? | → | I'd like to know whether _____ . |
| **g** What was the last thing you bought? | → | Do you know what _____ ? |

1.12 **Listen, check, and repeat the indirect questions.**

**2** **Work with a partner. What are the main differences between direct and indirect questions? Discuss the following.**

**a** word order **b** *do / does / did* **c** *if / whether* **d** formality

**3** **Complete these indirect questions. Then ask your partner.**

**a** Where is the cheapest clothing store in town? *Do you know ...?*
**b** Are cheap clothes good value for money? *Do you think ...?*
**c** Where is the best place to buy jeans? *Where do you think ...?*
**d** Have you ever sewn a button on a shirt? *I'd like to know ...*
**e** How much money would you spend on a leather jacket? *Do you mind telling me ...?*
**f** How many pairs of sneakers do you have? *Could you tell me ...?*
**g** Do clothes and fashion matter to you? *Would you say ...?*

**Use the indirect question beginnings to write three more questions to ask your partner.**

## VOCABULARY

**1** **Work with your partner. Note down items of clothing that have the following parts or accessories. Use your dictionary if necessary.**

**a** a belt: *pants, a skirt, a dress ...*
**b** a buckle
**c** buttons
**d** a collar
**e** cuffs
**f** a hem
**g** sleeves
**h** a zipper

**2** **Underline the correct alternative to complete these common idiomatic expressions. Discuss with your partner and use a dictionary if necessary. Which expressions are similar to ones in your language?**

**a** Tom is very funny. He's always coming out with amusing **off-the-cuff** / **off-the-sleeve** remarks.
**b** Richard is very lazy. He needs to **belt down** / **buckle down** soon if he wants to do anything with his life.
**c** Julie is very smart. She's **as bright as a button** / **as bright as a zipper** and always scores the highest on exams.
**d** Harry is very careful. He knows how to **tighten his belt** / **tighten his buttons** when he doesn't have much money.
**e** Zoë is very open. She wears her heart **on her hem** / **on her sleeve**, so you always know what she's feeling.

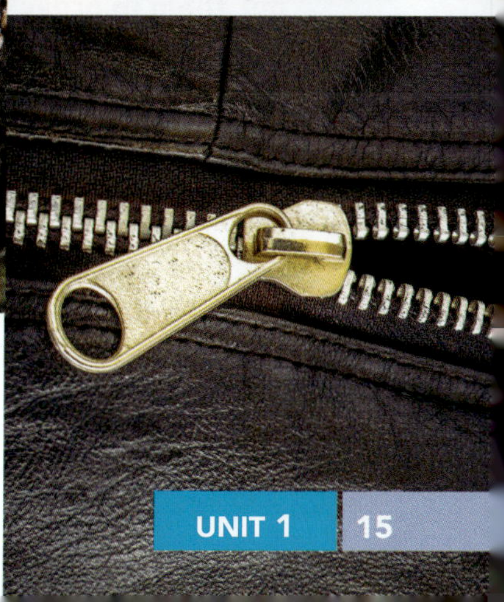

**Which descriptions could you use to describe people you know? Tell your partner.**

## LANGUAGE FOR LIFE

**1** ▶ 1.13 **Listen to the conversation and answer the questions.**

- **a** Where are Rosa, Ian, and Mike?
- **b** What are the relationships between them?
- **c** Who does Mike meet at the club?

**2 Match the useful phrases (a–f) used in the conversation with their function (1–6).**

| | |
|---|---|
| **a** Calm down. | **1** I'm going to tell you something surprising. |
| **b** You're so annoying. | **2** I think you're angry. |
| **c** You get worked up so easily. | **3** You make me angry. |
| **d** It can't be her. | **4** I'd like you to continue speaking. |
| **e** You'll never guess ... | **5** I'm sure it isn't her. |
| **f** You were saying? | **6** You get angry very quickly. |

**Who said the useful phrases (a–f)? Write *Rosa*, *Ian*, or *Mike* next to each expression. Listen again and check.**

**3 Work with a partner. Complete more useful phrases (a–j) from the conversation to talk about people's appearance. Use the phrases in the box.**

> a very   changed so   in the   look anything   looking woman   no resemblance
> spitting image   that smile   ~~that woman~~   the same

- **a** Look at that woman over there.
- **b** The one ______ white jacket?
- **c** She's the ______ of Gwyneth Paltrow.
- **d** She doesn't ______ like Gwyneth Paltrow.
- **e** She has ______ hair.
- **f** I'd recognize ______ anywhere.
- **g** She has ______ distinctive smile.
- **h** That woman bears absolutely ______ to Gwyneth Paltrow.
- **i** I saw this amazing-______ walking towards me.
- **j** I didn't recognize her. She's ______ much.

**4 Complete the second sentence so that it has a similar meaning to the first sentence, using the word in parentheses.**

- **a** I look exactly like my father. ➔ I'm the spitting image of him. (image)
- **b** Our eyes are identical. ➔ We've ______ . (same)
- **c** His way of walking is unusual. ➔ He has ______ . (distinctive)
- **d** I look very different from my mother. ➔ I don't look ______ . (like)
- **e** She looks completely different from the rest of the family. ➔ She bears ______ . (resemblance)
- **f** She was an extremely attractive woman when she was younger. ➔ She ______ . (amazing)

**Change the sentences to make them true for you and your family.**

### LIFE SKILLS: Communication

Making a good first impression

**1 There is an expression in English, "You never get a second chance to make a first impression." What is the meaning of this expression? Do you agree or disagree with it? Why?**

**2 Read the tips for creating a good first impression then put them in order from 1 (most important) to 8 (least important).**

- ☐ Show you're listening.
- ☐ Look your best.
- ☐ Don't try to fill all the silence.
- ☐ Pay attention to body language.
- ☐ Don't be afraid to start.
- ☐ Ask questions.
- ☐ Give an appropriate greeting.
- ☐ Don't reveal too much personal history too quickly.

**3 Work with a group. Did you have the same or different order? Can you think of any more tips to add to the list?**

MACMILLAN LIFE SKILLS

# 1 Writing Extra

## INTRODUCTION EMAILS

**1 Work with a partner and discuss these questions.**

- **a** Have you ever introduced yourself in an email? Why did you send this email?
- **b** What are some common situations when people send introduction emails?
- **c** What kind of language should you use in an introduction email?
- **d** Are there any differences between writing an email in English and writing an email in your own first language?

**2 Read this email from Fatima to Dmitri, the owner of a local gym. Do you think the language is appropriate and correct? Why / Why not?**

**3 The underlined words and expressions (1-12) make the email very informal in places. Replace these words and expressions with these more formal alternatives (a-l).**

1 – j, 2 – ...

- **a** have conducted research
- **b** speaks very highly of your business
- **c** I would be pleased to provide further details
- **d** Please do not hesitate to contact me
- **e** I am writing to you today to see whether
- **f** I believe you know my colleague
- **g** significantly
- **h** Kind regards
- **i** If you are interested in learning more
- **j** My name is
- **k** Because
- **l** I believe that with my assistance

mail

Compose
Inbox
Drafts
Sent
Spam
Trash

To: info@fitnesstime.com
From: fatima_partyallthetime_99@hotmail.com
Subject: A great idea

Hey,

**1** I'm Fatima Raheem and I am a social media consultant at E-Consultants, a company specializing in online consultancy. **2** You're friends with my buddy, Michael Beatty, who is a member of your gym and **3** says it's pretty cool.

**4** I'm checking if you might be interested in working together. Although your gym already has an excelent location, website, and facilities, we **5** checked it out and discovered that your business has very little online presence. Your name does not appear in searches for local gyms, and you do not seem to have any active company Facebook or Twitter accounts.

**6** You definitely need me and as an expert in social media, we would be able to **7** totally increase traffic to your website and location, ensuring that the local community is aware of the fantastic services you provide. **8** Cuz we realize how busy you must be as a business owner, we are intrested in a partnership in which we would take care of 100% of your ongoing social media activity.

**9** If that sounds good to you, **10** I'll give you more info about our work, experience, and what we can offer you. I would also be very happy to visit you at your busines in order to meet face-to-face to discuss this opportunity.

**11** Call me if you like, and I look forward to hearing from you.

**12** Peace,

Fatima

**Are there any other things in the letter that you would change in order to make it more formal?**

**4 Write an introduction email to someone you don't know. This can be someone you are interested in working with, someone you want to ask information, etc. Include information about the following.**

- Who you are
- Why you are writing
- What action you would like the person to take

**5 Exchange emails with another student in the class and write a reply. Imagine you are the person they were writing to and answer his or her questions.**

# 2 Generations

## READING & VOCABULARY

1 **Work with a partner. Decide what ages you think correspond to each stage in life.**

| Ages | Stages |
|---|---|
| 0 - ☐ | infancy |
| ☐ - ☐ | childhood |
| ☐ - ☐ | adolescence |
| ☐ - ☐ | adulthood |
| ☐ - ☐ | middle age |
| ☐ - ☐ | old age |

**Do the following tasks.**

**a** Match each of the important life events in the box with a stage in the table.

> buying a car   changing a baby's diaper   first words   a free bus pass   learning to swim   leaving home   retiring   school trips or international exchanges

**b** Think of other important life events associated with each stage.
**c** Decide which is the best age or stage to learn a foreign language.

2 **Read the article on page 19 about Antonio Souza's experience learning English with a pen pal. Answer the questions.**

**a** What was his pen pal's name and where was she from?
**b** Was Antonio able to learn English and speak fluently? What evidence do you have for your answer?
**c** What happened to his friendship with his pen pal over time?

3 **Look at the highlighted words and phrases in the article. Categorize them under the headings in the table. Use your dictionary if necessary.**

| Language learning | Relationships | Describing people |
|---|---|---|
| *pen pal* | | |

4 **Use a word or phrase from Exercise 3 to complete the comprehension questions.**

**a** What did Antonio's teachers do when they realized that he had a(n) _____ for languages?
**b** Why did Antonio find an Internet _____?
**c** Why were Hannah's brothers considered _____ and _____?
**d** Which sports did Hannah's _____ sisters play?
**e** Why did Hannah's parents _____ _____ Antonio and treat him like one of the family?
**f** Are Hannah and Antonio still _____ _____ with each other? How?
**g** What did Antonio do so that his English would not become _____?

**Answer the questions.**

5 **Work in small groups. Discuss the following questions.**

**a** What are the advantages and disadvantages of international exchanges or study abroad?
**b** Do you agree that "immersion is the only way to learn"? Why? / Why not?
**c** What are your own school-age experiences of learning languages?

- **Grammar:** Verb patterns (1). Adjective structures
- **Vocabulary:** Language learning. Relationships. Describing people. Sayings. Social register
- **Language for Life:** At home: showing someone around your home

https://blog.howilearntenglish.com/antoniosouza/personalexperience

# How I learnt English

I grew up in a small, remote town called Óbidos, in the north of Brazil, along the banks of the Amazon River. Having visitors from big cities like Manaus, Rio de Janeiro, or São Paulo was always an occasion, and if we had visitors from abroad, as we sometimes did, it was like Christmas. These new and exciting people, speaking with exotic accents and even different languages always used to set my imagination on fire. From as early as I can remember, I had wanted to learn foreign languages so I could communicate with these exotic visitors, and maybe even one day visit the cities they came from.

I was so fascinated with foreign languages that I was determined to start learning one. It would be the first step to achieving my dreams. Through the Internet and with the help of my teachers, I started to learn a few basic words and expressions in English. My teachers told me that I had an aptitude for languages and encouraged me to find internet pen pals so I could practice my new found language skills. Pretty soon, I became pen pals with Hannah from the United States. After two months of exchanging written messages and pictures with her, I decided to do video calls too. I knew that my English was getting better every day, but I also needed to improve my fluency. From the very beginning, Hannah was patient and kind and helped me with my pronunciation. But it was a two way street - I was learning English, and Hannah was learning Portuguese.

After we had been friends for a year, Hannah and her whole family came to Brazil. They spent a week on the beaches of Rio de Janeiro and a week touring the historic cities of Ouro Preto and Tiradentes before heading north to visit me in Óbidos. Hannah comes from a large family. Besides her mother and father, she has two hip, urban brothers who dressed fashionably and used all the latest slang. Her two sisters are very sporty. Both of them have played competitive basketball for their school teams. Hosting this huge family and speaking just English with them for a whole week was a true immersion in the language. Although their visit was a short one, we did a lot. I took them on a tour of the historical sites, where they learnt about our Portuguese architecture, we did some handcraft with jute, which grows abundantly in the region, and we even went fishing! Hannah's visit strengthened our friendship, and we promised each other that we would never grow apart.

After Hannah's visit we kept up our correspondence and on my sixteenth birthday, her parents invited me to visit them in the United States during my school holidays. What a gift!!! We started making plans right away. Being around Hannah and her friends, I could see how cool she was. Not only did my English improve immensely in this month, but I also learnt so much about American culture. Because I already knew the family so well, and because they didn't want me to get homesick, Hannah's parents doted on me - I was treated like one of the family.

Hannah and I are still in touch today. We write to each other on birthdays and special occasions like Easter and Christmas. I am happy that our friendship never soured as some relationships do. As people grow up, they change and lose touch with friends, and most pen pals barely speak to each other after a few years, but not Hannah and me. I have been back several times to visit her family, and Hannah spent one month traveling around Brazil and visited Óbidos during her gap year.

Thanks to the encouragement of my parents and teachers and the help of Hannah and her family, I was able to achieve my lifelong dream of learning a foreign language and traveling abroad. I had a strong foundation and continued to practice, so my English never got rusty. In fact, I also went on to learn Spanish and German. Today, I am completing my Master's Degree in International Relations, an area I might never have considered if I hadn't fallen in love with and learnt foreign languages as a child.

## READING

**1 Work with a partner. Look at the two pictures and discuss the questions.**

- **a** What generations do each of the two women belong to?
- **b** What similarities and differences are there between young people and their parents in terms of their upbringing, habits, and lifestyles?

**Read the profiles below. Which generation do you belong to?**

# The Generation Gap

### In this personal profile we look at Martha and her daughter Tiffany and their similarities and differences, which many attribute to the 'generation gap'.

**Martha is a Generation Xer. This generation came between the Baby Boomers and the Millennials and is called the 'Middle Child' generation. Once considered lazy, aimless, and unmotivated, today Generation X is taking charge. The people of this generation are increasingly becoming managers and running their own businesses - 55% of startups are run by Generation X people. This cohort has also become the epicenter of family life, which is increasingly becoming multi-generational. Generation Xers take care of their parents and their children, who either live with them or near-by.**

"My name is Martha. I was born in 1965. I am a divorced mother of two - Tiffany and Thomas. I grew up surrounded by my family, my mother and my father and my two sisters. At that time we didn't have computers, so we played outside with our neighborhood friends, made up our own games, and even made some of our own toys when we were in a creative mood. In the summers we rode our bikes, played catch, played baseball and softball in the park, and had swings in the backyard. In the winters there were snow fights and sledding. We spent a lot of time outdoors. As teenagers, while we continued to play sports, we were also into music and music videos. I feel like my children did much less of that. They spent more time indoors playing video games and board games, and reading. It makes me think that they missed out on the kind of childhood I had.

Nowadays, I am busier than I have ever been. I run my own engineering firm and manage fifteen employees. My daughter Tiffany has finished college and moved back home. She has a part-time job and is thinking about what to do next. Thomas is in his last year of college and will probably go straight to law school afterwards. My parents are getting on in age, so I asked them to move into an apartment nearby so I could help them with anything they need. Life is good, but I worry a lot about my family."

**Tiffany is a Millennial, which is the name given to people born from the early 1980s to 2000. This is the last generation to remember a time without computers and the Internet, but at the same time, they are very comfortable and familiar with technology and media. On the one hand, this generation is considered to be entitled and sheltered, but on the other hand, they are confident, team-oriented, and high achievers. Because of the Great Recession in the United States, this generation is seen as less well-off than their parents. After college they are flocking back to their parents' homes while they look for full-time employment or save to buy their own homes.**

"I am Tiffany. I was born in 1993. My childhood was a happy one. My brother and I played lots of video games at home or at our friends' homes. We had all the latest games, and our friends loved coming to our house. We were not really into sports, although I don't mind seeing a basketball game or football game on TV. We did read a lot though. Mom used to take us to the library every week, and she always emphasized the importance of reading and getting a good education.

I finished college two years ago. Nowadays, I work as a part-time secretary, but this is out of necessity rather than choice. Full-time jobs are difficult to come by. I studied political science in college, and there doesn't seem to be much demand for political scientists on the market, so I may go back to grad school and train to be a teacher, but I am still considering my options. In the meantime, I live with my mom as I can't afford the high rents downtown on my salary. I am happy to be near my family, but I know that my mom worries about my future. Maybe I should have studied something more practical. A lot of my friends are in a similar position - either back home with their parents, or sharing an apartment downtown. I don't like sharing, so I prefer to live with my mom. Eventually my generation will get itself sorted, but the economy is tough right now."

**2 Answer the questions about the article.**

- **a** What makes Martha feel that her children missed out on the kind of childhood she had?
- **b** Why did Martha encourage her parents to relocate to an apartment near her house?
- **c** Why did Tiffany's friends enjoy visiting her house.
- **d** Who likes watching a football or basketball game on TV?
- **e** Does Tiffany want to share an apartment with a friend?

**What other generations have you heard about? Tell your partner.**

## GRAMMAR & VOCABULARY

**1 Look at the underlined verb patterns in the article and in Exercise 2 on page 20. Record the different verb patterns in the appropriate boxes below.**

**a** verb + *to*-infinitive
get to do sth

**b** verb + object + *to*-infinitive

**c** verb + gerund

**d** verb + object + gerund

**e** verb + object + infinitive without *to*

"I said, would you mind turning down your fan?"

**Verb patterns (1)**

verb + *to*-infinitive
I didn't **want to dance**.

verb + object + *to*-infinitive
She **asked me to dance**.

verb + gerund
I **hate dancing**.

verb + object + gerund
I **watched her dancing**.

verb + object + infinitive without *to*
She **made me dance**.

**2 Work with a partner. Look at twenty more common verbs and verb phrases in the box. Categorize them according to the five patterns outlined in Exercise 1. Some verbs can belong to more than one category. Use a dictionary if necessary.**

aim allow arrange ask avoid can't afford decide expect finish encourage
help hope let (not) mind offer spend time teach tell urge warn (not)

**3 Complete the sentences with the correct form of the verb in parentheses.**

**a** My family always avoids (talk) _____ about politics or religion.
**b** My parents always encouraged me (save) _____ money for a rainy day.
**c** I don't mind (lend) _____ money to my brothers and sisters.
**d** My father taught me (drive) _____ .
**e** My parents always let me (stay out) _____ past midnight.
**f** When I finish (study) _____ I want to travel.
**g** I'd rather do something active than spend my time (sit) _____ at home (watch) _____ TV.
**h** I hope (start) _____ a family of my own one day.

**Which sentences are true for you? Compare with your partner.**

**4 Work with your partner. Match the sentence halves to make *sensible* pieces of advice for parents with teenagers.**

**a** You should help them
**b** You shouldn't let them
**c** You should make them
**d** You should tell them not
**e** You should warn them not
**f** You should encourage them
**g** You should ask them not
**h** You should expect them

**1** keep their rooms clean.
**2** to take drugs.
**3** smoke.
**4** to respect their elders.
**5** to stay healthy.
**6** to play their music too loud.
**7** do well at school.
**8** to believe everything they hear.

**What advice did your parents give you as a teenager? Tell your partner.**

**5** **Grammar Extra 2** page 140. Read the explanations and do Exercises 1 and 2.

## PRONUNCIATION & VOCABULARY

**1** 1.14 **Listen and repeat the single vowel sounds in English and the example words.**

**2** 1.15 **Listen and repeat these sayings about family and friendship. Write the correct phonetic symbol for the vowel sound in each underlined syllable.**

**a** Charity begins at home. /æ/ /ɪ/
**b** Blood is thicker than water.
**c** Home is where the heart is.
**d** Birds of a feather flock together.
**e** Two's company, three's a crowd.
**f** One good turn deserves another.

**3** **Match the sayings (a-f) in Exercise 2 with their meanings (1-6).**

**1** If someone does you a favor, you should do them a favor in return.
**2** People of a similar type often spend time with each other.
**3** Take care of your family and friends first.
**4** Two people can be happy together. A third can get in the way.
**5** Wherever your loved-ones are, that's where your home is.
**6** Family relationships are the most important.

**4** **Which of the sayings in Exercise 2 do you like best? Are there any similar sayings in your language? Discuss with a partner.**

**Single vowel sounds**

/ɪ/ big gym
/i/ green beans
/ʊ/ should look
/u/ blue moon
/e/ bed said
/ə/ about
/ɔ/ saw talk
/æ/ fat cat
/ʌ/ must come
/ɑ/ calm pasta

See Phonetic symbols & Spelling on page 174.

## SPEAKING & LISTENING

**1** **Work in groups. Which of these points do you think employers would consider important / not important in a future employee.**

**He or she should ...**

- have good manners
- be clean and nicely dressed
- be from a good family background
- be nice
- be good-looking
- have attended an excellent university
- have good academic qualifications
- like to participate in after-work activities with colleagues
- have suitable work experience
- have the same interests as other colleagues in the office
- use social media
- have previously worked for a competitor

**Do you think any of the points are more (or less) important for a future employee?**

**2** 1.16 **Listen to a prospective employer and the HR Manager talking about a prospective employee they are about to interview. Are the statements true or false?**

**a** The interviewers don't know anything about Andy.
**b** Andy has had many jobs before.
**c** The interviewers approve of Andy's previous work experience.
**d** Andy doesn't have the right qualifications for the job.
**e** This is the last stage of the hiring process.
**f** A strong work ethic is important to the employers.

Andy

**3** **Underline the correct verb form to complete the sentences from the conversation in Exercise 2.**

**a** I'm really looking forward to **meet** / **meeting** Andy again.
**b** It's difficult to **know** / **knowing** with the younger generation if they will stay in the company for long.
**c** It is essential for us to **have** / **having** a candidate with the right kind of experience.
**d** It's important for us to **find** / **finding** someone with the right balance of experience and qualifications.
**e** He needs to **be** / **being** a strong character to deal with the kind of clients we have.
**f** He is likely to **stay** / **staying** with us for three to five years.

**Listen again and check your answers.**

Interviewers

## LISTENING

1 1.17 **Listen to Andy explaining how he feels about going for his second interview for a new job. What reason does he give for looking for a new job?**

2 **Look at the box below. Which of the items mentioned by Andy do you think might give the wrong impression to his interviewers. Explain why.**

his shyness his conversation skills his background
his age his present job his education

**Listen again and check. How does he intend to make a *good* impression?**

## GRAMMAR & VOCABULARY

1 **Look at the extracts from the conversation between the two managers and with Andy. Underline the correct preposition in each extract.**

**a** ... he went to one of the best universities in the country. I was impressed **of** / **to** / **with** that.
**b** ... he will sit our internal exam, which will test his knowledge **in** / **on** / **of** the area.
**c** ... I decided to apply **for** / **to** / **at** a job in a new company.

**Who makes each of these statements?**

### Adjective structures

Adjective + *to*-infinitive
It's **difficult to understand**.
I find it **hard to imagine**.

Adjective + *for* + object + *to*-infinitive
It's **easy for you to talk**.

Adjective + prepositions
I'm **fed up with** TV.
I'm **terrible at** sports.
What are you **interested in**?

2 **Complete the sentences with the prepositions in the box. You can use each preposition only once.**

about about at for in of to with

**a** Were there any school subjects you were particularly bad ______ ?
**b** If you could be famous, what would you like to be famous ______ ?
**c** What kinds of things do you worry ______ ?
**d** Which insects or animals are you afraid ______ ?
**e** Is there anything you're allergic ______ ?
**f** What kinds of sports are you interested ______ ?
**g** Who was the last person you got angry ______ ?
**h** Is there anything you are particularly optimistic or pessimistic ______ ?

**Work with a partner. Ask and answer the questions.**

3 **Think about three different situations. On a piece of paper, write down how you feel about each one. Use sentence structures from the table or your own ideas.**
*It's amusing for me to look at pictures of myself as a child. OR*
*I find it amusing to look at pictures of myself as a child.*

| | | | |
|---|---|---|---|
| It's<br>It isn't | difficult<br>embarrassing<br>easy<br>boring<br>irritating<br>amusing | for me | to look at pictures of myself as a child.<br>to talk about relationships with my parents.<br>to discuss politics with my parents.<br>to see my parents dancing.<br>to annoy my brothers and sisters.<br>to visit relatives. |
| I find it<br>I don't find it | | – | |

4 **Fold your piece of paper and give it to your teacher. Then follow the instructions.**

- Take one of the pieces of paper with the sentences written by another student.
- Ask questions to find out which student it belongs to. Use the following question structure.

| ***Is it / Do you find it*** | **adjective** | ***to*-infinitive clause** |
|---|---|---|
| *Is it / Do you find it* | *amusing* | *to look at pictures of yourself as a child?* |

## READING & LISTENING

**1 Read the two conversations: the first between Andy and his friend Sarah before the interview; the second between Andy and the two managers. Choose the most appropriate option (a, b, or c) to complete each conversation.**

| | a | b | c |
|---|---|---|---|
| **1** | The door's open | Come in | Enter |
| **2** | Thank you | Greetings | That's great |
| **3** | How have you been | How's it going | What's the matter |
| **4** | beat | fine | full |
| **5** | What've you been up to | What have you been doing | What do you do |
| **6** | hurry up | relax | chill out |
| **7** | Do you want | Would you prefer | Are you looking forward to |
| **8** | Anyone | Whatever | I don't mind |
| **9** | I can't help it | I don't really know | No idea |
| **10** | a little old-fashioned | on my last legs | elderly |

### Conversation 1

*Sarah arrives at Andy's apartment and knocks on the door.*

**Sarah:** Hello!
**Andy:** Hi. (1) The door's open!
**Sarah:** Here, I remembered to bring you the book.
**Andy:** OK, (2) ______.
**Sarah:** So, (3) ______?
**Andy:** All right, but I'm (4) ______.
**Sarah:** Why? (5) ______?
**Andy:** Nothing - it's just that I worked late last night.
**Sarah:** Oh. Well, you'd better just (6) ______ this evening. (7) ______ to watch TV or watch something online?
**Andy:** (8) ______.
**Sarah:** Do you know what's on TV tonight?
**Andy:** (9) ______. Trash as usual.
**Sarah:** Oh, you're in a bad mood. You're not nervous about the interview this week, are you?
**Andy:** No, just tired. I feel like I'm (10) ______.
**Sarah:** Get some rest and don't worry. I'll make you a cup of coffee.

### Conversation 2

*Andy arrives at the office for the second interview. (HR is the human resources manager and EM is the employing manager)*

**EM:** Hello. Please, (1) come in!
**HR:** Welcome Andy, nice to see you again.
**Andy:** Good afternoon. (2) ______ for calling me back for a second interview.
**EM:** Shall we begin? Please have a seat here Andy.
**HR:** (3) ______ since our last interview?
**Andy:** (4) ______, thanks for asking.
**EM:** (5) ______?
**Andy:** Well, I have been working a lot lately, but that is normal at this time of the year, isn't it?
**HR:** Well, we hope you have found time to (6) ______ too.
**Andy:** Thanks.
**EM:** Just a reminder ... we'll be having a short written test after the interview. (7) ______ paper or computer?
**Andy:** (8) ______ doing it on the computer.
**HR:** Good. Let's get started. Andy, we are interested in your knowledge about the industry. What do you know about our Corporation?
**Andy:** Well, all I know is what is public knowledge, what appears in the media and on your website. I have studied it, but (9) ______ much more than this.
**EM:** Okay. I do know that you have worked at XYZ Ltd. What can you tell us about your time there?
**Andy:** I really enjoyed my time working there. I had several opportunities to grow which is always great because it prevents us from becoming (10) ______.
**HR:** I see. Last time, you spoke about ...

▶ 1.18-1.19 **Listen to each conversation and check your answers.**

**2 Discuss what advice you would give to a young person taking an interview.**

## LISTENING & SPEAKING

**1 Work with a partner. List the things you would expect to experience on a visit to the USA to learn English. Think about: the people, the food, the climate, the language, etc.**

**2** 1.20 **Listen to Rosa talking about the time she spent with a family in the United States. Are the statements true or false? Correct the false sentences.**

- **a** Rosa felt positive about her trip to the USA.
- **b** She was worried about the food.
- **c** She was hoping for hot weather.
- **d** Her host family didn't like talking about personal matters.
- **e** They made Rosa feel at home.

**3 Put Rosa's account of her stay in the correct order. Then listen again and check.**

[1] I knew there were a lot of things I would have to get used

[ ] on treating me like a member of the family. When I met them for the first time, they gave me a big hug and then asked me

[ ] about trying new things. Also, I hate warm winters, so I was dreaming

[2] to when I decided to go to the USA and stay with a family. But I was looking forward

[ ] of the typical gray days in Seattle, where the family lived. I was a little worried

[ ] with the language at first – I couldn't understand anything! But the family made me feel

[ ] about making new friends, and whether my host family would object

[ ] at home, and it was definitely the best way to improve my English. In a family situation, you have to sink or swim. It's as simple as that.

[ ] in turning Seattle into a tropical city! I had problems

[ ] to experiencing a new culture. I am not difficult when it comes to food, so I was excited

[ ] to having my friends in their home. But they insisted

[ ] about my family, my work, and even my boyfriend. The other surprise was the weather – I think global warming has succeeded

**4 Use the verb + preposition structures from Rosa's account to make true statements about yourself.**

- **a** I've always dreamed of ...
  *I've always dreamed of learning to fly.*
- **b** I'm looking forward to ...
- **c** I worry about ...
- **d** I don't object to ...
- **e** I always insist on ...
- **f** I've never succeeded in ...

**Discuss your sentences with your partner.**

## SPEAKING: ANECDOTE

**You're going to tell your partner about somebody's home you have stayed in.**

- Ask yourself the questions below.
- Think about *what* to say and *how* to say it.
- Tell your partner about somebody's home you have stayed in.

- **a** Whose home did you stay in? A relative's? A friend's? A family's? ...
- **b** When did you stay there and how long did you stay for?
- **c** What was the purpose of your stay?
- **d** How did you get there?
- **e** Who lived in the house and what were they like?
- **f** How did their lifestyle differ from yours?
- **g** What was the house / your room like?
- **h** What were the best / worst moments of your stay?
- **i** Would you like to stay there again? Why? / Why not?

## LANGUAGE FOR LIFE

1 1.21 **Listen to Jennifer Brown showing her new au pair, Maria, around her home. Answer the questions.**

- **a** How many children does Jennifer have?
- **b** Which is Jennifer's favorite room?
- **c** What color are the bathroom walls?

2 **Listen again and number the rooms in the order Jennifer shows them. Which three rooms does she not show?**

Maria's room the bathroom Ben's room Jennifer's room Katy's room
the dining room the kitchen the living room the study

3 **Match the two halves of the useful phrases that Jennifer uses to welcome Maria.**

| | | | |
|---|---|---|---|
| **a** | Did you have | **1** | holler. |
| **b** | Welcome to | **2** | you around. |
| **c** | Let me introduce you | **3** | our home. |
| **d** | Then I'll show | **4** | a pleasant flight? |
| **e** | Please call | **5** | coffee. |
| **f** | Help yourself to | **6** | at home. |
| **g** | Make yourself | **7** | to the rest of the family. |
| **h** | If there's anything you need, just | **8** | me Jennifer. |

1.22 **Listen, check, and repeat.**

### LIFE SKILLS: Communication

Intergenerational Communication

We are now seeing up to four generations interacting in the home or the workplace. Each generation grew up in a distinctly different era, with their own generational values, experiences, expectations, and communication styles.

- **Work together with a partner to suggest solutions to some of the communication problems which may occur due to these generational differences.**

| Generation | Characteristic | Behavior | Perceived Problem | Suggested Solution |
|---|---|---|---|---|
| Millennials and Generation Z | Very comfortable with technology and digital communication | Returns phone calls with texts and/or emails. | Not the best way to deal with urgent matters as texts and email could go unread. They are also more open to misinterpretation. Baby Boomers and Generation Xers may see this as a sign of disrespect. | |
| Generation X | Require constant feedback and validation | Seek guidance, feedback, and assurance. | Older generations see this behavior as needy and insecure. Younger generations feel adrift and unappreciated when they don't get constant feedback. | |
| Veterans and Baby Boomers | Formal and bound by rules | Value arriving on time and working '9 to 5'. | Younger generations value 'being there', quality time, and getting the job done, versus quantity of time and clocking in and clocking out. | |

Some rules for better intergenerational communication.

1. Be flexible. Understand that each generation has their own communication style which may be different from your own. Try to adapt where possible.
2. Don't judge. Different does not mean better or worse.
3. Set rules. If there are clear rules from the onset on what is expected, people are more likely to stick to the rules and work together more harmoniously.

# 2 Vocabulary Extra

## LEARNING ABOUT WORDS

**1 Work with a partner. Discuss the following questions.**

- **a** What does it mean to "know" a word?
- **b** How many words do you think you "know" in your language?
- **c** How many words do you think you "know" in English?

**2 Read the text about word frequency and answer the questions.**

**Word frequency**

It is a remarkable fact about all languages (not just English) that they consist of a small number of very frequent words, and a large number of very rare ones. As the graph shows, the hundred most frequent words in English make up about 45% of most texts. More importantly, the 7,500 most frequent words make up well over 90% of everything we read. This is important for language learning because a good working knowledge of these 7,500 common words provides a valuable basis for understanding what we read and hear.

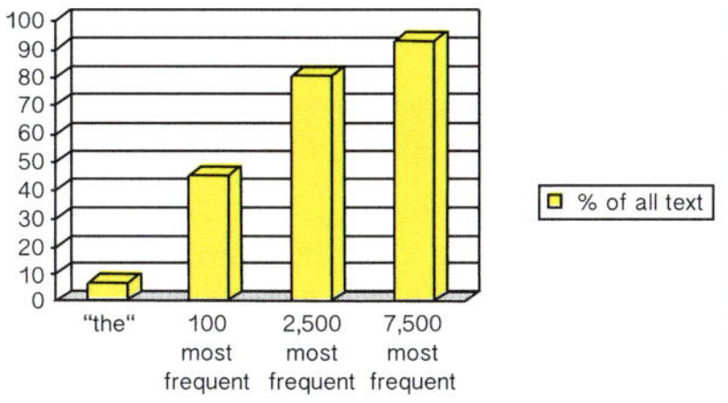


- **a** What is the most frequent word in the English language?
- **b** What percentage of text is made up of the most common 100 words?
- **c** If you know the 2,500 most common words, what percentage of most texts can you understand?
- **d** If you want to understand over 90% of all texts, how many of the most common words do you need to know?

**3 Most common words have more than one meaning. Look at the dictionary entry for *word* and answer the questions.**

- **a** How many main meanings of *word* as a noun are listed?
- **b** What is the third most common meaning of *word*?
- **c** What is the meaning of *word* when it is uncountable?
- **d** How many different phrases with *word* are listed?
- **e** How many phrases are you familiar with?

**4 Work with your partner. When might someone say the following?**

- **a** "Tell us in your own words how it happened."
- **b** "I don't know the words to this."
- **c** "I'd just like to say a few words."
- **d** "Can I have a word with you?"
- **e** "Keep it to yourself. You know how word spreads."

**5 Underline the correct verb to complete some common phrases.**

- **a** Just **say / tell** the word.
- **b** I always **hold / keep** my word.
- **c** I won't **hear / see** a word against him.
- **d** Don't **put / throw** words into my mouth.
- **e** **Have / Take** my word for it.
- **f** Words **fail / lose** me.

**Check your answers and the meaning of the phrases in the extract.**

**6 Check your own dictionary. How does it show information about word frequency? How does the entry for *word* differ from this extract?**

**Choose five useful phrases with *word* to learn.**

---

**word**[1] /w3rd/ noun ★★★

| | |
|---|---|
| **1** unit of language | **4** of advice/praise etc. |
| **2** short conversation/talk | **5** things sb says/sings |
| **3** news/information | + PHRASES |

**1** [C] a single unit of written or spoken language: *The Latin word for a table is "mensa."* ♦ *The first word that many babies can say is "Mama."* ♦ *Can you read the words on this page?*

**2** [singular] a short conversation or discussion, usually without other people listening: **want a word (with sb)** *David wants a word with you.* ♦ **have a word (with sb)** *Can I have a word with you?* **2a.** [C] a short speech on a particular subject: **say a few words** (=give a short speech) *I would just like to say a few words about our guest.* ♦ **+about/on** *Let me say a word on the subject of security.*

**3** [singular/U] news or information about someone or something: *We haven't received any word from Brian yet.* ♦ **word spreads** *Word of the incident spread quickly.* ♦ **send word** (=send a message) *He sent word by an army messenger that they had arrived in Jakarta.*

**4** [C usually singular] if someone gives you a word of something such as advice, praise, or warning, they advise, praise, or warn you: *A word of advice: Don't take anything Gina says too seriously.*

**5 words** [plural] someone's words are things they say: *I was remembering the words of my old friend.* ♦ **in your own words** *Tell us in your own words how the accident happened.* **5a.** used about the words of a song, rather than the music: *I can hum the tune, but I don't know the words.* → EAT, MARK[2]

**a dirty word** something that you do not like or do not approve of: *Vacation is a dirty word to most people in this office.* ♦ *As far as she is concerned, cooking is a dirty word!*
**from the word go** from the time when something starts: *We expected business would start slowly, but we were really busy from the word go.*
**give/say the word** to give someone an order to do something
**give (sb) your word** to promise to do something: *You gave me your word that you would take care of them.*
**have/exchange words (with sb)** to have an argument with someone
**keep your word** to do what you promised to do
**in a word** used for giving the shortest answer possible, without explaining anything: *"Did you like Vince?" "In a word, no."*
**in other words** used for introducing another way of saying or explaining something, especially a more simple way
**a man/woman of his/her word** a man or woman who does what he or she promises to do
**my word** or **upon my word** *old-fashioned* used for showing surprise or anger
**not have a good word for** to think that someone or something is not very good: *He never seems to have a good word for me.*
**not hear a word (said) against** or **not hear a bad word about** used for emphasizing that you think someone or something is extremely good: *Jan won't hear a word against him.*
**not hear/understand etc. a (single) word** used for emphasizing that someone does not hear/understand etc. anything that you say to them: *Jane could hardly understand a word Mervyn said.* ♦ *I don't believe a single word he told me.*
**not in so many words** used for saying that someone says something in a very indirect way: *"Did he say he was unhappy?" "Not in so many words."*
**put in a (good) word for sb** to tell someone about the good qualities that a particular person has, usually in order to get an advantage for that person
**put (sth) into words** to express something such as your feelings in words
**put words into sb's mouth** to claim that someone has said a particular thing, although they have not said it, or they did not mean what you say they meant
**take sb at their word** to do something as a result of what someone has said, even though they may not have meant exactly what they said
**take my word for it** *spoken* used for emphasizing that what you are saying is completely true: *Take my word for it, she still loves you.*
**too...for words** [plural] used for emphasizing a particular quality that someone or something has: *If her father came to pick her up, that would be too embarrassing for words!*
**word for word** if you repeat something word for word, you repeat it exactly as someone else said it or wrote it
**(the) word is that** used for telling someone what other people have said about something: *Word is that her latest book is the best yet.*
**word of mouth** communication that consists of comments that people make to each other in an informal way, not formal communication such as news reports and advertisements: *The book became a worldwide best-seller, largely by word of mouth.* ♦ *Most of our customers hear about us by word of mouth.*
**word up** *Am E very informal* used for saying "hello." This expression is used by young people.
**words fail me** *spoken* used for emphasizing that you are very pleased, surprised, or angry
**words to that effect** used for reporting the general meaning of what someone has said, rather than their exact words: *He told me, "Go away," or words to that effect.*
**your word (of honor)** a sincere promise that you make
→ GOOD[1], LAST WORD

From the *Macmillan English Dictionary (American edition)*

# 3 Gold

## READING

**1 Read the article and explain the links between the following.**

- California - golden - the Gold Rush
- James Marshall - Sutter's Mill - a discovery

# CALIFORNIA - THE GOLDEN STATE

The idea and image of gold has historically been associated with the state of California. The official nickname 'The Golden State' was perhaps inspired by the fields of golden flowers which bloom in spring and the gold discovered at Sutter's Mill in Coloma, which prompted the California Gold Rush from 1848 to 1855. Coincidently, in 1846, two years before gold was discovered in the territory, the narrow entrance to the San Francisco Bay was baptized 'The Golden Gate', a sign of things to come. Although that literal and figurative 'golden era' has long passed, California still captivates people's hearts and minds today through industries like film, television, and technology.

### SOME HISTORY

What is now the state of California was once part of Mexico and was ceded to the United States in 1848 at the end of the Mexican-American War. Up until this time, the land was a sparsely populated settlement, with a handful of immigrants arriving by sea or over land up until the 1840s. This all changed in 1848 when the discovery of a few nuggets of gold prompted a human deluge. People streamed west from across the United States and even from overseas in search of a fortune. The population exploded from a few thousand to over a quarter of a million in just a few years.

### THE GOLD RUSH

In January 1848, just days before Mexico was to cede the territory to the United States, James Marshall, working at Sutter's Mill in Coloma, noticed something gleaming in the river. His suspicions were confirmed - he had discovered gold. The news spread like wildfire, and by 1849 miners and prospectors were flooding into the new territory. Many took the risk of the dangerous cross-country trip and, despite having difficulties and the perils of disease and death, they had hope of finding fortune and riches. Called the 49ers in reference to the year in which the rush to California started in earnest, these adventurers came to California in search of opportunities to make a fortune for themselves and their families which they left behind back east.

The sudden and large influx of gold brought about by the Gold Rush transformed the American economy and forever changed the Californian landscape. At the center of this transformation was San Francisco, strategically located on the coast. What was little more than a crude village in 1848, was transformed by the 1860s into an important center for finance, trade, and manufacturing, with the opening of banks, the development of the San Francisco Port, and the completion of the Pacific Railway, which had its most westerly terminal in the city of San Francisco.

### CALIFORNIA TODAY

Today, the state of California continues to hold people's fascination. Although the Gold Rush ended in 1855, the state continued to be a magnet for those seeking fame, fortune, and success. Today, California is the home of Hollywood and the birthplace of the booming tech industry. It is the most populous state, with the largest Gross Domestic Product (GDP) in the United States. It is here where the hippy movement originated in the 1960s and is home to the best-known and prestigious public university system in the United States. This diversity of culture, business, education, entertainment, and innovation is a reflection of California's rich and varied history and peoples, which make the Golden State what it is today.

**Glossary**

**cede** verb [T]: to allow someone to take something such as power or land away from you

**sparsely** adjective: existing in small amounts, or a large distance apart

**deluge** noun [U]: large numbers of people or things that come at the same time and are difficult to deal with

**prospectors** noun [C]: someone who searches an area of land or water for gold, etc.

**perils** noun [U]: dangers

**crude** adjective: simple

**2 Which words would you use to describe the Forty-Niners?**

businessman conservative dreamer entrepreneur farmer opportunist risk-taker visionary

**Can you use any of these words to describe people you know? Tell a partner about them.**

- **Grammar:** Reported speech. Unreal conditionals
- **Vocabulary:** *have*, *make*, *take* collocations. Metaphor. Money expressions
- **Language for Life:** Shopping: money expressions. Explaining what you want

## LISTENING

1 ▶ 1.23 **Listen to the story of Sam Brannan – the first gold rush millionaire. What is the connection between the items in the picture of the Forty-Niner and Sam Brannan's fortune?**

Sam Brannan

2 **Work with a partner. Match the sentence beginnings (a–j) with the sentence endings (1–10) to retell the story of Sam Brannan.**

| | | | |
|---|---|---|---|
| a | Sam Brannan became ... | 1 | all the picks, shovels, and pans. |
| b | He was running ... | 2 | the laws of supply and demand. |
| c | He quickly recognized ... | 3 | a successful businessman in California. |
| d | He bought up ... | 4 | the market for picks, shovels, and pans. |
| e | He ran ... | 5 | his fortune and his health. |
| f | He cornered ... | 6 | the only store near the gold fields. |
| g | He really understood ... | 7 | an unnoticed death. |
| h | He made ... | 8 | a gap in the market. |
| i | In the end he lost ... | 9 | $36,000 in just nine weeks. |
| j | He died ... | 10 | up and down the streets shouting "Gold, gold, ..." |

**Listen again and check your ideas.**

A Forty-Niner with a pick, a prospecting pan, and a shovel

## VOCABULARY

1 **Look back through the article on page 28 to complete these verb-noun collocations with *have*, *make*, and *take*.**

a Many ______ the risk of the dangerous cross country trip ...
b The adventurers came to California to ______ a brighter future for themselves.
c ... they ______ hope of finding fortune and riches.

2 **Complete some more verb-noun collocations by adding *have*, *make*, or *take* to these lists.**

| a ______ | b ______ | c ______ |
|---|---|---|
| a fortune | action | difficulty |
| a fuss | advice | dinner |
| a living | a deep breath | a duty |
| a loss | an exam | fun |
| a mess | notes | hope |
| money | office | inspiration |
| a profit | place | a moment |
| sense | responsibility | a right |
| a start | a risk | a talk |
| way | sugar | a vision |

**Work with your partner. Check (✓) all the collocations you already know.**

3 **Complete the sentences with an appropriate noun from Exercise 2. Which sentences are true for you?**

a I always make a ______ when I cook.
b I don't understand my dreams. They never make ______ .
c The president of my country took ______ two years ago.
d I always have ______ finding somewhere to park near here.
e I don't take ______ in coffee or tea.
f In my job, I have a ______ to two weeks' vacation per year.

**Choose five other collocations from Exercise 2 that you think would be useful for you. Write example sentences for them. Use a dictionary if necessary.**

## VOCABULARY

**1 Look at the words in the dictionary definitions. What do they all have in common?**

**2 Work with a partner. Fill in the blanks with appropriate words from the dictionary definitions.**

- **a** "He [Sutter] had no idea that the ______ would become a ______ , a ______ of humanity that would destroy his dream."
- **b** "By the end of the year, whispers of a gold strike had ______ eastward across the country."
- **c** "They said their goodbyes and ______ west - thousands of young adventurers willing to take a chance on gold."

**3 Read the conversation between Martha and her dad. Use the words in the box to complete some expressions which illustrate two more metaphors: TIME = MONEY and IDEAS = FOOD.**

**Metaphor:**
**MOVEMENT = WATER**

**deluge** noun [singular]: a very heavy fall of rain → a huge number of people moving together

**drift** verb [I]: be pushed along slowly by air or water → to move somewhere slowly and randomly

**flood** noun [C]: a large amount of water that temporarily covers a dry area → a large number of people moving together

**stream** verb [I]: flow continuously → to move in large numbers

**trickle** noun [singular]: a small amount of liquid that flows slowly → a few people moving slowly

chewing digest food half-baked precious profitably running out ~~spare~~ spend wasting worth

**Martha:** Morning!
**Dad:** You're in a good mood today. Any particular reason?
**Martha:** Yes, there is. I've decided to become a millionaire.
**Dad:** You've decided to become a millionaire. I see. And how exactly do you propose to do that?
**Martha:** Well, if you can (1) **spare a couple of minutes**, I'll tell you.
**Dad:** Martha, you know how (2) ______ **my time is** ...
**Martha:** Dad, I promise you it will be (3) ______ **your while**.
**Dad:** Oh, OK - but just five minutes or I'll be late for work.
**Martha:** OK. I've got this idea for a website ...
**Dad:** Oh come on, you're (4) ______ **your time** if you think you can make money out of the internet. All the best ideas have been used up. You should be using your time more (5) ______ , getting a real job ...
**Martha:** I promise you it's not some (6) ______ **idea**. It's something I've been (7) ______ **over** for the last few weeks. Please just have a look at these plans, then tell me what you think.
**Dad:** Hm, yes, interesting. There's certainly (8) ______ **for thought** here. How are you going to find the money to do it?
**Martha:** Well, I was hoping you might help me. Will you?
**Dad:** Well, I can't tell you until I've had time to (9) ______ **all this information**. But you certainly have a good idea. Very original.
**Martha:** But we're (10) ______ **of time**. If we don't do it very soon, somebody else will.
**Dad:** Yes, you could be right. Look, I've got to go now, but as soon as I get back from work, I'll (11) ______ **the rest of the evening** looking at it. Have you told anybody else your idea?
**Martha:** No, not yet.
**Dad:** Well, don't ... I think you've really got something here.

1.24 **Listen and check your answers.**

**4 Complete the table with the expressions from the conversation. Do you have similar expressions based on the same metaphors in your language?**

| Time = money | Ideas = food |
|---|---|
| *to spare a couple of minutes* | |

**5 Look at the opinions. Complete the expressions with an appropriate word.**

- **a** Don't rush decision-making. Always take time to ______ things over.
- **b** The difficult thing about exams is that you always ______ out of time.
- **c** Going to the gym is a huge ______ of time.
- **d** It's best to read serious books. They give you ______ for thought.
- **e** Everyone should ______ at least one year living in a foreign country.

**Do you agree or disagree with the opinions? Tell your partner.**

## READING & GRAMMAR

**1 Work with a partner. Discuss the following questions.**

- **a** When was the last time you splashed out (spent a lot of money) on clothes, on a meal, on a gift, etc.?
- **b** When did you last feel guilty about spending money?
- **c** What is the most extravagant thing you've ever done?

**2 Read a newspaper report about a sixteen-year-old who goes shopping. Why did she have to do community service?**

# The News

## School's out for shopping!

**Teenager skips school to go on a shopping spree.**

An unidentified 16-year-old high school student played hooky from school yesterday when she decided she wanted some retail therapy instead. Just before the first bell she called up her best friend and told her that she was planning to skip school and go shopping instead. When her friend asked her where she got the money, she said that her grandparents had given her a large sum of money for her sixteenth birthday.

As customary when a student doesn't show up, the school called her parents to report her absence. It didn't take long for her mother to find her, but by then she had burnt through some of the money buying clothes and make-up. After having a serious talk, her mother said that they were going to see the school principal the following day. At the meeting, her mother told the school administration that she had punished her daughter by taking away the rest of the money and grounding her for a month. She said that her daughter had always been so responsible and that she was surprised that she would do something like this.

When asked for an explanation, the student said that she had needed a day off to relax because she had been studying so much and was stressed. Her friend said that although she had thought about joining in the fun, she decided against it because she didn't want to get into trouble at school and with her parents. The school administration reported that the student would have to do one hour of community service for a week for skipping school for such a futile reason. The school also put out a statement warning students against truancy and talking about the importance of staying in school.

**3 Look through the newspaper report again and <u>underline</u> examples of reported speech. Then answer the questions (a–f) by writing what each person probably said in direct speech.**

- **a** What did the teenager say to her friend? "I _____ to skip school today and go shopping."
- **b** What did her friend ask her? "Where _____ you _____ the money?"
- **c** What did she respond to her friend? "My grandparents _____ me money for my sixteenth birthday."
- **d** What did her mother say about the following day? "We _____ _____ to see the school principal tomorrow."
- **e** What did her mother tell the school administration? "I _____ my daughter by taking away the rest of the money."
- **f** What explanation did the student give for her actions? " I _____ a day off because I _____ so much."

> **Reported speech**
>
> I told her we **were having** a party **the following Saturday**.
> I said she **could come**.
> She asked me who else I **had invited**.

**4 Work with your partner. Find examples from Exercise 3 and the newspaper report of the changes (a–d) that usually occur when speech is reported.**

- **a** Tense changes: *was planning → had been planning*
- **b** Word order changes (questions): _____
- **c** Pronoun changes: _____
- **d** Time reference changes: _____

**5** **Grammar Extra 3, Part 1** page 142. Read the explanations and do Exercise 1.

## PRONUNCIATION

1 **Underline the correct word to complete this explanation about the schwa /ə/ sound.**

The schwa /ə/ is the most common (1) **vowel / consonant** sound in English. It is particularly common in (2) **stressed / unstressed** short words like *a*, *the*, *as*, *for*, and *your*. Stressed syllables within single words are (3) **never / always** pronounced with a schwa.

2 **Read the sayings about money and underline the vowel sounds that are pronounced using a schwa.**

- **a** Money makes the world go around.
- **b** There's no such thing as a free lunch.
- **c** Put your money where your mouth is.
- **d** The love of money is the root of all evil.

▶ 1.25 **Listen, check, and repeat.**

3 **Which of the sayings in Exercise 2 do you like best? Are there any similar sayings in your language? Discuss with a partner.**

## LISTENING & VOCABULARY

1 **Work in small groups. Think about the questions (a-f). Then discuss your answers.**

- **a** It's impossible to have too much money - do you agree?
- **b** Would you prefer fame or fortune?
- **c** Were you given or did you earn an allowance as a child?
- **d** What was the first thing you saved up for and bought yourself?
- **e** If you could buy yourself a skill or a talent, what would it be?
- **f** What can't money buy?

▶ 1.26 **Listen to Patti, Eric, and Lewis. Are any of their answers similar to yours?**

Patti

Eric

Lewis

2 **Who talks about the following things? Put P for Patti, E for Eric, or L for Lewis.**

- **a** being broke
- **b** soccer
- **c** happiness
- **d** being practical
- **e** a quarter a week
- **f** toy soldiers

3 **Patti, Eric, and Lewis then answered two more questions. Underline the correct alternative for each highlighted money expression in their answers. Who do you think gave each answer?**

**Question 1:** Does it matter if a wife earns more than her husband? How would you handle it?

- **a** "I would feel like a failure if my wife earned more than I did. It's a man's job to earn a **life / living**, and a woman's place is in the home."
- **b** "It wouldn't worry me. I know lots of couples where the woman is the main **breadwinner / breadbasket**. In fact, it would be really good to have a wife who was **loaded / full up**!"
- **c** "It wouldn't matter to me, but it might matter to my husband. It shouldn't matter, but human nature being what it is, it probably would."

**Question 2:** If you were given $1,000 to save, spend, or invest, what would you do?

- **a** "Uh, the sensible thing to do would be to save it for a **rainy / windy** day or pay off my **debt / debit**, but I think I'd rather splash **out / across** on a family vacation."
- **b** "Well, I certainly wouldn't save or invest it - I'd probably **throw / blow** it on a new music system and some massive speakers."
- **c** "I think I'd be tempted to get a new computer. Mine's getting a little slow. You can get them for **peanuts / doughnuts** these days, you know ..."

▶ 1.27 **Listen and check your ideas. What are your answers to these questions? Tell your partner.**

## GRAMMAR

**1 Look at these conditional sentences. Match the *if*-clauses with the main clauses.**

| *if*-clauses | Main clauses |
|---|---|
| **a** If you have dreams, ...<br>**b** If I were single with no kids and no responsibilities, ...<br>**c** If I didn't behave well, ...<br>**d** If I'd known that they would become valuable antiques, ...<br>**e** If I had to choose one sport I couldn't live without, ... | **1** I didn't get an allowance.<br>**2** it would have to be soccer.<br>**3** I'd want fame instead of fortune.<br>**4** I'd have kept them.<br>**5** money makes them possible. |

**Unreal conditionals**

**If I'd bought** it with my credit card, **I'd still be paying** for it now.

**Discuss these questions with a partner.**

**a** How many clauses do conditional sentences have? Can you put them in any order?
**b** Which two sentences talk about real situations (*real conditionals*)?
**c** Which three sentences talk about hypothetical situations (*unreal conditionals*)?
**d** Which auxiliary verb appears in the main clause of all the unreal conditionals?

**2 Look at the table below and explain what happens to the verb form when you move from a real situation to a hypothetical one.**

| Real situation | Hypothetical situation (Unreal condition) |
|---|---|
| **I'm not** single. | If **I were** single, I'd want fame instead of fortune. |
| **It's not raining**. | If **it were raining**, I'd have come here by car. |
| **I've been saving**. | If **I hadn't been saving**, I wouldn't be able to go on vacation. |
| **I left** home late. | If **I hadn't left** home late, I'd have arrived here on time. |

If I were single, ...

**In modern English all the following *if*-clauses are grammatically acceptable – except for one. Which one?**

**a** If I was single, ...
**b** If I was rich, ...
**c** If I was a child, ...
**d** If I was European, ...
**e** If I was you, ...

**3 Work in groups. Discuss the following situations.**

**If you governed your country, ...**

**a** where would you build your palace?
**b** what laws would you change?
**c** what new laws would you bring in?
**d** what would you spend the most money on?
**e** what would you tax?
**f** what would you ban?
**g** who would you appoint in your administration?
**h** what would you have named after you?

**4 Complete the sentences to make them true for you. Discuss your sentences with your partner.**

**a** If I'd been born in a different country, ...
**b** If I'd been born an animal, ...
**c** If I'd had famous parents, ...
**d** If I'd started learning English earlier in my life, ...
**e** If I'd listened to my parents' advice when I was younger, ...
**f** If I hadn't come to this English class today, ...

**5** **Grammar Extra 3, Part 2** page 142. Read the explanations and do Exercises 2 and 3.

## READING & VOCABULARY

**1 Work with a partner. Before you read, discuss the following questions.**

**a** Have you ever bought from a catalog? How about online?

**b** How long ago was a catalog first used? Make a guess.

**c** What do retailers do today to make you buy more?

**Read and compare your own answers with the answers given in the article.**

https://allaboutshopping.com/shop-till-you-drop-from-the-comfort-of-your-home

# Shop till you drop from the comfort of your home

Shopping from the comfort of one's home is not as new a concept as you may be inclined to believe. Before the advent of modern day e-commerce, catalog shopping and TV shopping channels embodied this same spirit of convenience.

Catalogs are said to date back to 1498 Venice, Italy. The invention and growth of the printing press saw increasing use of catalogs in the United Kingdom and Europe in the 17th and 18th centuries, before crossing the Atlantic in the 19th century.

Tiffany's Blue Book, introduced in 1845, was the first ever mail order catalog in the United States. Perhaps because of their popularity and quality, many mistakenly credit Sears and Roebuck with this feat, but their first catalog was published in 1894.

From this time onwards, the popularity and use of catalogs grew from strength to strength. Sales were spurred on by developments such as the railroad, the creation of the US Postal Service, and the credit card. Growth of the catalog mail order industry peaked in the 1980s, when it grew by around three hundred percent.

By 1977, when paper catalogs had been around for over a century, electronic home shopping was born, virtually by accident. Bud Paxon, at that time the owner of a radio station, and Bob Circosta were together responsible for starting and running what became the first home shopping network. Bud Paxon had found himself stuck with 112 can openers in lieu of payment for advertising and convinced his employee, radio talk show host Bob Circosta, to try selling the products on the radio. To their surprise, the products sold out in less than an hour.

Sensing an opportunity, Bud Paxon started the first home shopping channel on television, calling it the Home Shopping Network, with Bob Circosta as the host. Bob went on to sell over one billion dollars in products and easily became one of the most recognizable faces in television.

In 1994, technology was once again the springboard for new developments in home shopping. Soon after the Internet came into the public domain, Amazon, which started off as an online book store, was founded by Jeff Bezos. Despite the dire predictions of its eventual demise, and some rocky years from a commercial point of view, Amazon has now become the world's largest on-line retailer in terms of revenue and the second largest in total sales, after Alibaba Group, China's biggest online retail company.

In addition to the growth of the number of online retail outlets, marketers are continually coming up with innovative ways to get people to spend their money, either in stores or online. Perhaps the most notable approach in recent years is the creation of special days for which consumers are heavily encouraged to part with their hard-earned money to buy gifts or take advantage of special discounts and offers. These 'special days' are appearing all over the world as you can see below:

| Country | Special shopping day | When it takes place |
|---|---|---|
| United States | Black Friday | the day after Thanksgiving |
| Japan, South Korea, and Taiwan | White Day | one month after Valentine's day |
| India | Friendship Day | first Sunday in August |
| China | Singles Day | November 11th (11/11) |

Increasingly, sales on these special days take place online rather than in stores. Customers are using their mobile devices to rack up millions of dollars in sales, with over fifty percent of Black Friday sales in the United States coming from online purchases. In China, online sales run into the billions of dollars for Singles Day.

Although the brick and mortar shopping experience still persists today, we can see that shopping from home has had a long and prosperous life and will continue to evolve in step with technology. With the help of modern day marketing and unique days created especially to encourage even more spending, this phenomenon will continue for the foreseeable future.

### Glossary

**retail** adjective: the sale of goods directly to the public for their own use

**in lieu (of)**: instead, or instead of

**2 Decide whether the sentences are true or false. Correct the false sentences.**

- **a** The invention of the printing press was responsible for expanding the use of catalogs in Europe.
- **b** The popularity of catalogs grew more and more.
- **c** The growth in catalog sales was encouraged by developments in the railroads, the US Postal Service, and credit cards.
- **d** Electronic home shopping came into being in 1977.
- **e** The catalog mail order industry reached its highest point in the 1970s.
- **f** Amazon was first an online music store.
- **g** Marketers invented new ways for people to spend their money by creating days like Black Friday.

## LISTENING

**1** ▶ 1.28-1.30 **Listen to three people talking about their most treasured possessions. Match the possessions (a-c) with the notes about the stories (1-3).**

- **a** Chris' camera
- **b** Katie's cell phone
- **c** Heather's neck-warmer

1. expensive - GPS - addresses and numbers - three hundred people
2. vintage - South Africa - bargain - tax - family pictures - $70^{th}$ birthday
3. saved life - avalanche - over face - mouth and nose - breathe

Chris

Katie

Heather

**2 Work with your partner and try to reconstruct the stories using the notes in Exercise 1. Listen again and check.**

## SPEAKING: ANECDOTE

**You are going to tell your partner about your most treasured possession.**

- Ask yourself the questions below.
- Think about *what* to say and *how* to say it.
- Tell your partner about your most treasured possession.

- **a** What is your most treasured possession?
- **b** What's it made of?
- **c** How old is it?
- **d** How long have you had it?
- **e** Did somebody give it to you or did you acquire it yourself?
- **f** What special significance does it have?
- **g** Did it belong to somebody else before?
- **h** Does it remind you of a particular person? Who?
- **i** Does it remind you of a time, a place, or an even in the past? What?
- **j** Where do you keep your treasured possession?
- **k** Who will you leave it to when you die?

## LANGUAGE FOR LIFE

**1** 1.31 **Listen to a conversation between John and Cara. Answer the questions.**

- **a** Who's Julia?
- **b** What's John's original budget?
- **c** How much does he spend in the end?

**2** **Match each pair of useful phrases from the conversation with a suitable meaning (1-4).**

- **a** It wasn't worth much.
- **b** I just got something cheap.
- **c** I was really hard up at the time.
- **d** I'm not made of money.
- **e** You have to be prepared to splash out.
- **f** This is a time when you have to push the boat out.
- **g** My budget is three or four hundred dollars.
- **h** I could stretch to $1,000.

> **1** poor
> **2** spend a lot of money
> **3** the most I can pay is
> **4** inexpensive

**Listen again and number the useful phrases (a-h) in the order in which you hear them.**

**3** **What does John mean when he says, "They're a little out of my price range"? Choose the correct option.**

- **a** They're much too expensive.
- **b** They're a little too expensive.
- **c** They're not expensive enough.

**Put John's words in the correct order.**

1. I want a (much) bigger diamond. = "I was hoping for *a little / something / sparkly / more*."
2. I want something (much) cheaper. = "I guess I was thinking of *little / pricey / something / less / a*."

1.32 **Listen and check.**

**4** **Use the prompts to rewrite the following requests in less direct language.**

- **a** I want something less tight. (I was looking for / a little)
- **b** I want something more comfortable. (I'd prefer / a little)
- **c** I want something more fashionable. (I'm looking for / a little)
- **d** I want something more formal. (I'd like / a little)
- **e** I want something more stylish. (I was looking for / a little)
- **f** I want something less colorful. (I was wondering if you might have / a little)

1.33 **Listen, check, and repeat.**

### Life Skills: Social Skills

**Negotiating**

Here are some key expressions you can use in a more informal setting, such as buying or selling a car.

| NEGOTIATION STAGE | EXPRESSION |
|---|---|
| Opening negotiations | I'd like to propose ... |
| Making a counter proposal | I'd like to make a counter proposal ...<br>How about this ... |
| Listening and asking for proposal | What do you think about ... |
| Making a proposal | I propose (that) ... |
| Agreeing | That sounds great! |
| Compromising | How about ... instead of ... |
| Clarifying | Let me see if I understand ...<br>Do you mean ...? |

- **Work with a partner to practice your negotiation skills. One will take the role of A, the other will take the role of B.**

A: You are buying a used car. You really like the car and want to buy it, but the asking price is $1,000 more than you can afford. Negotiate with the seller to get a better price.

B: You are selling your car. You are asking for less than the market value of the car, because you really need to sell the car quickly and get the cash. The car is in great condition and has special features. You cannot lower your price. Negotiate with buyer to get the price you are asking.

MACMILLAN LIFE SKILLS

# 3 Writing Extra

## DESCRIPTION

**1 Read this description of an imaginary day in the life of a very wealthy person. Complete the description using appropriate linking words and expressions from the box. Use each word and expression only once.**

after as as soon as by the time during just as then until when while

## A day in my very wealthy life

The first thing I did (1) ______ I woke up in my favorite house this morning was to admire the *breathtaking* view from my bedroom window. **A** (2) ______ I did an hour of exercise with my personal fitness trainer (3) ______ my housekeeper prepared my breakfast. **B** (4) ______ a shower, I spent some time with my personal assistant and told her to send checks to all the charities I support. **C** (5) ______ I was leaving home, a special delivery arrived. It was a package from Paris. **D**

I didn't get to the airport (6) ______ noon, so I instructed the pilot to use our fastest plane and take me to my favorite city. **E** (7) ______ the flight, I had lunch and looked at pictures of my last vacation. **F** (8) ______ we'd landed, I contacted a friend who has just finished making her movie and arranged to meet her for dinner later. **G** I spent the rest of the afternoon doing what I love doing most. **H**

(9) ______ I met my friend at the restaurant I was famished, so I ordered all my favorite things on the menu. **I** (10) ______ we were leaving the restaurant, I spotted somebody I'd always wanted to meet. **J** It was the perfect end to a perfect day.

**2 Insert the adjectives and adverbs from the box into the description in appropriate places. Use the words in the order in which they appear in the box. Compare your ideas with a partner.**

~~breathtaking~~ vigorous luxurious extremely efficient huge a light close latest absolutely

**3 Imagine that this is a description of how a day might be in your life if you were very wealthy. Add the following details using your own ideas. Exchange descriptions with other students in the class.**

**A** Describe the view.
*Steps lead down from the house to the white sands of my private beach and in the distance I can see dolphins playing in the deep blue ocean.*
**B** What did you have for breakfast?
**C** Which charities?
**D** What was in the package?
**E** Which city?
**F** Describe your last vacation.
**G** Describe your friend.
**H** How did you spend the afternoon?
**I** What did you order?
**J** Who was it and what happened?

**4 Choose one of the titles below and write a description. Use all the linking words from the box in Exercise 1 and add adverbs and adjectives to make your description more interesting.**

A day in my life as a secret agent
A day in my life as a famous sports personality
A day in my life on a desert island
A day in my life as the leader of my country

**5 Exchange your description with other students and choose the most interesting description in the class.**

# Review A

▶ Grammar Extra **pages 140-143**

## GRAMMAR

**1 Underline the correct alternative.**

I (1) **'ve had** / **had** some great experiences in my life, especially since I (2) **'ve been working** / **worked** as a doctor here in Africa for the last ten years. I (3) **'ve met** / **am meeting** some wonderful people, and (4) **have traveled** / **was traveling** to some amazing places.

One date I will never forget is January 1, 2000. It (5) **was** / **has been** one of the most important days of my life! My wife, Cassie, and I (6) **were living** / **lived** in South Africa. Cassie (7) **expected** / **was expecting** our first baby, but the baby was late. We (8) **has been** / **had been** in the hospital for two days, and we (9) **are** / **were** feeling very tired and fed-up. All our friends and family (10) **were** / **have been** out celebrating the new millennium, but Cassie and I (11) **were having to** / **had to** stay inside, just waiting. Our son, Tom, was born just after midnight. I could hear the fireworks outside, but I didn't care! I (12) **had never seen** / **never saw** anything as beautiful as my new baby son.

**2 Match the sentences (a-f) with the responses (1-6).**

a I'm not interested in politics.
b I can speak Arabic.
c I really enjoyed the new James Bond movie.
d I've never seen a Shakespeare play.
e I've been to New York.
f I'd love to visit China one day.

1 So have I. 2 Neither am I. 3 So would I.
4 Neither have I. 5 So did I. 6 So can I.

**Give true responses to sentences (a-f). Compare with a partner.**

a *Neither am I. / I am.*

**3 Complete the tag questions with the words in the box.**

| aren't | do | don't | isn't |
|---|---|---|---|

a It's a beautiful day, _____ it?
b You like sushi, _____ you?
c You're coming to dinner tonight, _____ you?
d You don't live in Chicago, _____ you?

**4 Write the questions in the correct order.**

a what / you / tell / is / me / Could / time / it ?
b is / Do / station / know / where / the / you ?
c you / today / think / it's / to / Do / rain / going ?

**5 Complete the conversation with a gerund or a *to*-infinitive.**

**Len:** Would you mind (1 help) _____ me, Katy?
**Katy:** Sure. What's the matter?
**Len:** Sara asked me (2 go) _____ with her to Mexico.
**Katy:** That's great, isn't it?
**Len:** Yeah, but I can't afford (3 take) _____ a vacation this year. I was hoping (4 spend) _____ some time (5 work) _____ this summer to pay off my loan.
**Katy:** Oh, I see.
**Len:** Mom offered (6 lend) _____ me the money, but I can't borrow money from her again! She helped me (7 buy) _____ my car.
**Katy:** Well, I don't mind (8 lend) _____ you the money.
**Len:** Really? Wow. Thanks, Katy. You're a really great sister.
**Katy:** Yes. But I'll expect you (9 pay) _____ it back soon.
**Len:** No problem, sis!

**6 Write the sentences in reported speech.**

a "I've got an idea to make some money," said Jerry.
Jerry said that _____ .
b "I've been thinking about it for a long time," he added.
He added that _____ .
c "I want to open a store," he said.
He told me that _____ .

**7 Complete the conditional sentences with the correct form of the verbs in parentheses.**

a If I (be) _____ rich, I (buy) _____ a bigger house.
b If you (borrow) _____ my phone again without asking, I (be) _____ mad at you!
c If I (win) _____ a million dollars, I (not keep) _____ all the money. I (give) _____ a lot of it away.
d When I was a child, if you (not have) _____ the money for something, you (not buy) _____ it.
e If Julie (know) _____ about Paul's past, she (not marry) _____ him. But it's too late now.

## VOCABULARY

**1 Match the adjectives (a–f) with nouns (1–6) to make collocations.**

| | |
|---|---|
| **a** impassive | **1** clothes |
| **b** forced | **2** smile |
| **c** close-set | **3** voice |
| **d** husky | **4** hair |
| **e** tousled | **5** eyes |
| **f** scruffy | **6** face |

**2 Label the pictures (a–h) with the words in the box.**

belt buckle button collar cuff hem sleeve zipper

a

b
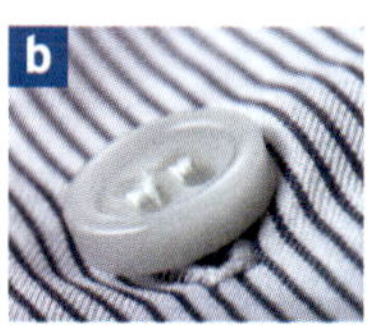
c
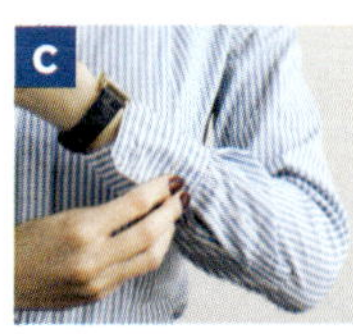
d

e

f

g

h
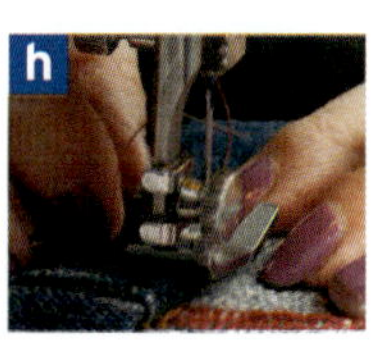

**3 Replace the words in bold with the words in the box.**

rearrange reconsider reconstruct relocate reword

**a** I'm going to **change the date of** the meeting next week.
**b** Joe asked me to **think again about** his big idea.
**c** Your report is good, but please **change** the last sentence.
**d** After the floods, they had to **build** the bridge **again**.
**e** Pam's company is going to **move** to Boston.

**4 Complete the text with the correct form of *have*, *make*, and *take*.**

Louise had been running a small business for two years, but had been (1) _____ difficulties for some time. Her bookstore should have been (2) _____ money, but it wasn't. In fact, the business was (3) _____ a loss. Louise was desperate, and she knew she had to (4) _____ action. She almost gave up and sold the business, but she decided she wanted to try to save the bookstore, so she asked a business advisor for help. The advisor visited Louise's store and spent two days talking to local people and (5) _____ notes. He realized that people didn't know about the store, and advised Louise to (6) _____ a look at ways of getting the store noticed. Louise (7) _____ his advice. She painted the store bright red and put advertising up all over town. Now the bookstore (8) _____ a fortune, and Louise is delighted.

## PRONUNCIATION

**1 Look at some words from Units 1–3. Say the words and add them to the table.**

~~advantages~~ appearance aptitude businessman decision designer embarrassing everything impression relationship spectacular talented

| A: □☐□ | B: ☐□□ | C: □☐□□ |
|---|---|---|
| | | *advantages* |

**2 Underline the stressed syllables.**

1.34 **Listen, check, and repeat.**

# 4 Challenge

## READING & VOCABULARY

**1 Look at the pictures on page 41 and discuss the questions with a partner.**

**a** What kind of trip do you think they are going on?
**b** What are the potential dangers they may face on this trip?
**c** What lessons might they learn from the trip?

**Read the article on page 41 and check your ideas.**

**2 Sentences (a-e) are from the article. Match them with the appropriate *places* (1-5) in the article.**

**a** The siblings ended their journey on schedule, on Victoria Island in British Columbia.
**b** "From the very first day, we were able to experience the kindness and generosity of Canadians."
**c** "I thought it would be impossible for them to survive on such a little bit of money."
**d** It would be a once in a lifetime opportunity.
**e** "I have learnt so much more about Canada than I ever have from a book."

Anthony (Tony) and Julia (Jules)

**3 Are these sentences true or false?**

**a** Anthony and Julia had <u>detailed plans</u> for their coast to coast expedition. (paragraph 1)
**b** The twins had a total <u>expenditure</u> of $200 for the duration of the trip. (paragraph 2)
**c** <u>The press</u> was present at the time they set off for the trip. (paragraph 2)
**d** People they met along the way showed <u>care and unselfishness</u> towards them. (paragraph 3)
**e** Tony and Jules only <u>thumbed rides</u> during their adventure. (paragraph 3)
**f** The <u>brother and sister</u> worked on a farm during their expedition. (paragraph 4)
**g** Tony found the Canadian <u>scenery</u> flat and boring. (paragraph 4)
**h** Antonia said, "The waiting and worrying was <u>intolerable</u>." (paragraph 5)

**Find the words or phrases in the article that mean the same as the <u>underlined</u> words.**

**4 Tony talks about "self belief" and expeditions that are "doable." Look at more examples of words formed with the prefix *self-* and the suffix *able*/*ible*, in the Word formation panel. Complete the sentences.**

**a** I feel very ______ when I speak English to a native speaker.
**b** I don't like working for other people - I'd rather be ______ .
**c** I have a friend who suffers from low ______ even though she's very successful.
**d** I never go to expensive restaurants. I prefer places where the food is good but prices are ______.
**e** I recently spent a very ______ evening with my old high school friends.
**f** I can't stand the summer. I find the heat and humidity ______.

**Are any of the sentences true for you?**

**5 Look up the list of nouns and adjectives with the prefix *self-* in your dictionary. Check (✓) the ones you know or can understand easily. Choose three more to learn. Write your own example sentences.**

**Word formation**

**self-** prefix relating to yourself: used with many nouns and adjectives: *self-belief, self-conscious, self-discipline, self-employed, self-esteem*

**able / ible** suffix to show something that can be done: used with many verbs to make adjectives: *accessible, doable, edible, enjoyable, reasonable, unbearable*

- **Grammar:** Narrative tenses. Future progressive and future perfect
- **Vocabulary:** Word formation. Collocations. Phrasal verbs
- **Language for Life:** Common ailments. Showing sympathy. Recommendations and advice

https://blog.tripexperience.com/cross-country-on-a-budget

# Cross country on a budget

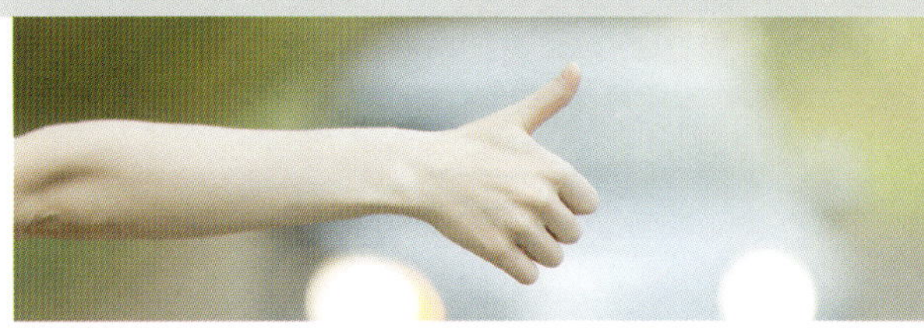

Eighteen-year-old twins Anthony and Julia Giles from Ontario, Canada had been discussing the idea of a gap year long before they even graduated from high school. They liked the idea of taking time off to travel and learn about different people and places, before embarking on their university studies. **1** Even though they knew that they wanted to travel, they didn't have an itinerary until it dawned on them that they would be graduating the same year that Canada celebrated its 150th anniversary. Because of this special commemoration, they decided to kick off their gap year by traveling across Canada, from coast to coast. "What better way to celebrate our country than by getting to know the places and people that make up Canada," pondered Anthony last week in a TV interview about their adventure.

In order to have the full experience they were looking for, Tony and Jules (as they are called) came up with one simple rule - to live on a budget of $200 each for the duration of the trip. Their mother, Antonia, was skeptical. **2** One week after graduating from high school, they set off from the most easterly tip of Canada, the lighthouse in Cape Spear, Newfoundland, with the goal of reaching the most westerly tip of Canada in two months. In this remote part of the country, such an unusual expedition caught the attention of the local media, who were out in full force to see them off. In an interview before setting off, Jules spoke to the local TV news. "We know that it's going to be difficult, but it is doable. Our parents brought us up to be self-sufficient, so we know how to camp, fish, and find edible berries and fruits in the woods. Most importantly, we are together and hope to have an enjoyable time getting to know our country."

Equipped with basic camping gear, a few changes of clothes, and some fruit and vegetables for their next meal, Tony and Jules set off from Cape Spear on foot. On their very first day, they were able to hitchhike a ride and camp in the fields of a cattle farm. The owners of the farm also offered them breakfast and some food to take along with them for lunch. **3** "It confirmed not just that our trip would be feasible, but that we would have the deep experience of getting to know people across the country and form friendships with fellow Canadians," said Tony. And so their trip went, from east to west, hitchhiking, trekking and taking the occasional bus; camping and even being invited into people's homes for meals and to sleep. As news spread of their adventure, people became even more willing to help. So much so, that by the end of their journey, they had only spent half of the money budgeted for the trip.

Staying more to the interior of the country rather than the big cities, the siblings traveled across seven Canadian provinces. "Our most exciting experiences were in the Prairies. There, we stayed with farming families and worked for two weeks on a wheat farm. It really gave us a greater appreciation for where our food comes from and how hard farmers work," remembered Jules. "The changing landscapes across Canada are absolutely fascinating. **4** I now feel ready to start university," said Tony, who intends to do a degree in Agricultural Science when he starts university. "I agree that this experience has certainly opened up our minds and shown us a different side of Canada and Canadians. I will enter university much more aware of the social and economic issues that affect Canadians across the country."

**5** Their relieved mother was there with an even bigger group of journalists to greet Tony and Jules at the end of their adventure. "The waiting and worrying was unbearable, but I am so proud of them," said Antonia from the stage which city officials had set up to welcome the adventurous duo. According to Jules, this adventure would be the first of many. "Now that we see that we can do it, we are already planning our trip across Europe next summer. This adventure has been a boost to my self-esteem. Now I know that I can achieve anything I set my mind to."

## LISTENING & VOCABULARY

**1 Work with a partner. Do you think these facts about Canada are true (T) or false (F)?**

- **a** Canada has only one official language.
- **b** Canada has 10 provinces and 3 territories.
- **c** The cultures of Canadians are quite similar across the country.
- **d** Agriculture is a big industry in Canada.
- **e** The weather is great all year long.

1.35 **Anthony and Julia went on a trip from one Canadian coast to the other after graduating from high school. Listen to the introduction to the interview and check your answers.**

**2** 1.36 **Listen to Tony and Jules' interview and answer the questions.**

- **a** Where were Julia and Anthony thinking of traveling to during their gap year?
- **b** Why did they travel on such a small budget?
- **c** Who was responsible for food and shelter?
- **d** What was the highlight of the trip for Julia?
- **e** How long had Anthony been in training before driving the combine?
- **f** How far from the barn did the combine stop?
- **g** What is the most important piece of advice for other young people who might want to do the same trip?

**Compare with a partner. Listen again and check your answers.**

**3 Read the extract from Jules' story of what happened on the farm. Which tenses are used for the verbs in bold?**

On this day, we (**wake**) up really early and (**head down**) to the fields to continue the harvest, ... this is the day he (**get**) to drive the combine by himself. All (**go**) well, when suddenly Anthony (**lose**) control and the combine (**race off**) across the fields. It almost (**crash**) into one of the barns, but luckily it (**stop**) just short of the barn and disaster (**is**) averted.

**Compare with a partner. Why do you think these tenses are used in this story? Discuss your ideas.**

**4 Complete the expressions from the story.**

- **a** It was a way to k_____ off our gap year.
- **b** They have enough on their p_____.
- **c** So, we didn't want to b_____ them even further.
- **d** We were each in c_____ of different tasks during the trip.
- **e** We knew from the o_____ that it would be impossible to travel through all 10 provinces.
- **f** If anyone wants to repeat our f_____ ...
- **g** We put some s_____ m_____ into place.
- **h** She definitely felt more at e_____ knowing that we were a phone call away.

**Check your answers in the Audioscript on page 152. Choose the three most useful expressions for you to learn. Write your own example sentences.**

## GRAMMAR

1 **Match the sentence endings (a–d) with the correct meaning (1–4).**

I got home yesterday and my father ...

**a** made dinner.

**b** was making dinner.

**c** had made dinner.

**d** had been making dinner.

**1** "Making dinner" happened **before** I got home. (a single completed action)

**2** "Making dinner" happened **after** I got home.

**3** "Making dinner" happened **before**, **while,** and **after** I got home.

**4** "Making dinner" started **before** I got home. (an action that was in progress but was not necessarily completed)

**Narrative tenses**

Simple past
She **came** into the room.

Past progressive
He **was standing** there.

Past perfect simple
She**'d never met** him before.

Past perfect progressive
He**'d been waiting** for ages.

**Name the tenses used in the sentence endings (a–d). Write the negative and question forms. Use each tense to make true statements about different situations when you got home yesterday. Tell a partner.**

2 **Grammar Extra 4, Part 1** page 142. Read the explanations and do Exercise 1.

## SPEAKING: ANECDOTE

1 **Work with your partner. Discuss which of the following challenges you think is the most daunting. How many of these challenges have you had to face?**

- taking part in a race or a competition
- doing an audition for a part in a play
- performing on stage (acting, singing, etc.)
- giving a speech or a presentation
- taking an exam or a driving test
- attending a job interview
- traveling abroad on your own
- cooking dinner for lots of people
- asking somebody out on a date
- meeting your boyfriend or girlfriend's parents

2 **You are going to tell your partner about a time when you did something challenging.**

- Ask yourself the questions below.
- Think about *what* to say and *how* to say it.
- Tell your partner about your experience.

**a** What did you do?
**b** Why did you decide to do it?
**c** Was it your first time?
**d** How did you prepare for it?
**e** What were you most afraid of?
**f** How did you feel while you were doing it?
**g** Did anything go wrong? What?
**h** How did you feel afterwards?
**i** Was it as challenging as you thought it would be?
**j** Would you do it again?

## READING

**1 Read the article and label the sections (a-e) with the headings in the box.**

Clothing   Fitness and training   The mind   ~~Charity Night Run~~   Nutrition

https://personalchallengesforcharity.com/marsha-miller-Charity-Night-Run-15k

# Personal challenges: Charity Night Run

Marsha Miller is aiming to raise money for a cancer charity by doing a "Charity Night Run." She will be joining 5000 other people in a 15k run at night on the university grounds in her city. She has two months to prepare. Here, she outlines her training plan.

**a** Charity Night Run?

The Charity Night Run is a 15K run set up by the local Cancer Society, a global charity that raises money for cancer treatment and awareness. Participants wear T-shirts with a white background and multicolored cancer ribbons to signify the fight against all types of cancer.

**b** ______

As you can see, I'm not a health nut, but for the Charity Night Run I need to be in good general health, so I'll be working on my stamina and general fitness levels. I'll be going to the gym four times a week, doing a combination of cardio, aerobics, and strength training.

**c** ______

I love to eat, so I'm a little worried about the diet. Apparently, carbohydrates are crucial for keeping energy levels up when you're training for a run like this, but they have to be the right carbs. I'll be supplementing my diet with protein drinks and vitamins. During the run it's important to maintain blood sugar levels, so I'll be eating energy bars, bananas, and other fruit snacks at regular intervals. Of course, it's also vital to stay hydrated, so I'll be drinking plenty of water along the way.

**d** ______

The right gear is also very important. Clothes must be light to allow the air to circulate and your skin to breath. I'll definitely be investing in a good pair of sneakers. Although a 15K is not as hard on the joints as a full marathon, it's still essential to have the right support for the soles of your feet and your ankles. Most of the heat from your body escapes from your head, so I'll be wearing a hat. And like everybody else, I'll be wearing the official event T-shirt.

**e** ______

Any exercise is a huge mental challenge for me. It's a constant battle for me to stay motivated enough to keep up with the training. I need to visualize myself reaching the finish line ... hopefully not on my hands and knees! Also, in the back of my mind I need to remember the reason for doing this: when I've completed this Charity Night Run I'll have contributed a sum of money to a very good cause, and that's what will keep me going.

**2 Underline the correct collocation to complete the comprehension questions. Look back at the article, if necessary.**

- **a** Which good cause does the Charity Night Run **earn** / **raise** money for?
- **b** What will Marsha be doing to improve her general **fitness** / **health** levels?
- **c** How will she be supplementing her **diet** / **food**?
- **d** Why will she need to eat snacks at **constant** / **regular** intervals during the walk?
- **e** Why will she be investing in a good **pair** / **set** of sneakers?
- **f** What will be in the back of her **brain** / **mind** when she is doing the Charity Night Run?

**Answer the questions.**

**Have you or has anyone you know ever done anything to raise money for a good cause? Tell a partner.**

## GRAMMAR

1 **Look back at the article about Marsha Miller on page 44. Find examples of the future progressive and the future perfect to add to the table. Then answer the questions *a* and *b*.**

| Things *she'll be doing to* prepare for the Charity Night Run | Things *she'll be doing* during the Charity Night Run | Something *she'll have done* when she's completed the Charity Night Run |
|---|---|---|
| She'll be working on her stamina and general fitness levels. | | |

**Future progressive and future perfect**

Future progressive
I'**ll be working** on that report tomorrow.

Future perfect
I'**ll have finished** it by 6:00 p.m.

a Which tense describes an action that will be *in progress at* a certain time in the future?
b Which tense describes an action that will be *completed by* a certain time in the future?

2 **Write future progressive sentences. Use *will* or *won't* with *probably* or *definitely* to make them true for you.**

a In about an hour from now, I (have) _____ lunch.
In about an hour from now, I'll probably be having lunch.
b In a few hours, I (drive) _____ home.
c At eight o'clock this evening, I (work out) _____ at the gym.
d At nine o'clock this evening, I (watch) _____ TV.
e This time next year, I (work) _____ in an office.
f Ten years from now, I (live) _____ at the same address.

3 **Think about things you will have done by the end of today. Write future perfect sentences using these prompts.**

By the end of today, ...

a spend / money I'll have spent $100.
b send / text messages
c speak to / people
d go into / stores
e do / exercise
f drive / kilometers
g eat / chocolate
h spend online / time
i say sorry / times

**Make questions using *How many ...?* or *How much ...?* Then ask a partner.**
By the end of today, how much money will you have spent?

4 **Grammar Extra 4, Part 2** page 142. Read the explanations and do Exercise 2.

## LISTENING & VOCABULARY

1 **Work with your partner. Look at the "Top ten" list and discuss the questions.**

**Top ten excuses for not doing exercise**

1 You hate it.
2 You can't afford a gym membership.
3 You're not motivated.
4 The weather's too bad.
5 You're too tired after work.
6 You don't know how to exercise.
7 It hurts.
8 You don't have time.
9 It doesn't make any difference.
10 You look terrible in Lycra.

a How much exercise do you do?
b What stops you from doing exercise?

2 1.37-1.40 **Listen to four people (Steve, Maria, Sam, and Tim) being asked the questions in Exercise 1. Which reasons do they give for not doing exercise?**

3 **Work with your partner. Go to the Additional material on page 136.**

## READING

**1 You are going to read a newspaper article about the challenges of becoming vegetarian and vegan. Think of ...**

- **a** three good reasons for becoming a vegetarian or vegan.
- **b** three reasons why people eat meat and other animal products such as dairy and eggs.
- **c** the challenges people may face when they give up meat and/or animal products.

**2 Read the article and find out ...**

- **a** Jessica's reasons for wanting to become a vegetarian.
- **b** Jessica's current diet.
- **c** what steps Richard recommends when changing one's diet?

**Do you think that Jessica is likely to become a vegetarian in the near future? Why / why not?**

# A change of habit

***More and more people are opting to change their eating habits. This article looks at vegetarianism and veganism, the reasons why people make these dietary choices, and the challenges they face when they do so.***

Recent research has shown a more than three-fold increase in the number of vegans in the United Kingdom in the last ten years, increasing to slightly over half a million. There are also reportedly more than one million vegetarians in the UK. Vegetarians do not eat meat or fish, while vegans do not eat anything made from animal products, including eggs, milk, and cheese.

These rising trends are being driven by three factors - concerns for personal health, the environment, and animal cruelty. In the past, there was an emphasis on the deficiencies vegetarians may suffer due to a restricted diet, but more recently focus has shifted to the benefits of a well-planned vegetarian diet, which can be healthy and nutritious. In fact, it has been found that a vegetarian diet provides health benefits such as a reduction in cardiovascular disease and chronic illnesses, due to the consumption of less saturated fats and more dietary fibers derived from a plant-based diet.

While many switch to vegetarianism due to a concern for their own health, many others do it out of a concern for the environment. Animal farming, especially on a large-scale, is harmful to the environment. Cattle production causes the emission of large quantities of greenhouse gases such as methane, which, in turn, are responsible for the rising global temperatures we have been witnessing in the last decade. And, at a time of increased pressure on natural resources, meat production uses one hundred times more water to produce one kilogram of meat than is required to produce one kilogram of wheat. Many vegetarians are concerned that we are wasting our resources and polluting the earth just to produce meat, when we can gain these nutrients from a plant-based diet with much less damage to our environment.

Concern about animal cruelty and compassion for animals is perhaps the main reason why some people opt to be vegans, avoiding all products derived from animals, including animal leather. In recent years, many documentaries have been made, exposing what actually happens to livestock on large industrialized farms from which we get most of our meat. As a result, not only are more and more people opting for veganism, but there is also a surge in animal rescue services and farm sanctuaries which save and protect animals from a life of cruelty.

But how does one go from eating meat to a plant-based diet. We spoke to Jessica who is considering making this transition. "I have been thinking about becoming a vegetarian, mainly because of the environment, but the problem is I love steaks and hamburgers. I have fish and chips every week. I am not sure if I would be able to give up eating meat!" Richard, who one year ago went from vegetarianism to veganism, advised "Take it step by step. If you really want to do this, then give up one thing at a time. If you stop everything at once it will be much more difficult." He also told her to look into different approaches suggested by advocacy groups on the internet. There are many ways to transition, and you should choose a path that will work for you.

Besides the transition itself, another challenge that some people face is finding suitable substitutes and preparing nutritionally balanced meals. "It might seem difficult at first, but you pick it up as you go along. The important thing is to be open to trying new things," says Richard. "And if you have any doubts, look up the available information. There is a lot of useful advice on the internet," he adds. According to nutritionists, vegetarians and vegans do face challenges such as getting enough variety on their plate and getting all the nutrients, vitamins, and minerals they need. One final challenge some vegans have reported is that, strange as it may seem, their lifestyle choice can sometimes drive friends away. "Some people that I used to frequently socialize with have disappeared. They are puzzled by what it means to be a vegan and since I don't eat hamburgers and a lot of snack available at bars, they find it hard to hang out with me," Richard reflects.

Despite all these challenges, as vegetarianism and veganism become a lifestyle choice for more and more people, supermarkets, restaurants, and bars are offering more choices to meet the needs of this growing segment of the population. Also, more people are coming to appreciate these choices, even if they don't make the same choices themselves.

## VOCABULARY

**1 Work with a partner. Discuss these questions about phrasal verbs. Use a dictionary if necessary.**

- **a** What is the difference in meaning between ***pick*** *a book* ***up*** and ***pick*** *a language* ***up***? Which meaning is idiomatic? Which meaning is literal?
- **b** What is the difference in meaning between *I* ***gave up*** and *I* ***gave*** *my independence* ***up***? Which verb is transitive? Which verb is intransitive?
- **c** ***Look sth up*** is transitive and separable. Which of the following patterns is not possible: *I looked up the word / I looked the word up / I looked up it / I looked it up*?
- **d** ***Look into sth*** is transitive and not separable. Which of these patterns are not possible: *I looked into the matter / I looked the matter into / I looked into it / I looked it into*?

**Identify all the phrasal verbs in the article on page 46. For each one, decide ...**

- if the meaning is literal or idiomatic.
- if the verb is transitive or intransitive.
- if the transitive verb is separable or not separable.

**2 Use an appropriate phrasal verb from the article to rewrite the underlined phrases in the sentences below.**

- **a** Jessica loves meat and fish. She's afraid that she won't be able to stop eating these foods. *she won't be able to give them up*
- **b** Richard told Jessica to investigate different approaches to changing her diet on the internet.
- **c** It might seem difficult at first but you learn as you go along.
- **d** Some people find it hard to socialize with vegans.
- **e** Richard advised Jessica to do some research if she had doubts about her choices.

**3 Complete the sentences by putting the object pronoun in parentheses in the correct position.**

- **a** I quit using the cell phone in gas stations when I saw an ad about it. It really put off. (me)
- **b** Whenever the flu is going around, I always seem to come down with. (it)
- **c** If I catch a cold in the winter, it usually takes me ages to shake off. (it)
- **d** My father has always been very healthy. It's a shame I don't take after. (him)
- **e** At the end of a day, the last thing I want to do is go running. I just don't feel up to. (it)
- **f** I don't need to do any exercise - my kids wear out. (me)

**Are any of these sentences true for you?**

## SPEAKING

**1 Identify the phrasal verbs in these statements about health. How many do you know? Look them up in a dictionary if necessary.**

- **a** I can't keep up with all the new diets that come out every year.
- **b** I know I need to lose weight, but I keep putting it off.
- **c** My problem is that I can't do without chocolate.
- **d** I wish someone would come up with a non-fattening chocolate that tastes as good as the real thing.
- **e** I'm also trying to cut down on caffeine.
- **f** I need to take up a new sport, but not one that takes up too much time.

**2 Work with a partner. Which of these statements do you relate to most? Tell your partner.**

**Phrasal verbs**

**come down with sth** become sick

**feel up to sth** feel strong enough to do sth

**put sb off** make sb dislike sth

**shake sth off** get rid of sth, e.g. an illness

**take after sb** be like an older relative

**wear sb out** make sb feel very tired

## LANGUAGE FOR LIFE & PRONUNCIATION

1 **Read the conversations and match an ailment with each one.**

difficulty sleeping   hay fever   a sore throat   a splitting headache   sunburn   a twisted ankle

**a**

**A:** Oh, no – you look like death warmed over! Late night last night?
**B:** No, not really. But I couldn't sleep. I don't think I slept a wink, and now I feel exhausted.
**A:** Oh, it's horrible when that happens. You should try ...

**b**

**C:** Oh, no! What happened?
**D:** I did something to my ankle. It's killing me!
**C:** You poor thing! It looks really swollen.
**D:** I know, and it's getting worse.
**C:** If you ask me, you need to ...

**c**

**E:** Ugh! I can't swallow anything.
**F:** Oh, yes, I know what you mean. I was the same last week. I could only eat ice cream!
**E:** So, what did you do?
**F:** Well, you could try this. ...

**d**

**G:** Don't touch my back!
**H:** Why? What's wrong?
**G:** I wanted to get a tan quickly, so I didn't bother to put any sunblock on.
**H:** Oh well, it serves you right then, doesn't it?
**G:** It really stings.
**H:** Have you tried ...

**e**

**I:** When did it start?
**J:** After I'd been playing computer games for a few hours. I feel as if my head's going to explode!
**I:** Oh well, you've only got yourself to blame.
**J:** I know, I know. But I've taken some aspirin, and it hasn't worked.
**I:** Well, you could try ...

**f**

**K:** Do you have a cold?
**L:** No, I'm all right – I always get a runny nose and red eyes at this time of the year.
**K:** That must be awful. If I were you, I'd ...

2 **Work with a partner. Look at the conversations in Exercise 1 and complete each one with your own advice.**

1.41 **Listen and compare your ideas with the original conversations.**

3 1.42 **Read and listen to the highlighted useful phrases in the conversations. Are the listeners being sympathetic or unsympathetic?**

**Practice the useful phrases with your partner. Try to use the same stress and intonation as the recording.**

4 **Work with your partner. Student A look at your problems on page 136. Student B look at your problems on page 139. Follow the instructions.**

### LIFE SKILLS: SOCIAL SKILLS

Advice on dealing with challenges

According to the Macmillan Dictionary, a proverb is "a short, well-known statement that gives practical advice about life." A quote is "someone else's words, which can sometimes be used as advice or words of wisdom."

Proverbs and quotes can sometimes provide us with "food for thought" or even help us through challenging moments.

- **Read two proverbs and a quotation related to overcoming challenges and difficulties. Write your interpretations individually and then compare with a partner.**

| Proverb | Your interpretation |
|---|---|
| Nothing is so difficult that diligence cannot master it. Malagasy Proverb | |
| When one is prepared, difficulties do not come. Traditional Proverb | |

| Quote | Your interpretation |
|---|---|
| "The ultimate measure of a man is not where he stands in moments of comfort and convenience, but where he stands at times of challenge and controversy." Martin Luther King Jr. | |

# 4 Vocabulary Extra

## PHRASAL VERBS

**1 Work with a partner. The diagrams show combinations of the two most common verbs with the six most common particles found in phrasal verbs.**

- Choose six from the twelve possible phrasal verbs and think of a meaning for each one.
- Decide if the phrasal verbs you chose are transitive [T] e.g. *I took off my coat*, or intransitive [I] e.g. *The plane took off*.
- Write a "vocabulary entry" showing the grammar, the definition, and an example sentence. Use a dictionary if necessary.

take sth up [T] = start doing something new – "I just took up jogging."

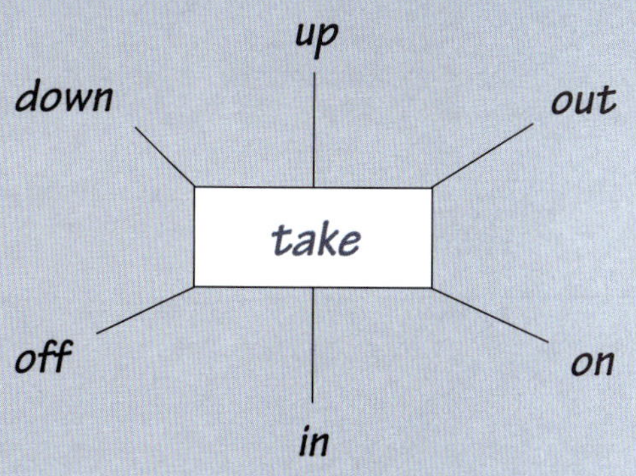


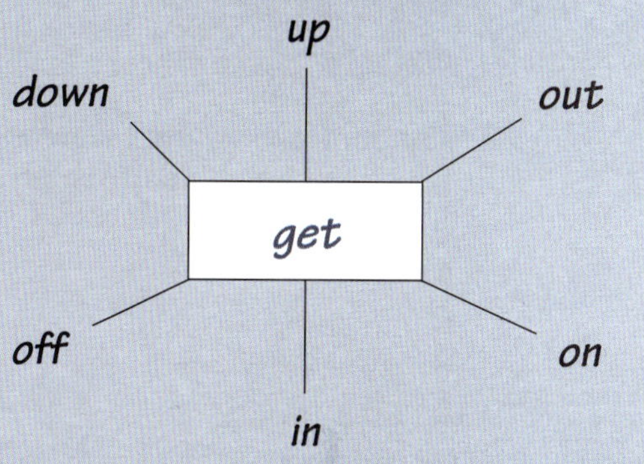


**2 Complete the following questions with *take* or *get*.**

a What time do you ______ up during the week?
b Do you always ______ out travel insurance when you go abroad?
c Clare wants to ______ on the basketball team.
d Do you find that grammar rules are easy to ______ in?
e What time do you usually ______ off work?
f What kinds of things ______ you down?

**Ask your partner the questions.**

**3 *Take*, *get*, *put*, *come*, *go*, and *set* are the six most common verbs found in phrasal verbs. Decide which common phrasal verb is being defined by each of the "meaning menus" A–F.**

a <u>come</u> up c ______ on e ______ off
b ______ on d ______ up f ______ on

**4 Replace the <u>underlined</u> words or phrases in sentences a–f with the correct form of an appropriate phrasal verb from Exercise 3.**

a I never miss the news. I like to know what's <u>happening</u> in the world.
b I always try to <u>leave</u> early when I've got a long way to drive.
c I buy a lottery ticket every week but my numbers never <u>win</u>.
d Daniel <u>was chosen to be part of</u> the soccer team.
e I'm so busy. I can't <u>accept</u> any more work right now.
f My apartment is pretty small, so when I <u>let people stay</u> they have to sleep on the couch.

**Are any of the sentences true for you? Compare with your partner.**

**5 Work with your partner. Some phrasal verbs are made up of a verb and two particles. Add *at*, *for*, *on*, or *with* to complete these sentences. Use your dictionary if necessary.**

a "Is that the best you can come up ______ ?"
b "When does it come up ______ renewal?"
c "Just get on ______ it. We don't have all day!"
d "Stop going on ______ me, will you?"
e "I can't put up ______ this any longer."
f "I might take you up ______ that one of these days."

**Decide in what context somebody might say these sentences.**

**6 Check your own dictionary. Look up phrasal verbs under the entries for *come*, *get*, *go*, *put*, *set*, and *take*. Choose five new phrasal verbs to learn.**

**A**

1 go to speak to sb
2 become available
3 need to be dealt with
4 travel further north
5 about information
6 to higher point/level
7 appear in sky
8 win money with a ticket
9 about plants
10 be judged in court
\+ PHRASES

**B**

1 get into the bus, etc.
2 continue doing sth
3 be chosen for group, etc.
4 appear on a show
5 asking how well sb did sth
6 finally do sth
\+ PHRASES

**C**

1 continue happening
2 happen
3 begin an activity/state
4 electricity, etc.: work
5 talk too much/again
6 do sth after
7 base an opinion on sth
8 go to a place before sb
9 walk on stage, etc.
\+ PHRASES

**D**

1 build a wall, etc.
2 fix sth to a wall/post
3 give money
4 let sb stay in your house
5 raise sth
6 suggest sb for a position
7 suggest sth/sb
8 try to achieve/prevent sth
\+ PHRASES

**E**

1 leave on a trip
2 make sth start working
3 make sth explode
4 cause sth accidentally
5 make sb/sth look attractive
6 make sb laugh/cry/talk a lot

**F**

1 employ sb
2 develop character, etc.
3 accept work/responsibility
4 fight/compete against sb
5 decide to do sth

From the *Macmillan English Dictionary (American and British editions)*

# 5 Ritual

## READING

1 **Work with a partner. In your opinion, what are the keys to success? Put the factors below in order of importance.**

Luck Natural talent Hard work Good habits
Great teachers Perfect timing Charisma Destiny

**Which of these factors is the most important according to the author of the text?**

2 **The famous people below are all mentioned in the article on page 51. Take turns telling the class what you know about them.**

- **a** Serena Williams
- **b** Michael Jordan
- **c** Benjamin Franklin
- **d** Oprah Winfrey
- **e** Steve Jobs

3 **Read the text and answer:**

- **a** Which of the factors from Exercise 1 is the most important according to the author of the text?
- **b** Is there anything you did not know about the famous people above?

## VOCABULARY

1 **Read the article on page 51 again and underline words or phrases that you don't know. Then answer the questions:**

- **a** Is the unknown word or phrase a verb, a noun, an adjective, ...?
- **b** Is it similar to another English word or a word in your language?
- **c** Can the context - the words in the surrounding text - help you guess the meaning of the unknown word?

2 **Complete the glossary below with words or phrases from the article.**

**Glossary**

1 **jump to conclusions** phrase: make a judgment before learning all the facts

2 ______ (adj.): very many; too many to be counted

3 ______ (phrase): to help sby or sth to be very successful or to cause them to fail completely

4 ______ (noun) [C]: way of considering or doing something

5 ______ (noun) [C]: a thick, solid piece; a unit of information

6 ______ (noun) [C]: sth that has been achieved successfully

7 ______ (adj.) [I]: able to continue over a period of time

8 ______ (phrase): prepare or arrange for use

9 ______ (noun) [C]: the state or condition of not being strong.

10 ______ (noun) [C]: the quality or state of being strong

11 ______ (verb) [T]: exceed a target or limit

12 ______ (adj.): unclear

13 ______ (noun) [C]: a thing made for a particular purpose, often a piece of electronic equipment.

14 ______ (adj.): having a serious, important, or useful quality or purpose.

**How many of the words or phrases you underlined in Exercise 1 are included in the glossary? Write glossary definitions for any other words. Use your dictionary if necessary.**

- **Grammar:** *will, would, used to* for present and past habits. Verb patterns (2)
- **Vocabulary:** Guessing from context. Collocations. Weddings
- **Language for Life:** Annoying habits

# The Morning Ritual

"I count him braver who conquers his desires than him who conquers his enemies; for the hardest victory is the victory over self." ~ Aristotle

It is easy to look at others who are successful and make the mistake of thinking that they are successful because they are lucky or have natural talent. But before you jump to conclusions, you should ask them if they agree. Ask Serena Williams, arguably the greatest tennis player of all time: "Luck has nothing to do with it, because I have spent many, many hours, countless hours, on the court working for my one moment in time, not knowing when it would come." Ask Michael Jordan, perhaps the greatest basketball player ever: "Maybe it's my fault. Maybe I led you to believe it was easy, when it wasn't ... Maybe I led you to believe that basketball was a God-given gift, and not something I worked for every single day of my life." What is the secret to success according to Michael and Serena? Hard work and good habits.

I know, it's not what you wanted to hear, I mean, hard work is so ... hard, ... and good habits? That sounds boring. So, how do we convince ourselves to do things that are hard and boring? One approach is to start out small and build up. As they say, a journey of a thousand miles begins with a single step. A good way to take those first steps is by setting up a simple routine that we can do every day. A routine is nothing more than a series of habits that we group together into a chunk and perform as a unit. Nowadays they call it "habit stacking." There are many powerful benefits to organizing habits this way: a series of habits is harder to forget; the feeling of accomplishment of getting a number of things done is more intense; you can prioritize diverse activities; doing a little every day is more sustainable.

My favorite routine is the morning ritual. There are a number of successful people, past and present, with strong morning rituals, from Steve Jobs to Oprah Winfrey to Benjamin Franklin, who had a morning ritual that took three hours before he started work. He woke up at 5:00 a.m., washed and then prayed. Afterwards, he asked himself the same question every day, "What good shall I do today?" He then made a plan for his day, followed by his personal studies (Franklin had many interests). Finally, he had breakfast, and at 8:00 a.m. he began his work day.

But you don't need three hours to have an effective ritual. Here are some ideas on how to set up a simple morning routine:

- Respect yourself – Instead of trying to correct your weaknesses, build a routine based on your strengths. Better not to force yourself to get up at 5:00 if you are not a morning person. Love yoga? Let that be the anchor of your routine.
- Don't overshoot – Try not to do too much. Instead of an hour of daily meditation, why not five minutes per day.
- Be specific – Know exactly what it is that you expect from yourself. Replace vague goals like "learn French" with "listen to one French podcast per day."
- Mix it up – If all your habits are very similar, you might get bored and give up. Mix and match things like meditation, organizing your schedule, reading a book, getting some exercise, and having a healthy breakfast. As they say, "Variety is the spice of life."
- Prepare the night before – Set yourself up for success by getting gear together the night before; you don't want to be stressed out looking for equipment in the morning.
- Turn off devices – If you keep the devices off until after you finish your ritual, you'll feel better about yourself when you check in on your social media.
- Make it meaningful - Steve Jobs had a morning routine that consisted of asking himself the same question each morning: *"If today were the last day of my life, would I want to do what I'm about to do today?"* If not, why keep doing it?

Serena Williams

Michael Jordan

Benjamin Franklin

Oprah Winfrey

Steve Jobs

## SPEAKING

1 **Work with a partner. What other examples of a personal ritual can you think of? Think about the following situations.**

a Before taking an exam
b Before a job interview
c Before taking part in a sporting competition
d Before leaving home every morning
e Before setting off on a long trip
f Before going out on a Saturday night
g Before sitting down to start working or studying

2 **Tell your partner about your own rituals or the rituals of people you know.**

## LISTENING & VOCABULARY

1 1.43 **Listen to Laura talking about her dad and his car. Are these statements true or false?**

a Laura's dad is very fond of his car and treats it better than a pet.
b When Laura was a child, her dad often took the family out in the car.
c Laura's sisters vandalized the seats and damaged the car doors.
d Her dad has always gone through exactly the same procedure before setting off.
e He backs out of the driveway very carefully and very slowly.
f Laura thinks he probably used to go through a similar ritual before taking off in a plane.

2 **Match words from column *A* with words from column *B* to make collocations from the recording.**

| A | B |
|---|---|
| a domestic | 1 Force |
| b a cozy | 2 speed |
| c a sudden | 3 animals |
| d slam | 4 blanket |
| e a box of | 5 urge |
| f first | 6 the door |
| g breakneck | 7 try |
| h the Air | 8 matches |

**Listen again and check the collocations. With a partner, use the collocations to describe the relationship between Laura's dad and his car.**

3 **Do you know anybody who is very attached to their car (or motorcycle, or computer, or any other piece of equipment)? Tell your partner about them.**

4 **Use some of the collocations from Exercise 2 to complete the sentences.**

a My father used to be a pilot in ______.
b I hate it when people drive down residential roads at ______.
c Every so often, I get ______ to quit my job and do something completely different.
d I didn't pass my driving test on the ______.

5 **Are any of these sentences true for you?**

## GRAMMAR

1 **Look at the verb structures in these extracts from the listening on page 52. Discuss the questions (a–d) with a partner.**

*He will start the engine ...* *He'll pick up the newspaper ...*
*He'll fold it perfectly ...* *He'll take the handbrake off ...*

- **a** Which modal verb is used?
- **b** Are the extracts about present habits, future habits, or past habits?
- **c** Does the main verb describe a repeated action or a state?
- **d** Are the actions characteristic of Laura's dad or unusual for him?

**Present and past habits**

These days he**'ll clean** his car once a year.
When it was new, he**'d clean** it every Sunday.
He **used to love** that car.

2 **Read the description of a family's morning routines. If possible, and without changing the meaning, replace the verbs in bold with *'ll* (*will*) + verb.**

My dad (1) **gets up** around seven o'clock. He (2) **hates** wasting time in bed. He (3) **has** two cups of coffee and a slice of toast before driving off to work. Dad (4) **'s** never late. My mom (5) **doesn't usually get ready** for work till after breakfast. She (6) **likes** to take her time in the morning. Mom (7) **'s got** a part-time job and she (8) **always leaves** it till the last minute before running out of the house. As for me, my morning routine (9) **varies** from day to day. It (10) **usually depends** on what I've been doing the night before!

3 **Prepare a similar text using *'ll* (*will*) + verb where possible to describe the morning routines of members of your own family. Read your text to your partner and compare your routines.**

4 **Now think about your life when you were twelve. Complete sentences (a–l) and then compare them with your partner.**

| My daily routine | My thoughts and feelings |
|---|---|
| **a** Before setting out for school, I'd ______ . | **g** My favorite subject used to be ______ . |
| **b** At break time, I'd ______ . | **h** I used to love ______ . |
| **c** During English classes, I'd ______ . | **i** I didn't use to enjoy ______ . |
| **d** At lunchtime, I used to ______ . | **j** I used to have ______ . |
| **e** After school, I'd ______ . | **k** I used to believe ______ . |
| **f** Before going to bed, I used to ______ . | **l** I didn't use to understand ______ . |

5 **Complete the statements with *used to*, *will*, and *would*.**

- **a** You can use ______ + verb to talk about present habits.
- **b** You can use ______ + verb to talk about past habits.
- **c** You can use ______ + verb to talk about past habits and past states.

6 **Grammar Extra 5, Part 1** page 144. Read the explanations and do Exercise 1.

## SPEAKING

1 **Write five sentences – four true and one false – describing ways in which your life was different ten years ago compared to now.**

- **a** *I didn't use to have a car.*
- **b** *I'd wear sneakers all the time.*
- **c** *I used to be blond.*
- **d** *I ...*
- **e** ...

2 **Read your five sentences. Your partner has to guess which sentence is false.**

## READING & VOCABULARY

**1 Work with a partner. Look at the picture and talk about how technology has changed marriage ceremonies for better or for worse. Make a list of all the services (flowers, dress, etc.) that go into a great wedding. Which of those services would you get online and which ones would you not? Explain.**

**2 Read a bride's account of her wedding. Answer the questions.**

- **a** Where did Bill propose to the author of the story?
- **b** Where did their wedding take place? What about the reception?
- **c** Why did they decide to "flip" their wedding?

# Falling in Love and Making Ends Meet

I met my husband when we were both in our senior year in college. I knew that I had met the one for me and that it was just a matter of time before we got married.

He comes from a big family, and, being an only child, I loved going to family get-togethers and meeting the endless stream of brothers, sisters, boyfriends, fiancées, uncles, cousins, family friends, and assorted others. They would have these huge bashes that ended at three in the morning with dancing, singing, karaoke, and games. Never a dull moment.

The year after college, Bill proposed to me in the middle of one of these family events with everybody watching. I didn't think twice and accepted on the spot. A huge cheer went up at the party. I've never hugged so many people in such a short period of time.

Planning the wedding was a nightmare: the invitations, the photographer, the deejay, the flowers, the caterer, the cake, the rehearsal dinner ... Bill wanted to have a theme wedding: the bridesmaids would be dressed as super heroes and the ushers as villains. Just no, Bill! But the biggest problem was the money; there was just no way to invite everybody we wanted to invite and have the kind of wedding we wanted to have. It would cost us money we just didn't have, especially because we both had student loans to pay off. That would mean no traveling, no Hawaii, no fun. And forget about having our own house!

We planned and re-planned for months, but we just couldn't fit everything into our budget. Not even close. Then we had an epiphany. Why not flip our wedding? Instead of having a wedding and then a honeymoon, we could go on our honeymoon and get married there. We would live stream the wedding so we wouldn't have to decide who to invite; we could invite everyone. And that's how we decided to elope. We sent out virtual invitations to our wedding and took off on our honeymoon. The ceremony, with the Pacific Ocean as a backdrop, was just the two of us, a justice of the peace, two witnesses (the receptionist and the hotel manager), and more than 200 virtual guests watching the wedding online as the sun set!

The sweetest thing was when we got back, Bill's brother picked us up at the airport, but instead of taking us back to our apartment, we went straight to a surprise wedding reception that the family had put together for us at Bill's parent's house! But that's another story!

That's how I had the best wedding ever but still had money left over for my student loans.

**3 Are these sentences true or false? Correct the false sentences.**

- **a** The couple met after their final year of university.
- **b** They had the sudden brilliant idea of inviting all of their guests to come to the wedding in Hawaii.
- **c** Typically there was a limited number of people at the parties her boyfriend's family hosted.
- **d** The bride didn't like the groom's idea for the wedding because she was worried about paying back the money she had borrowed to pay for her education.
- **e** Bill was in a bad mood for a while but came out of it when they came up with the plan to run away and get married.
- **f** There were only two people at the wedding which took place with the hotel reception as the setting.
- **g** They were worried about having space for the people invited to the wedding so they decided to live stream the event.

**Find words or phrases in the article that mean the same as the underlined words in the true/false sentences.**

**a** *final year = senior year*

### Glossary

**assorted** adjective: consisting of different or various kinds; miscellaneous

**flip** verb [I/T]: to turn (sth) over

**elope** [I]: to run off secretly to be married

**justice of the peace** noun [C]: a local public officer authorized to perform marriages

**backdrop** noun [C]: the background of an event; setting

## LISTENING & VOCABULARY

**1 Read these descriptions of wedding rituals. Are any of them common in your country?**

- **a** The bride and groom cut the wedding cake together.
- **b** The groom gives the bride gold coins during the church ceremony.
- **c** The bride has her hands and feet decorated in henna designs.
- **d** Guests pin money on the bridegroom's suit during the reception.
- **e** Guests throw rice over the bride and groom as they leave the church.
- **f** An older person holds a black umbrella over the bride's head as she leaves her home to go to the groom's house.
- **g** The bride throws her bouquet of flowers over her shoulder into the crowd of guests.
- **h** The father of the bride, the groom, and the best man make speeches at the reception.

**2** 1.44-1.47 **Listen to four people talking about wedding rituals. Match a ritual (a-h) from Exercise 1 with a person (1-4). What is the meaning of each ritual?**

Jorge 

Sandra 

Ilhan 

Laila 

**3 Look at the words and phrases in the box, which you can use to describe weddings in the USA. Now complete the task.**

aisle best man bouquet of flowers bridesmaid church confetti
honeymoon photographer priest propose a toast reception rice
ring speech veil vows wedding cake wedding presents

- **a** (Circle) the words and phrases that you don't know and look them up.
- **b** Underline the stress in each word and practice saying all of the words and phrases.
- **c** ~~Cross out~~ the words that you *wouldn't* use to describe a wedding in your country.
- **d** Write a brief description of a typical wedding ritual in your country.
- **e** Read, compare, and comment on your partner's description.

## SPEAKING: ANECDOTE

**You are going to tell a partner about a wedding you have been to.**

- Ask yourself the questions below.
- Think about *what* to say and *how* to say it.
- Tell your partner about your experience.

- **a** Who was getting married and how did you know them?
- **b** Where, when, and what time of year did the ceremony take place?
- **c** What was the weather like?
- **d** What were you wearing?
- **e** What did the bride and groom wear?
- **f** How many people did you know at the wedding?
- **g** Where was the reception held?
- **h** What did you have to eat and drink?
- **i** Did anybody give any speeches? Who?
- **j** Did the guests give the bride and groom presents?
- **k** How did the day end?
- **l** Did you enjoy the wedding?

## READING & VOCABULARY

**1 If you're not organized when traveling, there are many things that can go wrong! Do you have any rituals to prevent problems with any of the following?**

- Packing your bags
- Closing your house
- Organizing documents

**What do you think went wrong with the people in the pictures?**

**2 Work with a partner. Imagine that you just got married and are headed off on your honeymoon. Look at the list below and talk about the activities that you ...**

**a** would hate to do.
**b** would really enjoy participating in.
**c** would love to try doing.
**d** think that you might regret doing.

- Lie on tropical beaches
- Explore cultural destinations
- Go to museums
- Ride roller coasters
- Go on sightseeing tours
- Dance at nightclubs
- Do adventure sports
- Dine at gourmet restaurants
- Relax at the pool
- Sleep until noon

**3 Read the story about a calamitous honeymoon and complete it with the correct forms of the verbs. Then, compare it with a partner.**

https://blog.mylifeexperience.com/how-i-survived-my-honeymoon-and-lived-to-tell-the-story

# Whatever Can Go Wrong, Will Go Wrong

### How I survived my honeymoon and lived to tell the story

My "perfect" Caribbean honeymoon started at the airport. I can't help (1) (laugh) ______ at our bad luck, it was so horrible, but so funny in a very unfunny way. First, my husband forgot (2) (bring) ______ his passport. I always tell him he has to check three things: passport, wallet, and tickets. He said that he remembered (3) (put) ______ it in his backpack, but he didn't. He had to go all the way back to the house to get it. "I remembered to bring my passport. Here it is." I thought. By the time he got back, we had missed our flight. I'll never forget looking at his frustrated face and thinking "It's my honeymoon. Everything is going to be okay". We did manage (4) (get) ______ another flight but it would mean arriving at 11:00 p.m. instead of 11:00 a.m. I wanted (5) (sit) ______ in a window seat, but the only seats they had were in the middle seats. I had intended (6) (sleep) ______ on the way, but we sat next to a very noisy family. I can't stand flying with crying kids!

We had expected (7) (take) ______ a limo from the airport, but there were none available at that hour, so we rented a car instead. It was hard to find the hotel and we had to stop (8) (ask) ______ for directions a couple of times. By the time we got to the hotel it was 2:30 in the morning. The receptionist said that they couldn't hold our reservation and there were no more rooms with an ocean view. The one room they had was small, dark and had a great view of the parking lot. We tried (9) (convince) ______ him to help us, that it was our honeymoon, but he said there was nothing he could do about it. To top it all off, Mike forgot (10) (close) ______ the shampoo bottle completely, and there was shampoo everywhere when I opened the suitcase.

Mike enjoys (11) (be) ______ active, while I prefer to take it easy, so I watched him taking surfing lessons from a lounge chair on the beach. "The important thing when you're trying (12) (get) ______ up on the board is to keep (13) (paddle) ______ . Otherwise, you'll never catch a wave," said the tanned instructor. Well, he stopped paddling too soon, got clobbered by a huge wave, and threw his back out. We didn't feel like (14) (go out) ______ for dinner after all that, and decided (15) (order) ______ room service. Something I ate did not agree with me, of course, and I was sick all night.

I had wanted an unforgettable honeymoon. I guess I should be careful of what I ask for. It was forgettable and regrettable! But though I may regret (16) (eat) ______ that shrimp cocktail, I'm happy to be married.

Now, we deserve (17) (have) ______ another vacation! We should try spending a romantic weekend ... Maybe we'll make it a staycation!

**4** 1.48 **Listen and check. Have you ever had any of the problems mentioned in the story? Talk about them with your partner.**

## VOCABULARY & GRAMMAR

1 **Look at the text on page 56 and identify the verbs that can be followed by both a *to*-infinitive or a gerund.**

2 **Complete the table with the verb patterns and example sentences you have identified in Exercise 1.**

| Verb pattern | Use | Examples |
|---|---|---|
| a *remember doing sth* | remember a definite past event | 1 *He remembered putting the passport in his backpack.* |
| b *remember to do sth* | remember sth you are/were supposed to do | 2 *I remembered to bring my passport. Here it is.* |
| c _____ | (never) forget a definite past event | 3 _____ |
| d _____ | forget sth you are/were supposed to do | 4 _____ |
| e _____ | say that an activity stops | 5 _____ |
| f _____ | say why an activity stops | 6 _____ |
| g _____ | try sth and see what happens | 7 _____ |
| h _____ | try sth and not be able to do it | 8 _____ |

3 **Underline the correct verb structure in these sentences.**

a I remember **buying** / **to buy** my first English dictionary.
b I remembered **bringing** / **to bring** my English dictionary today.
c I'll never forget **traveling** / **to travel** abroad for the first time.
d I usually forget **packing** / **to pack** something important when I go abroad.
e I had a really busy morning. I didn't even stop **having** / **to have** coffee.
f I stopped **eating** / **to eat** meat when I was a teenager.
g I've tried **coming** / **to come** into town by bus, but I prefer using my car.
h I tried **taking** / **to take** the bus this morning, but it was completely full so I drove.

**Verb patterns (2)**

verb + *to*-infinitive or verb + gerund?
He **stopped to smoke.**
He **stopped smoking.**

**Check (✓) any sentences that are true for you. Rewrite the sentences so that they are true for you and compare with a partner.**

4 **Grammar Extra 5, Part 2** page 144. Read the explanations and do Exercise 2.

## LISTENING

1 1.49 **Listen to four people who were asked the question, "Do you think you're romantic?" Put them in order: *1* = most romantic; *4* = least romantic.**

a b c d

2 **Work with your partner. Complete the verb patterns and then put each comment in an appropriate column in the table.**

a Try (remember) _____ his/her birthday.
b Stop (buy) _____ him/her flowers occasionally.
c Remember (meet) _____ him/her for the first time.
d Forget (say) _____ nice things to him/her.
e Stop (look) _____ at other women/men.
f Try (make) _____ him/her give up things he/she enjoys.

"The best way to remember your wife's birthday is to forget it once."
*H.V. Prochnow*

| How to be romantic | |
|---|---|
| *Do ...* | *Don't ...* |

**What other *dos* and *don'ts* can you think of? Add them to the table.**

## LANGUAGE FOR LIFE & PRONUNCIATION

**1** 1.50 **Read and listen to people talking about things that really annoy them. Match the picture with one of the people (1-6).**
**Which of the habits mentioned would annoy you most?**

**1 Naomi**
"I hate it when men wear too much aftershave. My brother-in-law, for example. He (insist on) _____ covering himself in this really strong aftershave - it makes me sneeze."

**2 Kevin**
"There are so many things that annoy me! But I think the thing that annoys me most is when I watch a movie with my girlfriend. She (always ask) _____ me questions about what's happening: 'Who's this? What happened there? Why did he do that?' Argh. That really gets on my nerves."

**3 Roz**
"It really annoys me when people talk about how fat they are when they are stick thin! I've got this friend who's really slim - much slimmer than me. But she (go on about) _____ being fat. It's so annoying."

**4 Dan**
"It really annoys me when my brother and his girlfriend are together. They (forever hug and kiss) _____ in front of me! Urgh - it makes me sick!"

**5 Sally**
"I can't stand it when people say they haven't done any work for an exam, and then they get the highest score. One of my friends is like that. She (always tell) _____ us how worried she is because she hasn't done any work, but then she gets 90%."

**6 Martin**
"I find it irritating when people keep losing things. For example, my mom (always lose) _____ her glasses. Why doesn't she put them on a chain? Or get a spare pair? She drives me crazy."

**2** **Listen again. Complete the highlighted description of the annoying habit with the correct verb structure.**

**3** 1.51 **Listen and repeat the highlighted useful phrases from Exercise 2. Mark the stressed words and note the intonation used. Practice them with a partner. Sound as annoyed as you can!**

### LIFE SKILLS: Communication
**The Practice of Gratitude**

All too often in these accelerated times, we focus on the negative around us, whether it be in work and personal relationships or the little stresses of parking our cars, shopping for food, or getting a cup of coffee. Everybody has a story to tell.

Unfortunately, what can get lost are all the good moments: an unexpected call from an old friend; the quiet cool of an early morning walk; the new recipe that came out perfectly; a loved one announcing that she is engaged to be married. If we pay attention, these moments are there, every day.

**1** **With a partner, make a list of a few other happy moments that we neglect every day.**

**2** 1.52 **Now, listen to this extract about the Three Good Things exercise and number the sentences in the order you hear them.**

**a** _____ Describe what happened in detail.
**b** _____ Decide a specific number of days for the practice.
**c** _____ Give your good thing a title.
**d** _____ Include how you feel about it.
**e** _____ Explain the cause of the good thing.

**3** **On a separate slip of paper, practice writing something for which you are grateful.**

MACMILLAN LIFE SKILLS

# 5 Writing Extra

## ARTICLE: EXPRESSING AN OPINION

**1 Read the article and choose the best title.**

- **a** Weddings are a waste of money
- **b** Weddings are for the family
- **c** Weddings are a chance to escape

These days, the traditional white wedding in a church, with guests wearing silly hats, is going out of fashion. Many couples now prefer to get married abroad and the more exotic or eccentric the location, the better. But are they making a terrible mistake? First and foremost, a wedding, with all its traditions and rituals, is a rite of passage to be shared with family and close friends. Understandably, there are those who want to avoid the stress and expense of a big wedding and opt instead for a low-key affair. I have no problem with that - it's a matter of personal choice. But in my view, a couple who opt for a vacation instead of a wedding are running away from reality. Celebrities are renowned for their short-lived marriages, but not surprisingly, marriages that began in exotic locations appear to have even less chances of surviving. Britney Spears, for instance, married a childhood friend in the Little White Wedding Chapel in Las Vegas and their marriage was annulled after 55 hours. Pictures of Renée Zellweger and her country singer groom exchanging vows on a Caribbean beach looked idyllic, but they separated after four months. It is worth considering the list of top wedding destinations - Cyprus, Italy, Greek islands, the Caribbean, Mauritius. What strikes me is that these are honeymoon destinations, and, personally, I think that the honeymoon has a completely different function from the wedding. Honeymoons are for the couple, a welcome escape from everyday life, a once-in-a-lifetime vacation. A wedding, on the other hand, is all about family and friends. In my opinion, marriages for life need to be rooted in life, not in fantasy. However lavish or modest the wedding, it has no meaning if the people who are there for you every day of your life cannot afford the airfare to the chosen exotic location. My advice to a couple who is tempted to tie the knot on a Caribbean beach is this: don't do it unless you can afford to pay for your nearest and dearest to go with you.

**2 The article was originally written in five paragraphs as follows.**

**paragraph 1** introduces the subject of the article
**paragraph 2** the writer states her opinion
**paragraph 3** she gives examples
**paragraph 4** she develops her ideas
**paragraph 5** she sums up her opinion and leaves the reader with food for thought

**Mark where you think each new paragraph begins.**

**3 Look at the highlighted expressions in the article and find the following.**

- **a** two expressions that mean "I think"
- **b** one way of giving an example
- **c** one direct question
- **d** three adverbs or adverbial phrases that show the writer's attitude
- **e** three phrases that introduce a new point

**4 Write an article giving your opinion on one of the following subjects.**

- Christmas has lost its meaning
- Traditions should be kept alive
- Marriage is an outdated institution

# 6 Eat

## READING & SPEAKING

**1** 1.53 **Read and listen to this description of a bad experience in a restaurant. What makes Jeff a bad waiter?**

https://www.restaurantexperiences.com

I am not quite sure if he was the worst waiter I have ever encountered, but he was comically bad. To this day, every time we meet someone named Jeff, we start laughing. It's a running joke in our family. A couple of years ago my wife Jesse and I went to this fancy little restaurant that had just opened in our neighborhood. We were greeted by Jeff.

**Waiter:** Good evening, my name is Jeff. I'll be your server this evening. Can I take your drink order?

**Me:** Give us a couple of minutes to sit down and take a look at the menu, please.

He gave us a big smile and bounced back toward the kitchen. A couple of minutes later, Jeff was back.

**Me:** Jeff, are there any specials today?

**Waiter:** Today we have a lovely grilled branzino with a caper and butter sauce. It comes with pan-roasted baby vegetables and is served on a bed of wild rice.

**Jesse:** Sounds wonderful, I'll have the special.

**Me:** Make that two.

After a few minutes, he returned.

**Waiter:** Oh, I'm sorry, we're all out of the special. You missed out!

Bizarrely enough, Jesse kept smiling like it was completely normal and seemed not to notice anything strange in his behavior. When I finally recovered, I ordered a carbonara and Jesse, not at all upset, the smoked salmon.

**Waiter:** Would you like that hot?

**Jesse:** You mean spicy hot?

**Waiter:** No, hot hot.

**Jesse:** I'm sorry, I don't understand.

**Waiter:** Some people like to eat their salmon cold.

**Jesse:** Um, I ...

**Waiter:** Hey, my shift is over. Could you repeat your order to Melissa? She'll be your server. Have a great night, folks!

Without saying anything else, and just very naturally, he bounced off before we could say a word, leaving us absolutely speechless and terribly hungry.

**Imagine you were the customer in this situation. How would you have reacted?**

**2 Read the questions about restaurant experiences and think about your answers.**

**Have you ever ...**

- **a** had problems with a waiter?
- **b** sent the meal back?
- **c** told the waiter the food was good, but in fact it wasn't very good?
- **d** refused to pay for a meal?
- **e** flirted with the waiter or waitress?
- **f** asked the waiter to send your compliments to the chef?
- **g** decided not to tip the waiter?
- **h** felt annoyed by noisy children sitting near you?
- **i** pointed at the menu to indicate what you wanted because you couldn't pronounce it?
- **j** taken a seat in a restaurant, looked at the menu, realized it was too expensive, and left?

**Discuss the questions with a partner.**

- **Grammar:** Present perfect: simple and progressive. Passives review
- **Vocabulary:** Food collocations. Guessing from context. Linkers. Numbers
- **Language for Life:** Complaints in a restaurant. Food idioms

## READING & VOCABULARY

**1 Read the article and answer: What is the main topic of the text?**

a Ordering food in different countries
b Customs at the table around the world
c Exotic foods and the gourmand

When I was growing up, my mom would give me a hard time about putting my elbows on the table. Little did she know that in France it is considered good table manners. OK, not really good, but accepted if you are conversing between courses. There, they expect you to keep your hands on the table, never under the table or in your lap. Turns out that wherever you go it's a good idea to read up on the dos and don'ts. They vary quite a bit from country to country.
Please be seated, you are about to be served a meal of etiquette!

**1** ______ First of all let's look at utensils, or the lack of utensils in a number of countries. Countries across Africa, the Middle East, and Asia eat with their hands. Be careful to eat with your right hand and never your left hand, which is considered unclean. While there are certain foods that people in the US eat with their hands, like sandwiches and pizza, be aware that it might not be OK in countries that have otherwise similar customs. In Brazil, for instance, pizza is eaten with a knife and fork, and a sandwich needs to be wrapped in a napkin before you pick it up. In Thailand, most food is already bite size and is eaten with a fork and a spoon. The fork guides the food, and the spoon goes to the mouth. When eating noodles, they use chopsticks.

**2** ______ This may seem simple, but it is not always so straightforward. In most countries in the West, the host or honored guest is seated at the head of the table. However, in Japan, the guest of honor sits at the center of the table furthest from the door. If you are in Saudi Arabia, you need to pay attention: some restaurants have family sections where women, children, and men with their families are seated separately from the all-male section. In some African countries, as well as Japan and India, your seat is on the floor. No slouching!

**3** ______ Slurping is considered a compliment in Hong Kong and Japan. And don't be afraid to burp in China, it shows that you are satisfied with the meal. To show your host your appreciation for a good meal in India, lick your fingers! Often a clean plate shows your host that you enjoyed the meal, but this is not a good idea in every culture; in China, it is considered bad manners and a signal to your host that you are still hungry. You should also be very careful about refusing food in many countries across the Middle East, as it is considered offensive.

**4** ______ When the time comes to pick up the check, who pays? Contrary to popular belief, the Dutch do not always "go dutch", or split the bill, but they do most of the time. Countries throughout the globe seem divided about who pays. There are countries like Holland, the US, and Germany where splitting the bill is typical. On the other hand, in Mexico, China, Italy, and Ireland, it is good form to argue over who gets to pay. However you do it, don't leave a tip when you're in Japan or Korea as it is an insult.

**5** ______ Keep in mind that these tips are generalizations and prone to situations that prove to be exceptions to the rule. The best policy is to do some research before you travel, and if you're not sure, you can always ask!

**2 Read the text again and match the paragraph headings below with the numbered paragraphs.**

a Compliments to the Chef!
b The Tools We Use
c When in Doubt, Ask
d Having a Seat
e No Free Lunches

**3 How do you show your appreciation for a good meal in your country? Which ways mentioned in the text would be bad manners where you live?**

### Glossary

**lack** noun [U]: the state of being without, not having
**chopsticks** noun [C]: a pair of small, thin sticks of wood used as eating utensils
**straightforward** adjective: uncomplicated and easy to do or understand.
**slouch** verb [T]: stand, move, or sit in a lazy way; have bad posture
**slurp** verb [T]: eat or drink something, usually liquid, with a loud sloppy sucking noise
**burp** verb [I]: noisily release air from the stomach through the mouth.
**lick** verb [T]: pass the tongue over something, in order to taste or clean it

## LISTENING & VOCABULARY

**1** **Work with a partner. You're going to listen to an interview with Jean Crowshaw, restaurant critic for *The Washington Times*. Think about what her job involves and discuss whether you think the following statements are true or false.**

- **a** She eats out every night of the week.
- **b** She never finishes everything on her plate.
- **c** She takes notes about the restaurant at the table.
- **d** She wears a wig to disguise herself.
- **e** She enjoys writing bad reviews most.
- **f** She always pays for her own meals.
- **g** She doesn't think waiters should ask you if everything's all right.
- **h** She likes waiters who tell you about their favorite items on the menu.
- **i** She enjoyed her best meal ever in an expensive restaurant downtown.

1.54 **Listen and check your ideas.**

**2** **Correct the false statements in Exercise 1. Listen again and check.**

**3** **Jean Crowshaw used the words in the box to talk about her job. Match each word with the appropriate adjective list (a–f) to make typical noun-adjective collocations.**

dish flavor food meal menu plate

- **a** fast / fresh / organic / plain / rich / stodgy / vegetarian _____
- **b** gourmet / heavy / light / ready-made / square / three-course / vegetarian _____
- **c** cold / fish / local / main / regional / serving / vegetarian _____
- **d** clean / dessert / dinner / dirty / paper / plastic / side _____
- **e** bland / distinctive / mild / strong / subtle / unique / unmistakable _____
- **f** à la carte / extensive / lunch / set / varied / vegetarian _____

**Circle the collocations you don't know. Write example sentences for them using a dictionary if necessary.**

*stodgy food = In the winter, I tend to eat more stodgy food, so I always go on a diet in the spring.*

**4** **Work with your partner. Decide which is the best and which is the worst restaurant in your area. Give reasons for your choices.**

## SPEAKING: ANECDOTE

**You are going to tell your partner about your favorite restaurant.**

- Ask yourself the questions below.
- Think about *what* to say and *how* to say it.
- Tell your partner about your favorite restaurant.

- **a** What's the restaurant called and where is it?
- **b** What type of restaurant is it: a family business? A chain ...?
- **c** What's the interior like?
- **d** What's the atmosphere like?
- **e** What do the waiters and waitresses wear?
- **f** What kind of food do they serve?
- **g** What's the service like?
- **h** How often do you go there?
- **i** When was the last time you went?
- **j** Who did you go with and what did you have?

## GRAMMAR

1 **Look at this extract from the interview with Jean Crowshaw on page 62. Name the tenses of the verbs in bold and choose the best description (a–c) for each one.**

*Well, I've **been working** for newspapers for more than twenty years. I **started** out as a journalist when I was twenty-three, and I**'ve worked** for several newspapers since then ...*

- **a** The action is **finished**. It happened at a **specified point** in the past. You **know** exactly **when**.
- **b** The action is **finished**. It happened at an **unspecified point** in the past. You **don't know** exactly **when**.
- **c** The action is **unfinished**. It started in the past and is **in progress** now. You usually know **how long**.

2 **Use the same tense sequence as the extract in Exercise 1 to make three sentences about yourself: two true sentences and one false one. Write about your work, your studies, your hobbies, your habits, etc.**

I ... (something you've been doing).

I ... (when or how you started).

I ... (a thing or things you've done – or haven't done – in that time).

*I've been driving for several years. I got my driver's license when I was eighteen. I've never driven abroad.*

**Work with a partner. Read your sentences out. Your partner guesses which is the false sentence.**

**Present perfect: simple and progressive**

Verbs describing actions or processes.
I**'ve made** dinner.
I**'ve been making** dinner.

Verbs describing single actions.
I**'ve cut** myself. (NOT ~~I've been cutting myself.~~)

Verbs describing states.
I**'ve had** that knife for years. (NOT ~~I've been having that knife for years.~~)

3 **Look at these sentence pairs. Underline the most appropriate form in each case. Discuss your answers with your partner.**

1 **a** I've **learned** / **been learning** how to make paella. It comes out perfectly every time.
  **b** I've **learned** / **been learning** how to make paella. But I still overcook the rice.

2 **a** I've **read** / **been reading** that new diet book. You can borrow it if you want.
  **b** I've **read** / **been reading** that new diet book. I'm on the last chapter.

3 **a** Have you **eaten** / **been eating** my birthday cake? There's only a tiny bit left!
  **b** Have you **eaten** / **been eating** my birthday cake? There's none left!

4 **a** I've **worked** / **been working** in a grocery store. I didn't like it very much.
  **b** I've **worked** / **been working** in a grocery store. I need the extra cash.

4 **The present perfect progressive can also describe an action which has *just* finished, especially when the results of the action are still evident. Look at the pictures (a–d) and describe what has been happening.**

a

b

c

d

5 **Verbs describing single actions or states are very rare in the progressive form. Discuss why the following sentences sound strange or wrong.**

- **a** **I've always been hating** mushrooms. I just can't eat them.
- **b** **I've been stopping** watching TV shows about food.
- **c** **I've been deciding** I should try and eat more healthily.
- **d** **I've been cutting myself** several times with the bread knife over the years.
- **e** **I've been having** the same dining table and chairs for years now.
- **f** **I've never been understanding** why people become vegetarian.

**Rewrite the sentences using the simple form. Are any of the sentences true for you?**

6 **Grammar Extra 6, Part 1** page 144. Read the explanations and do Exercises 1 and 2.

## READING & VOCABULARY

**1 Work in small groups and make a list of how you think food and food customs will change in the future. Think about the following questions:**

- **a** Are there foods that have become more or less popular in your lifetime?
- **b** Considering the impact of technology, globalization, and health, how do you think food might change in the future?
- **c** Which is more important, having access to exotic foods from around the world or having access to fresh locally-grown foods?

# Food Trends

We live at a time when we've come to expect novelty in our daily lives. This goes for the world of food, too, resulting in food trends from the exotic to the down-to-earth, from 100% natural to high-tech, from the brilliant to the questionable. Let's look at what to expect this year in the world of food.

An idea that has been growing in popularity over the past decade is farm-to-table dining. Instead of purchasing food from large corporations, restaurants are involved in the entire process of putting food on your plate. In other words, restaurants grow their own food or source in-season produce from small local growers, guaranteeing the freshest food. What's more, farm-to-table is sustainable as it eliminates the need for long distance transportation. Another environmentally friendly trend is the creative use of food that would typically be lost or wasted to create viable gourmet dishes. This could include using "trash fish" or traditionally unpopular fish which fisherman discard, or re-purposing stale popcorn to make popcorn ice cream.

The world of technology will change the food of the future, but it's already hitting home today. Concerned about your weight, but not

ready to give up your French fries? Many are turning to hot air fryers. The device creates a crunchy outer layer without using oil. As a result, you can have the fried foods you love without the calories or the cholesterol. The next big technological advance may be printed food. That's right, the technology to print food using a 3D printer with edible paste as "ink" already exists. Why would you want to print food? First and foremost, convenience. You get home at the end of long day and, instead of spending an hour making dinner, you push a button and presto! Secondly, the possibility of customization at the touch of a finger will make special orders a snap. In fact, pizza, crackers, and baked goods have already been successfully printed.

Closer to the present, other food trends are re-defining our relationship to food and to each other. Some restaurants are experimenting with a return to the past by seating customers communally, that is, sharing tables. This is already a fairly common practice in Japan and Germany. Not only does this permit restaurants to fully use the available space, but it also allows for interesting opportunities for interaction between strangers. Yet another trend that may seem strange to others is tactile food. We have always wanted our food to taste delicious and for a long time have liked our food to be beautiful, but does it also feel and sound good? The movement for tactile food aims to involve all the senses. What's more, tactile food is also seen to have therapeutic applications for children who are picky eaters.

Finally, a food trend that has been picking up speed recently is the raw water trend. Raw water is water that is untreated, unfiltered, and unsterilized. Proponents of the trend say that the water not only tastes better and is more refreshing, but it also provides important minerals and bacteria without chemicals like chlorine and fluoride. However, the jury is still out on raw water. Some critics worry that untreated water could carry harmful bacteria, viruses, parasites, and carcinogens. They also contend that fluoride is essential to good dental health.

In summary, the future holds many intriguing possibilities for the gourmand and the common consumer alike. Only time will tell which trends are here to stay.

### Glossary

- **a** **trend** noun [C]: a general direction in which something is developing or changing
- **b** ______ adjective: making a sharp noise when bitten or crushed
- **c** ______ phrase: a decision has not yet been reached on a controversial subject
- **d** ______ adjective: of or connected with the sense of touch
- **e** ______ noun [U]: things that have been produced or grown, especially by farming
- **f** ______ adjective: uncooked or unprocessed
- **g** ______ adjective: capable of working successfully
- **h** ______ adjective: no longer fresh and good to eat; hard or dry
- **i** ______ noun [C]: an easy task
- **j** ______ adjective: liking only a few things; difficult to please
- **k** ______ verb [T]: get rid of something that is no longer useful or desirable
- **l** ______ noun [C]: the quality of being new, original, or unusual

**2 Look at the words and phrases highlighted in yellow in the article. Try to guess the meaning from the context and then complete the glossary.**

**3 Which of the trends are being adopted in your country? Which of the trends do you find strange and which do you think are useful? Discuss with a partner.**

## VOCABULARY & WRITING

**1 Use all the linkers in the table below to complete the summary of the article on page 64. Some linkers can go in more than one place.**

| Organizing ideas | Adding more information | Connecting or contrasting ideas | Showing cause and effect | Concluding |
|---|---|---|---|---|
| | Furthermore | however<br>even though<br>Although | so<br>Consequently | To sum up |

The author writes about the latest food trends. He says that farm-to-table restaurants focus on serving fresh food. **a** ______, they cut down on pollution and transportation costs as the food is grown locally.
Another trend is air fryers, which are replacing frying with oil. **b** ______ , people don't have to sacrifice fried foods in order to reduce their cholesterol intake. **c** ______ 3D food printing will allow users to print food instantly and make specialized orders easily, at present it is still limited in use. With respect to the social aspects of food, communal seating involves using all available space by seating strangers together **d** ______ restaurants can maximize profits and provide a unique dining experience. Tactile eating promises to engage all the consumer's senses in the eating experience, **e** ______ it might not be for everyone. Finally, he addresses the question of raw water. **f** ______ some say that raw water tastes great and is good for you; others question if that is really the case. **g** ______, food trends present some interesting possibilities but they may not last.

**2 There are ten more linkers highlighted in blue in the article on page 64. Add each of them to an appropriate column in the table in Exercise 1.**

**3 Read this article about becoming a vegetarian and underline the correct linker (a–k).**

https://foodchoices.com

I have always known that I could become a vegetarian if I wanted to. I'm not a big meat person. If you ask me where I want to eat tonight, a steakhouse would be right down at the bottom of the list. **a However / Furthermore**, thinking about giving up meat and actually doing it are two different things. Recently, I've decided to take the plunge and try it. I've been looking into the subject and here are my main reasons for giving up meat.

**b In other words / The first reason** is the question of sustainability. Compared to growing grain, raising beef costs much more per kilo, and requires much more land. Cattle also expel vast quantities of methane. **c As a result, / Although** the production of beef has an extremely negative impact on the environment. **d What's more / So,** the consumption of beef worldwide is on the rise, which suggests that the impact will only grow over time. **e Even though / In other words,** giving up meat is the same as being kind to the environment.

**f Secondly / On the other hand,** there is the question of cruelty to animals. You don't have to look very far to find horrible examples of animal cruelty. There have been a number of documentaries in recent years that focus on what happens behind the scenes in the slaughterhouses because people just don't know the reality. **g In fact / However,** most of us have so little understanding of how animals are slaughtered that we don't associate eating meat with killing an animal.

**h Finally / To sum up,** in my view being a vegetarian is better for my health. Vegetarians generally consume less saturated fat , so their cholesterol levels tend to be lower than those who eat meat.

**i Furthermore / So,** vegetarians tend to have lower blood pressure and a lower body mass index. All of this is correlated with living longer.

**j Consequently, / But** there are some things that vegetarians need to keep in mind. Certain vitamins, like Vitamin B12, are only found in animal products, so it is suggested that vegetarians take a supplement. Other substances that should be monitored are protein, iron, zinc, and omega 3. Fortunately, there is almost always a way a vegetarian can supplement a deficiency and keep to a vegetarian diet.

**k As a result / To sum up,** there are many good reasons to become a vegetarian.

**Glossary**

**take the plunge** phrase: commit oneself to a course of action about which one is nervous.

**cattle** noun [U]: large farm animals, domesticated for meat or milk

**slaughterhouse** noun [C]: a place where animals are killed for food.

# What a Waste!

It has never been easier to eat whatever you want whenever you want. But, here's something that might make you lose your appetite: the amount of food that is wasted. Here are a few numbers to chew on:

- Every year roughly 990 billion dollars of food is wasted or lost globally.
- Approximately one-third of all food that is produced is lost or wasted, including 45% of fruits, vegetables, roots, and tubers.
- On average, 10 billion apples and 2.7 million bags of potatoes are thrown away per day.
- 8% of all fish caught, mostly dead or damaged, is thrown right back into the sea, and in total 35% is lost or wasted.
- The food wasted in Latin America could feed 300 million people. For comparison, the population of Brazil, the 5$^{th}$ most populous country in the world, is 209 million.

The problem in the developing world is food loss. This is when food is lost due to problems during harvesting and processing, perhaps because of equipment problems, or during transportation because of poor infrastructure. Food loss is unintentional. These countries have extremely low levels of food waste. In wealthy countries, food loss is low but food waste is high. Food waste results from the consumer throwing out unwanted food, or from supermarkets refusing food that does not meet aesthetic standards or throwing out food that is past its use-by date, which is a result of overstocking. In the US, Canada, Australia, and New Zealand, 39% of all food is wasted.

It should come as no surprise that these distinct realities create distinct health problems. For example, the number of undernourished people in the world is on the rise again, after a long period of decline. In 2016, 815 million people, or 10.8% of people on the planet, fell into this category. That is up from 777 million people in 2015. When we break the undernourishment rates down, there is a glaring disparity: in North America and Europe the rate is under 5%, whereas in Sub-Saharan Africa almost 19% of the population is undernourished.

On the other hand, global obesity is at an all-time high at 12.8%. When we pull these numbers apart, we see that the obesity rate in Asia is 7.4%, compared to 27.7% in Europe and North America. If we look just at the United States, the adult obesity rate jumps to 36.5%.

What can we conclude about how to combat food waste and loss? Evidently, food loss demands a different approach from food waste. In the developing world, the problems are much more significant because of their impact on the nourishment of the population, and potentially costly because solutions would require investment all along the food supply chain in areas such as infrastructure, transportation, storage, and market facilities.

In wealthy countries, combatting food waste is potentially trickier because a large percentage of initiative involves increasing awareness across entire populations, that is, they require the participation of everyone. Some specific solutions include:

- educational campaigns to change consumers' attitudes to food and create better food habits
- redirecting food that would be wasted from producers and supermarkets to needy populations
- continued development of apps that connect farmers, producers, and restaurants with charitable organizations
- re-thinking and improving use-by dates on packages

Are you ready to play your part?

## READING

1 **Work with a partner. Read the statistics about food waste on page 66 and guess which is the correct number in each case.**

1 The fraction of food produced in the world which is wasted or lost:
**a** 1/4 **b** 1/3 **c** 1/2

2 The value of food wasted or lost globally per year:
**a** $90 billion **b** $990 billion **c** $9 trillion

3 The percentage of adults classified as obese in the United States:
**a** less than 20% **b** around 35% **c** more than 40%

4 The number of apples thrown away around the globe every day:
**a** 10 billion **b** 15 billion **c** 18 billion

5 The number of people who could be fed with the food wasted or lost in Latin America:
**a** 800,000 **b** 3,000,000 **c** 300,000,000

**Read the article and check your ideas.**

2 **Work in groups. Discuss the questions.**

**a** What kinds of food do people throw away and what happens to the waste in your country?
**b** How much food does your own family throw away in a typical week?
**c** What do you think you can do in your day-to-day life to reduce food waste?

## GRAMMAR

1 **Use the words in the box to complete the information from the article on page 66.**

lose day date tubers sea

The study found that ...

**a** people most commonly wasted fruits, vegetables, roots, and ______.
**b** people threw away 10 billion apples on average each ______.
**c** people throw about 8% of all fish directly back into the ______.
**d** people in Canada, New Zealand, Australia, and the US wasted 39% of food in part because it was past it's "use-by" ______.
**e** people waste or ______ roughly 990 billion dollars of food a year.

**Rewrite the information using passive structures for the underlined verbs. Check your ideas in the article. Why are passive structures preferred in the article?**

**Passives review**

*be* + past participle

It**'s being wasted.**
It**'s been thrown away.**
It **could have been recycled.**

2 **Grammar Extra 6, Part 2** page 144. Read the explanations and do Exercise 3.

## PRONUNCIATION & VOCABULARY

1 **Say the numbers in the box and categorize them in the table.**

01/01/1901 99.9 4/5 246,813,579 207-419-3211 53rd

| Cardinal numbers | Ordinal numbers | Fractions | Decimals | Dates | Telephone numbers |
|---|---|---|---|---|---|
| | | | | | |

1.55 **Listen, check, and repeat.**

2 1.56 **Listen and write one more number in each column in the table in Exercise 1. Practice saying them.**

3 1.57 **Listen and write down three different ways of saying *O*. Match each way of saying *O* with an appropriate situation (1–3).**

**1** the temperature **2** a year **3** a tennis match score

**Numbers review**

Cardinal: **1,234,567**
Ordinal: **42nd**
Fraction: **1/2**
Decimal: **0.125**
Date: **11/27/01**
Telephone: **307-918-7791**

Ways of saying *O*: **love, oh, zero.**
Years: **2009** (two thousand and nine OR twenty oh nine). BUT 2010 = two thousand and ten OR twenty ten.

## LANGUAGE FOR LIFE

**1 What kinds of things do people complain about in restaurants? Match the items (a–d) with words from the box. Use your dictionary if necessary.**

- **a** The service
- **b** The lighting
- **c** The food
- **d** The other customers

> bland bright dark (un)helpful noisy bad overcooked overdone rude slow

1.58 **Listen to the conversation and note any of the complaints you thought of.**

**2 Complete the useful phrases with words from the box in Exercise 1.**

- **a** The service is very _____ this evening.
- **b** It's so _____ in here that we can't read the menu.
- **c** I'm afraid this steak is _____ .
- **d** I think the scallops are _____ .

1.59 **Listen and repeat. Have you ever complained about anything in a restaurant? Tell your partner about it.**

**3 Replace the underlined phrases (a–e) with the idioms (1–5) from the conversation.**

- **a** He's an important person in the hotel industry.
- **b** If you're really nice to him, he'll give you a nice big tip.
- **c** He thinks he's the best.
- **d** I feel like I need to be really careful.
- **e** You have to give it all less importance.

1. you butter him up
2. take it all with a grain of salt
3. I'm walking on eggshells
4. the greatest thing since sliced bread
5. a big cheese

**Check your answers in the Audioscript on page 152.**

**4 Tell your partner about ...**

- someone who's a big cheese in your world.
- a time when you had to butter someone up.
- the kind of thing that makes you turn as red as a beet.
- someone you know who's a smart cookie.

### LIFE SKILLS: Empathy

**Turning off and Tuning in**

It is not uncommon nowadays to see people walking down the street or driving their cars and messaging at the same time. Or we can be talking to a friend, and at the same time they are surfing the internet. Not all lack of attention, however, can be blamed on technology. Have you ever found yourself preparing what you are going to say next instead of really listening to what is being said? Or maybe you have given someone the "uh huh" treatment when they were telling you a story. It has become a challenge to slow down and be truly present instead of jumping ahead or jumping to conclusions. We need to turn off our electronic devices and learn to listen fully and intently, without distracting thoughts – to give others our complete and undivided attention. Have you ever assumed the worst about someone, only to find out later that there was a perfectly good reason for why they were doing what they were doing?

- **Try this exercise in giving people the benefit of the doubt. For each of the situations suggest an alternative and more understanding explanation for why someone has done something to annoy you. Work in pairs.**

| The Situation | Initial Impression | Other Possible Explanations |
| --- | --- | --- |
| Guy who cut you off in traffic. | *He's a jerk!* | *He's having a medical emergency.* |
| Doctor is late for appointment. | | |
| Student has not done his homework. | | |
| Partner forgot your birthday. | | |

**Think of some annoying situations that have happened to you and see if you can find an alternative explanation.**

MACMILLAN LIFE SKILLS

# 6 Writing Extra

## EXPLORING SYNONYMS

1 **Work with a partner. Look at these ways of saying that you're hungry. Order each expression from *least* hungry (1) to *most* hungry (4).**

☐ "I'm absolutely ravenous."  ☐ "I'm famished."

☐ "I'm hungry."  ☐ "I'm starving."

**Read the dictionary extract to check your ideas.**

2 **Which two verbs in the box go with all six noun phrases (a–f)?**

chew eat grab have munch nibble

a ______ breakfast
b ______ lunch
c ______ dinner
d ______ a snack
e ______ something to eat
f ______ a bite (to eat)

**Which verb would you use to suggest that you only have a short time to eat?**

3 **Think of three ...**

a items of food you would never have for breakfast.
b places nearby where you could grab a bite if you were in a hurry.
c items of food you can nibble.
d items of food you can chew.
e items of food you can munch.
f times of year when some people might "stuff themselves."

**Compare your ideas with your partner.**

4 **Think of other ways of saying *fat* and *thin*. Complete the table based on the information in the dictionary extracts.**

| FAT | | THIN | |
|---|---|---|---|
| **positive** | **negative** | **positive** | **negative** |
| plump | big, large | slim | skinny |
| ______ | ______ | ______ | ______ |
| | ______ | ______ | ______ |
| | ______ | ______ | ______ |
| | | | ______ |

5 **Work with your partner. Decide which word or words in the table in Exercise 4 you might use to describe ...**

a a healthy baby.
b an extreme medical condition.
c somebody who looks good because of exercise.
d somebody who looks extremely thin because of illness or lack of food.

6 **Check your own dictionary. Which synonyms does it give for *hungry*, *eat*, *fat*, and *thin*? Look for other ways of saying *cook*.**

### Other ways of saying **hungry**

**starving** or **starved** (*informal*) very hungry and wanting to eat immediately: *Have you got any bread? I'm starving!*

**ravenous** extremely hungry, especially because you have not eaten for a long time or you have been doing a lot of physical work: *The kids are always ravenous after swimming practice.*

**famished** extremely hungry, especially because you have not eaten for a long time: *Can we order now? I'm famished.*

### Other ways of saying **eat**

**have breakfast/lunch/dinner** to eat a particular meal: *Have you had breakfast yet?* ♦ *He called while we were having lunch.*

**have something to eat** to eat something or to have a meal: *We'll stop and have something to eat when we get into town.*

**snack/have a snack** to eat something small between your main meals: *We usually have a drink and a snack around 11.* ♦ *No snacking, now!*

**grab a bite (to eat)** (*informal*) to eat a snack or small meal when you do not have much time: *Maybe we could grab a bite at Charlie's before the movie.*

**eat up** to finish all the food you have been given: *Eat up! There's plenty more.*

**nibble (at)** to take very small bites from your food: *She nibbled at her sandwich politely, waiting for the others to arrive.*

**chew (on)** to use your teeth to break food up slowly in your mouth: *He was chewing on a piece of celery.*

**munch** to eat something noisily and enthusiastically: *The kids were munching potato chips in front of the TV.*

**stuff yourself** (*informal*) to eat so much that you feel sick or uncomfortable: *I'm not surprised you feel lousy, the way you stuffed yourself last night.*

### Other ways of saying **fat**

**plump** slightly fat in a way that looks nice: *a plump friendly-looking man in his forties*

**chubby** used especially for describing babies and children who look fat in a healthy attractive way: *a chubby little boy*

**big** or **large** used for suggesting that someone is a little fatter than they should be or than they usually are, especially if they are also tall: *The driver was a big man with bright red hair.*

**dumpy** short and fat: *But I look so plain and dumpy in the uniform!*

**overweight** fatter than doctors think is healthy for someone of a particular height: *You risk heart disease if you are overweight and don't exercise regularly.*

**obese** very fat, especially in a way that might be dangerous to your health: *In some parts of the country, 15% of the population is now considered to be obese.*

### Other ways of saying **thin**

**slim** thin in an attractive way: *He was looking much slimmer after his vacation.*

**slender** thin in a graceful way: *a tall slender woman in her late 40s*

**skinny** (*informal*) too thin: *a skinny little boy of about eight*

**anorexic** extremely thin in a way that does not look healthy, also used by doctors to describe someone who has the illness ANOREXIA NERVOSA: *He must have been dieting – he was looking positively anorexic!*

**lean** thin and strong: *a lean man wearing a cowboy hat*

**emaciated** extremely thin because you have been sick or do not have enough to eat: *emaciated children holding out bowls for food*

**trim** thin in a way that suggests you are careful about what you eat and how much you exercise: *His trim figure made him look younger than he was.*

**gaunt** so thin that people can see your bones under your skin: *His face was gaunt with lack of sleep.*

**bony** so thin that people can see your bones under your skin: *long bony limbs that never seemed to fit his clothes*

From the *Macmillan English Dictionary (American edition)*

# Review B

▶ Grammar Extra pages 142-145

## GRAMMAR

**1 Underline the correct alternatives.**

Some friends and I (1) **were deciding / decided** to explore the forest on the north-east coast of Australia. I was the experienced one - I (2) **traveled / had traveled** around the world, and my friends (3) **were counting / had counted** on me. After all, I (4) **was living / had been living** in Australia for ages.

As soon as we arrived, I (5) **picked / had picked** up a long stick and marched purposefully into the rainforest. As I (6) **was cutting / had been cutting** my way through the forest, I (7) **heard / had heard** the sound of a large animal. And it (8) **was coming / had been coming** towards me! Was it a wild pig? Or a crocodile!? Suddenly, it appeared - a giant lizard. My friend and I (9) **looked / had looked** at each other for one second. Our other friends, who (10) **put / had been putting** up the tent, (11) **were hearing / heard** me before they (12) **were seeing / saw** me. I came running out of the forest screaming like a baby, effectively ending my reputation as an intrepid explorer.

**2 Make true sentences about what you will be doing at these times tomorrow. Use the future progressive.**

- **a** 7:15 a.m.
- **b** 10:20 a.m.
- **c** 1:20 p.m.
- **d** 8:10 p.m.
- **e** 1:10 a.m. (of the following day)

**Compare your sentences with a partner. How many of your sentences are the same?**

**3 Check (✓) the sentences in which the bold words are possible. Correct the sentences which are not possible.**

- **a** I**'ll** often go out for a walk with friends.
- **b** I**'d** have blond, curly hair when I was a baby.
- **c** Most days I **used to** work until 8:00 p.m. I'm always exhausted.
- **d** When I was younger, I**'d** go out every evening.
- **e** I**'ll** like watching horror movies.
- **f** I **didn't use to** like spinach, but I do now.

**Which sentences are true for you? Compare with your partner.**

**4 Complete the sentences with the verbs in parentheses in the gerund or infinitive form.**

- **a** I'll never forget (see) _____ the first moon landing.
- **b** I always stop (buy) _____ a newspaper before my English class.
- **c** I never forget (call) _____ my mom on her birthday.
- **d** I've tried (eat) _____ seafood, but I really don't like it.

**Check (✓) the sentences that are true for you.**

**5 Read the conversation between an interviewer (I) and Chef Louis (CL). Underline the correct uses of the present perfect progressive. Change the incorrect uses to the simple form.**

**I:** Chef Louis, good job on your new restaurant.

**CL:** Thank you. (1) **I've been dreaming** of this day for a very long time. Yes, (2) **I've been working** for some of the best chefs in the world and now, finally, I have my own place.

**I:** When and where did you start your career?

**CL:** I started in a small restaurant in France when I was just sixteen. You know, (3) **I've been cooking** for a very long time.

**I:** Tell me: what's the worst accident that (4) **has been happening** to you in all that time?

**CL:** Well, nothing disastrous fortunately, but (5) **I've been cutting** my finger more times than I can remember!

**I:** Tell us about your life in the USA.

**CL:** Well, (6) **I've been living** here since 1992. And in that time (7) **I've been having** some wonderful experiences. I'm very happy here.

**I:** And so tell us about your restaurant.

**CL:** (8) **I've always been loving** food. It's my passion. In my restaurant we have food from all over the world. I have a new chef, Yoshi Ikeda. (9) **He's been teaching** me some techniques from Japan. And (10) **I've been having** lessons from another fantastic chef from Thailand. Come and try our new dishes!

**I:** I'd love to. Chef Louis, (11) **I've been enjoying** talking to you today. Thank you for your time.

## VOCABULARY

**1 Match each word part with the prefix *self-* or the suffix *ible/able* to form words.**

| | | |
|---|---|---|
| self- | **a** conscious<br>**b** reason<br>**c** employed<br>**d** vis<br>**e** do<br>**f** unbear<br>**g** discipline<br>**h** ed | ible / able |

**2 Complete the sentences with the verbs in the box in the correct tense.**

> call feel get give
> keep let pick take

**a** It took Neil a long time to ______ over being sick.
**b** I was counting on him, but he really ______ me down.
**c** I'm going to ______ up tennis. I need to get in shape again.
**d** I hate it when you leave someone a message and they don't ______ you back.
**e** I never had formal guitar classes. I just ______ it up.
**f** I'm getting old. I can't ______ up with the new fashions.
**g** She's become a vegetarian. She's ______ up eating meat and fish completely.
**h** I don't ______ up to going to the gym today.

**3 Complete the words associated with weddings.**

**a** b r__d__
**b** g r___m
**c** b__s t m__n
**d** c__n f__t t__
**e** v___l
**f** h__n__y m___n
**g** b r__d__s m___d
**h** v__w s
**i** p r__p__s__ a t___s t
**j** w__d d__n g c__k__
**k** b___q___t __f f l__w__r s

**4 Underline the correct verbs.**

**a** **Raise** / **Stick** your tongue out.
**b** **Hold** / **Clench** your hand up.
**c** **Stick** / **Bend** your knees.
**d** **Bend** / **Shake** your head.

**5 ~~Cross out~~ the incorrect adjective in each sentence.**

**a** I usually eat **gourmet** / **three-course** / **vegetarian** food.
**b** I don't like food with a **bland** / **hard** / **strong** flavor.
**c** When I travel, I always like to try out the **local** / **regional** / **unmistakable** dishes.
**d** The restaurant has a **set** / **fast** / **varied** menu.

**Change the adjectives to make the sentences true for you. Compare with your partner.**

**6 Write an answer to each question.**

**a** When is your birthday? (*day/month/year*)
**b** How many children do your parents have? (*cardinal number*) What position do you come in the family? (*ordinal number*)
**c** What's your cell phone number?
**d** What's the population of your country?
**e** As a fraction, what is the number of left-handed people in your family (e.g. 1 in 4 = $^1/_4$)? What is this as a percentage (e.g. 1 in 4 = 25%)?

**Work with your partner. Read out your answers to each other.**

## PRONUNCIATION

**1 Look at some words from Units 4-6. Say the words and add them to the table.**

> ~~candlelight~~ competition expedition
> hazardous however invitation
> neighborhood organic organized
> reception superstitious tomato

| A: □□□ | B: □□□ | C: □□□□ |
|---|---|---|
| candlelight | | – |

**2 Underline the stressed syllable.**

1.60 **Listen, check, and repeat.**

# 7 Escape

## READING & VOCABULARY

**1 Work in small groups. Discuss the questions.**

- **a** What words and images do you associate with the word *beach*?
- **b** Have you ever lived on or near the beach? Where? When?
- **c** What kinds of things might spoil living on or near the beach? Make a list.

**Read the personal account of a family's decision on whether to live on the beach or not on page 73. How many of the things you listed in *c* above does the author mention?**

**2 Are the statements true or false? Compare your answers with a partner.**

- **a** The author ...
  - enjoys the prospect of living near the beach.
  - doesn't want to move to Barbados.
  - is originally from Scotland.
- **b** The author's wife ...
  - wants to move to Barbados.
  - is supportive of her daughter's idea.
  - grew up near the beach.
- **c** The author's daughter Amanda ...
  - enjoys the prospect of living near the beach.
  - hates the cold.
  - finally gets her way and moves to Barbados.

**3 Read each definition and complete the corresponding phrase from the extract. Check the text if necessary.**

- **a** Go for a quick swim = go for a d_____
- **b** Refuse very firmly to do something = put your f_____ d_____
- **c** Think of a solution that both sides would accept = to come up with a c_____
- **d** A small flat boat you fill with air = an inflatable r_____
- **e** Eat something by taking a lot of small bites = n_____ on (a piece of fresh fruit)
- **f** Take a short sleep during the day = take a n_____

**Write your own example sentence for each phrase. Use a dictionary if necessary.**

**4 Is your attitude toward beaches similar to a) the author's or b) the author's daughter's attitude? Discuss with your partner.**

- **Grammar:** Reporting verbs. Past modals. Articles
- **Vocabulary:** Beach vacations. Reporting verbs. Word formation. Spoken discourse markers
- **Language for Life:** Advice and recommendations

https://mypersonalblog.lifeeverywhere.com/life-on-the-beach476&89

# Life on the Beach

*A little over a year ago, my then twelve-year-old daughter soberly said that she would be moving to Barbados to live with her grandparents. After taking a micro-second to compose myself, I decided to tread lightly until I could better understand what had prompted such a radical announcement. "Really Amanda? Why?" I asked nonchalantly.*

*"It's just too cold here; I can't stand it anymore!" responded my Scottish born and bred daughter. Except for our annual two-week vacations in Barbados with my parents and one week somewhere like Spain, Italy, or Greece in the summer, Amanda has known nothing but the cold and rainy weather in Scotland her whole life. "It's just that growing up on the beach is so much fun … and warm!" she said.*

*I understand the allure of the warm weather and growing up by the beach. Long, lazy days, going for a dip in the ocean before heading to school, nibbling on a piece of fresh fruit, and taking a nap to the sound of the surf are just a few of the delights of living near the beach. I grew up in Barbados after all, so I know what I'm talking about. And while it might seem like paradise on earth, Amanda needed to consider the cons as well.*

*"OK, I understand your point of view, but don't you think it's a bit radical for us to move to Barbados? Have you thought about the implications?"*

*Having lived in Barbados until twenty years of age, I knew that life near the beach was not as idyllic as it may seem on TV, in a magazine, or even on a two-week vacation. First of all, in warm, tropical places there are lots of bugs and insects. Because of the salt from the sea, houses, cars, and furniture corrode much more easily, so there is a lot of work to keep everything free of salt. The cost of living can be higher, especially during the high season when we have a lot of tourists. Most importantly however, there is always the risk of hurricanes. While my fear may seem irrational, I lived through Hurricane Ivan in 2004. For others it may have been just a slightly more serious weather event, but for me it was a life changing experience. To see the roofs blown off houses and everything my parents had worked for destroyed in a matter of hours affected me so deeply that I moved abroad in a matter of months.*

*But of course, my daughters and my wife had never experienced anything like this, and pretty soon Amanda's idea of moving to Barbados became the hot topic at home. Even my wife was thinking seriously about the possibility. At that point I put my foot down - there would be no move to Barbados. Despite the wonderful warm weather and the chance to be closer to family, a move would be too expensive, too disruptive, and for me, at least, the disadvantages of living by the beach outweighed the advantages. But I also understood Amanda's point of view, so we came up with a compromise. Starting the following summer, Amanda and her sister would spend the entire two month school break in Barbados. And we would continue to spend our Christmases there as well. This way, the girls could be closer to their cousins and get to experience beach life without having to permanently move there.*

*After that initial scary announcement last year and the ensuing discussions and negotiations, the girls have just returned from their first summer in Barbados. They have a greater appreciation for family and island living. To my surprise, Amanda immediately complained that the island was absolutely run over with British tourists (did she think she was a local?), that their lovely ice creams had become more expensive in August (what did she expect?), and that it was more difficult to get into the teen matinee that they frequented on the weekends. Chuckling to myself I thought "Nothing like experience to open one's eyes."*

*As for me though, their excitement, and even their complaints, brought back some of the best memories of my own teenage years. Who knows, maybe next year you might even see me relaxing on one of those calm beaches, floating away on an inflatable raft, sunglasses on, icy fruit juice in one hand and the latest best-seller in the other. Maybe!*

## VOCABULARY & GRAMMAR

**1 Look at this summary of the personal account on page 73. Put the lines in the correct order.**

- [ ] the cons of living near the beach. I **explained** my
- [1] A little over a year ago, my twelve-year-old daughter **announced**
- [ ] that she could understand my point of view as well.
- [ ] own experience of growing up on the beach, but in the end, came up with a compromise by **suggesting**
- [ ] Scotland was too cold and rainy.
- [ ] her, but also felt it necessary to **mention**
- [2] that she would be moving to Barbados. She **insisted** that
- [ ] that she spend the summer holidays in Barbados. After her return, my daughter **confessed**
- [ ] me. I understood her point of view, I **reassured**
- [ ] "Growing up on the beach is more fun," she tried to **persuade**

**2 All of the verbs in bold in Exercise 1 are used to report messages. Divide them into list A and list B according to the headings.**

| **A** "*tell* verbs": where the hearer is usually the direct object | **B** "*say* verbs": where the hearer is not usually the direct object |
|---|---|
| ... persuade me to ... | ... mentioned that ... |

**3 Add more reporting verbs from the box to the appropriate column in the table in Exercise 2. Check the verb patterns in your dictionary if necessary.**

admit advise assure claim confirm convince encourage

2.02 **Listen to five people talking about their favorite beach. Notice how the verbs in the box are used and confirm your answers.**

## SPEAKING: ANECDOTE

**You are going to tell your partner about a family vacation you went on as a child.**

- Ask yourself the questions below.
- Think about *what* to say and *how* to say it.
- Tell your partner about the family vacation.

**a** Where did you go?
**b** Who chose the destination?
**c** Had you been to the same place before?
**d** Who went on this vacation with you?
**e** How did you get there and how long did it take?
**f** Where did you stay?
**g** Was it a good place for a vacation? Why? / Why not?
**h** How did you spend your time there?
**i** Who enjoyed the vacation most?
**j** Have you been back to the same place since you were a child?

## LISTENING & GRAMMAR

**1 Work with a partner. Look at the pictures of three different vacations and discuss what kind of things might go wrong on vacations like these.**

Sarah and Paul in Canada

Amy and Josh in Guatemala

Rachel in Spain

2.03-2.05 **Listen to the three experiences and compare your ideas with what actually happened. Answer the questions.**

**a** Who shouldn't have ignored expert advice?
**b** Who should have checked the weather forecast?
**c** Who should have double-checked their travel itinerary?

**2 Work with your partner. Underline the two modal verbs or phrases (*a*, *b*, or *c*) which are appropriate to complete each sentence. ~~Cross out~~ the answer which is not appropriate.**

**1** Sarah and Paul _____ go skiing on the black runs.
**a** couldn't **b** weren't allowed to **c** didn't need to
**2** Sarah and Paul _____ get up early to go skiing.
**a** weren't allowed to **b** didn't have to **c** didn't need to
**3** Amy _____ go on vacation to Guatemala alone.
**a** wasn't allowed to **b** couldn't **c** didn't have to
**4** Amy and Josh _____ return to Miami before they could fly to Guatemala.
**a** needed to **b** could **c** had to
**5** Rachel didn't think she _____ buy a pair of padded cycling shorts.
**a** was allowed to **b** had to **c** needed to
**6** Rachel _____ have listened to the man in the bike store.
**a** should **b** ought to **c** shouldn't

**Past modals**

We **had to go** via Miami.

We **couldn't take** much luggage.

You **didn't need to fly**.

You **should have come** by train.

We **weren't allowed to change** our tickets.

We **ought to have booked** earlier.

**Listen again and check your answers. Check (✓) the modal verb or phrase (*a*, *b*, or *c*) that is actually used in the recordings.**

**3 Which modal verbs or phrases in Exercise 1 and 2 can you use to say it was ...**

**a** necessary for you to do something?
*I had to / needed to ...*
**b** not necessary for you to do something?
**c** permitted for you to do something?
**d** not permitted for you to do something?
**e** wrong for you to do something?
**f** wrong for you not to do something?

**4 Think about a recent travel experience. Make as many true sentences as you can using the following prompts.**

Think about ...

**a** something you had to do.
**b** something you couldn't do.
**c** something you didn't have to do.
**d** something you could do.
**e** something you shouldn't have done.
**f** something you should have done.

**Tell your partner.**

**5** **Grammar Extra 7, Part 1** page 146. Read the explanations and do Exercise 1.

## READING

**1 Work with a partner. Discuss the questions.**

- **a** When was the last time you posted a vacation photo on social media?
- **b** Which of the photos (1-5) would you be most likely to post?
- **c** If you had to post these particular photos, who would you tag in each one? Why?

1

2

3

4

5

**2 Read the article below and match the character types (A-E) with the pictures (1-5) in Exercise 1.**

# EVERY PHOTO TELLS A STORY

Did you know that the type of photo you post, together with the message you write, reveals more about your personality than the place you're describing? Flowery, long-winded descriptions often come from the indecisive person who loves the sound of their own voice and is incapable of summarizing. On the other hand, short, sharp phrases (or none at all) are probably the work of the impatient, time-conscious, no-nonsense-taker. Then there's the choice of photo itself. Do you choose something jokey, a historical monument, or tasteful local artwork? Look at the examples on this page and choose the type that fits you best.

**A: The culture vulture** Sightseeing is a way of life for this person. This traveler takes life – at home and away – too seriously. A bookish kind of person who likes to be well-informed about the places he visits. This person can be a little humorless at times.

**B: The joker** This person posts the kind of photo that is bound to raise a smile but it gives no idea at all of what the vacation is really like. He is a cheerful kind of person, more interested in having fun than soaking up the local lifestyle and culture.

**C: The indecisive type** This poster combines lots of different photos in one picture, with a view to pleasing everyone. They are thoughtful and caring, but through their desire to please everyone, they run the risk of being unadventurous or even uninteresting.

**D: The artsy type** The poster of this tasteful scene is typical of style gurus, even on vacation. Image-conscious and stylish (some may say snobby), they're often dissatisfied with the usual attractions and will go out of their way to find unusual ones. This traveler does not want to be mistaken for one of the crowd.

**E: The totally tasteless type** The irresistible, tacky photo is a genuine, unselfconscious choice. This traveler has a sunny, positive outlook and is happy to share it with friends back home.

Answers: A3, B4, C5, D2, E1

**3 Think of people you know who fit the character types in the article. Tell your partner about them.**

## VOCABULARY

**1** **Reread the article on page 76 and <u>underline</u> all the adjectives with the suffixes *ful*, *less*, or *ish*. Which suffix means: (a) has this quality; (b) doesn't have this quality?**

**2** **Which suffix (*ful*, *less*, or *ish*) can combine with all the words in each list (a–c) to form adjectives?**

**a** care / end / home / relent / taste / use
**b** bull / child / devil / fool / hell / self
**c** doubt / help / pain / stress / tear / thought

**Check your ideas in the Word formation panel. Check (✓) the adjectives you know. Choose three more to learn. Write your own example sentences.**

**3** **Look again at the article on page 76 and find ten adjectives beginning with the prefixes in the table. Add each adjective to the correct column.**

| dis- | il- | im- | in- | ir- | un- |
|---|---|---|---|---|---|
| | | | indecisive | | |

**Complete the table with the negative version of the adjectives in the box. Use your dictionary if necessary.**

adequate appropriate divided honest legal literate
logical loyal mature moral obedient
polite rational relevant responsible willing

**4** **Read the story carefully. Use the words in bold at the end of some lines to form words that fit in the blanks on the same lines.**

# Never **AGAIN!**

I hate traveling. It's not that I'm (1) ______ . It's just that I have a problem. **willing**
Four problems actually, and they're named Max, Charlie, Ella, and Jack.
Ranging in age from five down to six months, they're (2) ______ when they're **resist**
asleep. But when they're awake, they're (3) ______ . Individually they're hard **relent**
work; in twos they're a handful; all together, they're a nightmare. More often
than not, they're (4) ______ and seem to have endless competitions to see who **obedient**
can behave in the most (5) ______ way. On top of that, they all want my **devil**
(6) ______ attention at the same time. **divide**
Under these (7) ______ circumstances, you may think that it would be **stress**
foolish of me to even consider traveling alone with my children. Well, I know
now that it wasn't just foolish, but downright (8) ______ . **response**
I wanted to visit my parents. My husband couldn't come, so I set off on
the five-hour train journey with a bagful of toys, a pocketful of candy, and a
headful of songs, stories, and games.
But regardless of my (9) ______ preparations, it was a (10) ______ trip. In **care** **hell**
fact, it was one of the worst experiences of my life. The final straw was when
I arrived, exhausted and (11) ______ , at my parents' house. Instead of being **tear**
sympathetic, they took great delight in telling me how awful I had been as a
child. Thanks, Mom and Dad, that was really (12) ______ ! **help**

2.06 **Listen and check.**

**5** **Did you enjoy traveling as a child? Tell your partner.**

### Word formation

**ful** suffix: with this quality: used with many nouns: *careful, cheerful, doubtful, helpful, painful, stressful, tasteful, tearful, thoughtful, useful*

**ish** suffix: with this quality: used with some nouns: *bullish, childish, devilish, foolish, hellish, selfish*

**less** suffix: without this quality: used with many nouns: *careless, childless, doubtless, endless, helpless, homeless, humorless, painless, relentless, selfless, tasteless, thoughtless, useless*

## LISTENING & SPEAKING

1 **Have you ever met anybody while on vacation and then stayed in touch with them?**

"... we eventually lost touch," says Anna Kenny.

2 2.07 **Listen to Anna talking about her friendship with Paulo and answer the questions.**

a What was Anna doing when she met Paulo?
b Why did she return to Texas?
c Where does Paulo live now?

3 **Listen again and complete the extracts with a single word.**

a I have **actually** ... many years _____
b **Come to think of it**, he was very _____
c **Anyway**, it was the beginning of a great _____
d **Do you know what I mean?** ... **In fact**, I thought we would be friends _____
e **Basically**, we wrote to each other less and less until we eventually lost _____
f **In the end** I reconnected with him on social _____
g **To tell you the truth**, social media certainly has its _____

4 **Match each of the discourse markers in bold in Exercise 3 with its interpretation below.**

1 the final result was
2 Do you understand?
3 although this may surprise you
4 I've just remembered this
5 To be more precise
6 Let's get back to the subject
7 I really am being honest
8 To put it simply

5 **Gill's summer friendship was more long-lasting than Anna's. Complete her story by underlining the appropriate discourse markers from Exercise 3.**

"We had similar hobbies," says Gill May.

**Tony:** Have you ever made a friend while on vacation and kept in touch long after you parted ways?
**Gill:** (1) **Actually** / **Basically**, I have. In fact my best friend and I met while on vacation.
**Tony:** No!
**Gill:** Yes, it's true. I went camping in Yosemite with some college friends, and Ashley came along at the last minute.
**Tony:** Camping in Yosemite? Not exactly tropical ...
**Gill:** No, (2) **in the end** / **come to think of it**, it was a little cold at times. (3) **To tell the truth** / **Anyway**, as soon as I met her I thought, "Wow, we have so much in common." (4) **Do you know what I mean?** / **Come to think of it**.
**Tony:** Oh, yes, I do ... I do.
**Gill:** But then I found out that she would only be staying a few days because she was moving to Europe the following week.
**Tony:** Oh no!
**Gill:** (5) **Basically** / **Actually** there were only four days before she left and I might never see her again.
**Tony:** Weren't you more interested in spending time with your closest friends than this virtual stranger?
**Gill:** I was, at first, but (6) **anyway** / **to tell the truth**, I was becoming bored with them. Ashley was so much more fun. We had similar hobbies, were both studying medicine, and our birthdays were only two days apart. By the second day, we were spending most of our time together. (7) **In fact** / **Actually**, we were inseparable.
**Tony:** What happened after she left?
**Gill:** Well, it was really sad because we had developed such a close bond that we felt like long lost sisters, but we exchanged email addresses and promised to keep in touch online.
**Tony:** Was it a long time before you got to see each other again?
**Gill:** Yes, we didn't see each other again for almost two years, but it all worked out well (8) **in the end** / **to tell the truth**. Now, although we live far apart from each other, we vacation together at least once a year.

2.08 **Listen and check. Practice the conversation with a partner. Concentrate on the correct stress and intonation. Take turns being Gill.**

6 **Work with your partner. Write a similar conversation about meeting somebody on vacation. Include as many discourse markers as you can. Practice your conversation and perform it for the rest of the class.**

## READING & GRAMMAR

1 **Complete the story with *a*, *an*, *the*, or put a dash ( - ) if no article is necessary.**

### Articles

The indefinite article ***a/an***: **a** hunter, **a** man, **an** idea

The definite article ***the***:
**The** tourist was from **the** USA.
**The** man was from Monaco.
**The** idea wasn't very good.

### The Treasure Hunter

(1) ______ poor treasure hunter was using (2) ______ metal detector to search for valuables on (3) ______ beach in (4) ______ Monaco. He had searched for hours but only found (5) ______ old rusty key. Tired and disappointed, he sat down to rest when he heard sounds of distress. (6) ______ cries were coming from (7) ______ cove close by. He waded into (8) ______ water and saw to his surprise that it was (9) ______ mermaid. Her tail was caught in (10) ______ discarded fishing net, and she could not free herself. When he rescued her, (11) ______ mermaid was so grateful she said, "Because you have saved me I will grant you (12) ______ one wish." He could not believe his luck. As he looked out into (13) ______ harbor, sounds of (14) ______ party were coming from (15) ______ largest yacht that he had ever seen. It belonged to (16) ______ successful millionaire businessman, (17) ______ richest man in Monaco. "I want everything (18) ______ owner of that yacht has!" he said.

"Go home, your wish has been granted," she said, and she dived into (19) ______ surf and disappeared.

He hurried home and, to his amazement, (20) ______ tiny shack he lived in had been transformed into (21) ______ mansion with (22) ______ garage full of (23) ______ expensive cars. As he approached, (24) ______ door opened and his wife came out, with (25) ______ huge smile on her face.

"Isn't it wonderful, my love?" (26) ______ man asked. "We are now very rich and can afford all (27) ______ things we ever wanted."

"Yes," she exclaimed. "Including (28) ______ zoo out back. We now have all (29) ______ animals we have ever wanted, including (30) ______ giraffe."

2.09 **Listen and check your answers. What is the moral of the story?**

2 **We do not use articles in generalizations. Here are some general rules for using articles. Find an example of each rule in the text in Exercise 1.**

**a/an**
- **a** Use the indefinite article to introduce new information.
- **b** DON'T use the indefinite article with plurals or uncountable nouns.

**the**
- **c** Use the definite article to refer to things that have already been introduced.
- **d** Use the definite article when the listener knows the answer to "which one?"
- **e** Use the definite article when there is only one.
- **f** DON'T use the definite article with continents, most countries, cities, lakes, and mountains.

3 **Grammar Extra 7, Part 2** page 146. Read the explanations and do Exercises 2 and 3.

## PRONUNCIATION

1 2.10 **Listen and repeat the place names. What is the difference between the pronunciation of *the* in box *A* and box *B*? Why?**

**A** the Danube the Panama Canal the Himalayas the Mississippi the Yucatán Peninsula

**B** the Andes the Eiffel Tower the Empire State Building the Indian Ocean the Orinoco

2 **Have you ever seen, visited, or traveled through any of these places? Add your own examples to boxes *A* and *B*. Find the pronunciation in your dictionary.**

## LANGUAGE FOR LIFE

1 **Work with a partner. Imagine you were visiting Paris for the first time. Which sights would you want to see?**

2.11 **Listen to the conversation. How many museums are mentioned?**

2 **Match the sentence halves to complete the useful phrases from the conversation.**

| | | | |
|---|---|---|---|
| **a** | I'd definitely | **1** | to avoid it. |
| **b** | The views | **2** | be disappointed. |
| **c** | That sounds like | **3** | to the Musée d'Orsay. |
| **d** | It's probably best | **4** | place for seafood. |
| **e** | Make sure you go | **5** | it. |
| **f** | It's worth | **6** | recommend the Eiffel Tower. |
| **g** | You should go to | **7** | I'd use the buses or the metro. |
| **h** | You won't | **8** | the Picasso museum. |
| **i** | If I were you, | **9** | are spectacular. |
| **j** | Whatever you do, | **10** | a must. |
| **k** | It's the best | **11** | don't leave Paris without tasting the oysters. |

2.12 **Listen, check, and repeat.**

3 **Complete the following tips from a travel website using words from the useful phrases.**

**a** If you're feeling energetic, you can hike up Table Mountain, but if I were you, I'd take the cable car. At the top, the _____ are _____.

**b** Whatever _____ do, _____ leave _____ a trip to the Sagrada Familia. It is Gaudi's most famous legacy to the city, and he is buried there.

**c** The _____ place _____ food is on the streets. If you pass a street stall and see lots of Thai people tucking in, you _____ stop and try some of the delicious dishes.

**d** While you're there, _____ sure _____ go for a walk along the oceanfront. From the right-hand edge of Bondi beach as you look at the ocean, you'll find a path that goes all the way to Coogee. It's quite a walk, but you _____ be _____.

**e** It's probably _____ to _____ the city in August, since it's so hot, but if you're there in the summer, I'd recommend a walk in Central Park. You can sit in the shade and watch the world go by.

**f** While you're there, a visit to the ancient city of Teotihuacan is _____ must. You can climb pyramids that were built 1,000 years before the Aztecs arrived in the area. There's a lot of walking and climbing involved, but it's _____ it.

**Match each tip with a city in the box.**

Bangkok Barcelona Cape Town Mexico City New York Sydney

4 **Work with your partner. Write some tips for your own city.**

### LIFE SKILLS: Stress Management

**Ways to Relieve Stress**

2.13 Listen to the radio program Health Watch where Dr. Julia John gives some tips for escaping from it all and reducing stress.

1 **Have you ever used any of these techniques? How did they make you feel?**

2 **What other techniques can be used for stress reduction? Which ones do you think Dr. John will talk about in tomorrow's program?**

3 **Listen again and complete the table below with information from the listening.**

| Stress Reduction Technique | Benefits |
|---|---|
| Meditation | 1 _____ 2_____ |
| Strengthen social circles | 1 _____ 2_____ |
| Laughing | 1 _____ 2_____ |

**Work in pairs - *A* and *B*. *A* should discuss one or two factors that cause stress and anxiety in their lives and how they feel. *B* should use the information from the listening to give advice on what can be done to reduce stress and the benefits obtained from this stress reduction activity. At the end of the activity, students switch roles.**

# 7 Writing Extra

## TRAVEL GUIDE

**1 Work with a partner and answer the questions.**

a Have you ever been or would you like to go to any of the cities in the pictures?

b What do you know about them?

**2 Look at the guide. Match each paragraph with the correct city in Exercise 1.**

### Insider's Guide to Five Exciting Cities

**1 What's it like to drive around?**

It is best to avoid driving into the city because of the narrow winding streets and very expensive parking rates. But if you do, you will need to look out for bicycles and pedestrians. They are everywhere! They always have the right of way and they know it. Even local people complain about parking restrictions – it can take up to four years to get a parking permit if you live by one of the famous canals.

**2 _____ ?**

There's a local saying: "Nine months of winter and three months of hell." This is not strictly true but the summer months of July and August tend to be very hot. However, the air is dry and, consequently, it doesn't feel as hot as it could. This heat tends to drive most city dwellers to the coast during the month of August, creating a quiet time of the year in the city. The weather in winter can be very cold, but there are often blue skies and some sunshine, and in general there is not too much rain.

**3 _____ ?**

If you aren't into theater, opera, art shows, shopping, or Asian cuisine, you can head out of the city. North, you'll find fields of pampered vines where many well-known wines come from. Alternatively, if you go south, you'll see stretches of spectacular Pacific coastline. There is also deep-sea fishing to the west of the city, redwood forests inland, and a very pleasant climate that's eternally spring.

**4 _____ ?**

Nowhere will you find bigger, better, juicier, tastier, and more tender steaks than in the steak houses of this elegant city. But it is surprising to find that, in a city where the majority of people are slim and chic, desserts are very popular – in particular, a sweet substance called *dulce de leche*, a sort of caramel and toffee spread. It's very addictive.

**5 What do people do on the weekend?**

If you're into music, ballet, or opera, get yourselves down to the wonderful, unique Opera House. But don't worry if you can't get tickets – there are plenty of other places in and around the city to visit, whatever the season. In spite of the fact that the city boasts the famous Bondi beach, in the summer, people head for the south coast where very white beaches back onto state forests and national parks. In the winter, the Blue Mountains are the ideal location for some excellent walks and crisp mountain air.

Buenos Aires

San Francisco

Amsterdam

Sydney

Madrid

**3 Write questions as suitable headings for paragraphs *2*, *3*, and *4*. Compare with your partner.**

**4 Match the highlighted words in the guide with the synonyms below.**

| Saying how things usually are | Linking words |
|---|---|
| is sometimes normally most are usually | owing to Despite this Even though Or else |

**5 Find all the examples of the word *very* in the guide and replace each one with an appropriate alternative from the box to make new adverb + adjective combinations. Use each word only once.**

bitterly dazzlingly ~~extortionately~~ extremely particularly surprisingly totally

*extortionately expensive*

**6 Write a guide about your own city or a city you know. Use linking words and adverb + adjective combinations to make your guide sound more interesting.**

# 8 Attraction

## LISTENING & VOCABULARY

**1 Work in small groups and discuss these questions.**

- **a** Who do you think is the most handsome man in the world?
- **b** Who do you think is the most beautiful woman in the world?
- **c** What makes them more attractive than other men and women?

**2 Five people were asked to describe what features make a face attractive. Complete the collocations (a–l) to describe some of the facial features they mention. Choose the most suitable words from the box. Sometimes more than one answer is possible.**

bone structure cheekbones eyebrows eyes eyes
in the cheeks jaw lips nose skin smile teeth

- **a** smooth _____
- **b** good _____
- **c** white _____
- **d** sparkling _____
- **e** a square _____
- **f** big _____
- **g** full _____
- **h** a big _____
- **i** a turned-up _____
- **j** high _____
- **k** arched _____
- **l** dimples _____

2.14 **Listen and check. Do you agree with any of their opinions?**

**3 Think about people that you know with interesting faces. Describe them to your partner. Try to use words from Exercise 2.**

## READING

**1 Work with a partner. Look at the statements (a–e) about the nature of beauty. Decide whether you agree or disagree.**

- **a** Beauty is just skin deep.
- **b** There are some common traits that all beautiful people share.
- **c** Some elements of beauty, such as symmetry, are valued only by humans.
- **d** The focal point for judging beauty is the face.
- **e** There are benefits to being beautiful.

**Read the article on page 83 and find out whether the statements are true or false.**

**2 Read the article on page 83 again and <u>underline</u> words or phrases that you don't know.**

- Try to guess the meaning from context.
- Complete the glossary – how many of the words you <u>underlined</u> are included?
- Add any other words and write your own definitions. Use a dictionary if necessary.

### Glossary

**a** _____ noun [U] the commonly held ideas typical of a particular time and expressed in the culture

**b** _____ noun [U] an extremely large number of people or things

**c** _____ adejctive: existing at a particular time or in a particular place

**d** _____ adejctive: slightly fat in a pleasant way

**e** _____ adejctive: thin in an attractive way

**f** _____ adejctive: a woman with a small waist and large breasts and hips

**g** _____ noun [C]: the muscle between your shoulder and elbow on the front of your arm

**h** _____ noun [C]: (inf) stomach muscles that are very well developed.

**i** _____ adejctive: important and noticeable

**j** _____ phrasal verb: to have a good quality or ability

- **Grammar:** Passive report structures. *have/get something done*. Unreal conditionals
- **Vocabulary:** Parts of the body. Body collocations. Appearance and character. Compound adjectives. Word-building
- **Language for Life:** Body idioms

# Is Beauty *Just Skin Deep?*

*What does this saying mean and is there any truth to it? This article will examine beauty and importance placed on beauty in society.*

People Magazine comes out with an annual list of the "Most Beautiful People in the World." A quick look at the covers of this annual special edition, from their first issue in 1990 to the present day, reveals the changing styles and tastes of the cultural zeitgeist. Over the years, covers have featured fair-haired, dark-haired and red-haried people, with long hair and short hair, curly hair and straight hair and all the lengths and textures between. There have been people with brown eyes, green eyes, and blue eyes - and the list goes on. There is a myriad of combinations, but they are all considered 'beautiful' or 'attractive'. What is it about all these different people, each with their own features, that makes them beautiful?

A quick look back at history shows that each era and culture has had their own prevailing views of what was beautiful. Up until the beginning of the 20th century, a plumper, fuller look for women was appreciated. The twentieth century, generally speaking, saw a slimmer look dictate beauty norms, although from the 1930s to the 1950s a more curvaceous figure ruled. After this, slim was in and has remained so, though to varying degrees. Since the 2000s, a healthy look with more variety in body types and shapes has been seen in the media. These beauty standards are mirrored in many ways for men as well, who have slimmed down over the years. An attractive man today has a toned body and a six-pack. More than body type and shape however, it is usually the face that is the focal point when judging beauty. As we can see from the "Most Beautiful" magazine covers over the years, many combinations of hair, eyes, and face shapes have been considered beautiful. Independent of era and culture, smooth skin and symmetry have remained consistent standards of beauty. According to scientists, these two features are "biological advertisements" of good health - an indication to prospective partners of good genes which can be passed down to future generations. The attractiveness of symmetry is seen not just in humans, but throughout the animal kingdom. Birds, for example, seek partners with symmetrical tail feathers, and fish seek partners with symmetrical stripes on their sides.

So what does this all mean? Besides appearing on magazine covers, there are real life consequences to the perception of beauty. Research has shown that people who are seen as beautiful are considered to be healthier and happier. Economist Daniel Hamermesh has measured the payoffs of being beautiful. His research has found that attractive people get higher salaries, better terms on loans, and more beautiful and successful partners. So, while some may say that beauty is just skin deep, research suggests that beauty sends out powerful messages to the world. Whereas in the past it was thought that one had to be born with it, today physical exercise and treatments make beauty accessible to everyone. Now, everyone can reap the benefits of beauty.

## GRAMMAR

**1 Look at an active and passive version of the same sentence. Answer the questions.**

1 For more than a century, people thought that a beautiful face was appealing because ...
For more than a century, it was thought that a beautiful face was appealing because ...

2 Do people all over the world consider the same features to be attractive?
Are the same features considered to be attractive all over the world?

a Which structure - active or passive - is more formal?
b Which structure is more likely to be found in written reports?
c Which structure is used in the article on page 83?

**Passive report structures**

**Formal (passive)**
**It was thought that** the world was flat.
**Bananas are said** to give you energy.

**Informal (active)**
**People thought that** the world was flat.
**They say that** bananas give you energy.

**2 Put the missing word in parentheses in the correct position in the sentence.**

a Chocolate thought to be bad for your skin. (is)
b It has suggested that you should drink at least two liters of water a day. (been)
c It used to assumed that carrots were good for your eyesight. (be)
d It said that reading in a dim light can damage your eyes. (is)
e Shaving body hair widely believed to make it grow back thicker and faster. (is)
f It often said that we only use 10% of our brains. (is)

**3 Rewrite the statements in Exercise 2 in a more informal style.**

a People ...
b Some doctors ...
c People ...
d They ...
e Many people ...
f They ...

a *People say that chocolate is bad for your skin.*

**Work with a partner. Do people believe that the same things are true in your country?**

## LISTENING

**1 Look at the pictures of three people who took part in a radio show about cosmetic surgery. Match each person (*Jean*, *Rita*, or *Michael*) with an opinion (a–c) you think they might have.**

a "I really don't think there's anything wrong with trying to improve on what nature has given us."
b "I think we should be grateful for what we have."
c "Personally, I'm dead set against cosmetic surgery of any kind."

2.15 **Listen and check your ideas.**

Jean Oldham, beauty editor

**2 Complete the extracts from the radio show with words from the box.**

ask believe frankly have point trying

a I ____ to say that the most beautiful women I know are not models.
b I ____ that true beauty comes from within.
c The ____ is, it's selfish and indulgent of people to spend vast amounts of money on superficial improvements.
d Quite ____, cosmetic surgery can do more for you than a vacation, because the benefits last longer.
e I guess what I'm ____ to say is that cosmetic surgery nowadays is almost as routine as going on vacation.
f If you ____ me, what we need to accept is that we can't look young forever.

Rita Taylor, cosmetic surgeon

**Do you think cosmetic surgery is a good or a bad thing? Tell your partner.**

**3 What are your opinions about the topics in the box?**

botox piercing size zero models tattoos liposuction

Michael Hirst, journalist

**Tell your partner about your opinions. Use as many of the highlighted expressions in Exercise 2 as you can.**

## READING & GRAMMAR

**1 Cindy Jackson has had a total makeover. What has she had changed?**

**Read her account and check your ideas. Complete the text with *had*, *have*, or *having*.**

# Total Makeover Changed my Life!

"I am forty-five years old. Divided between my family and my career, I neglected to look after myself along the way. One year ago, I took a long, hard look in the mirror and realized that my hairstyle and clothes were tired and outdated. I needed to make some changes.

First, I (1) had had my hair cut and colored. I hadn't been to a hairdresser in years. The results were absolutely amazing - I looked years younger, as if I (2) _____ had a facelift. Next, I (3) _____ my colors done. This is a consultation which tells you the best colors and combinations for your clothes and makeup. I then set out, over several weekends and trips to many different stores, to build up a decent wardrobe. To get the best look possible, I (4) _____ some of the clothes adjusted, taken in at the waist, or shortened to suit me better. To complete the process, I (5) _____ my teeth whitened over a three month period. My doctor also recommended that I (6) _____ my skin treated with a chemical peel, but I (7) _____ had that done yet. Finally, I went down to the mall and (8) _____ my makeup done by a professional.

Before the makeover, I was invisible. I hadn't really invested time and money to look good. Now, I look and feel ten years younger. I feel energetic and hopeful. Who would guess that a simple makeover could do that."

**What does Cindy Jackson identify as the main change in her life after the makeover? What do you think about her comments?**

**2 What is the difference in meaning between *I cut my hair* and *I had/got my hair cut*? When do you use the structure *have/get* + object + past participle?**

> ***have/get* something done**
>
> ***have/get*** + object + past participle
>
> She **had** her hair **colored**.
> He's **getting** his teeth **straightened**.

**3 Write the sentences in the correct order.**

- **a** get / every six months / serviced / my car / I
- **b** redecorated / my house / four years ago / had / I
- **c** my hair / once a month / I / cut / get
- **d** installed / had / a burglar alarm / I
- **e** last month / my blood pressure / checked / I / had
- **f** had / I've / my nails / never / done

**Make questions based on the sentences (a–f) using *How often …?*, or *Have you ever …?*, or *When was the last time …?*, as appropriate.**

**Ask and answer the questions with a partner.**

**4 How well do you know the town or city you are in? Work with your partner and take turns asking each other where the best place is to have/get things done. Use the verbs / objects in the box or your own ideas.**

> clean / a winter jacket   color / hair   cut / a key   do / a tattoo
> reheel / shoes   repair / a TV   take / a passport picture   test / eyes

*Where is the best place to get a winter jacket cleaned?*

**5** **Grammar Extra 8, Part 1** page 146. Read the explanations and do Exercise 1.

## READING & SPEAKING

1 **Work in small groups. Discuss the questions.**

a What is the minimum time you need to know if you will be friends with someone?
b What in your eyes makes someone attractive?
c What situation or behavior would give you a negative impression of someone?

2 **Read the article on page 87 about the friendship experiment. Make a note of each person's experience, and then answer the questions below.**

a Who were the two most popular people?
b Who was the least popular person?
c Who made friends with Maria?
d Who didn't get along with Fernando?

## VOCABULARY

1 **Decide if these words, highlighted in blue in the text, usually have positive or negative meanings. Check your answers in the article on page 87.**

a self-centered (lines 34-35)
b enigmatic (line 27)
c down-to-earth (lines 3-4)
d sensible (line 54)
e stand-offish (line 5)
f sensitive (line 20)
g trustworthy (line 40)
h open-minded (line 10)
i uptight (line 64)
j mature (line 17)
k laid-back (line 41)

2 **Choose words from the list in Exercise 1 which best replace the words in bold in these sentences.**

a My ideal friend would have to be someone **caring** and **dependable**.
b I think I'm a **level-headed** kind of person. I haven't done anything crazy yet, anyway!
c I'd say I feel **relaxed** about work – I never let things bother me.
d People think I'm **unfriendly**, but actually, I'm just really shy.
e I wish my parents were more **tolerant**. It shouldn't be a problem if I go out at night.
f I prefer to be friends with people older than me. You can have more interesting conversations with somebody with is **experienced** and **grown-up**.
g I know somebody who likes to think she's **mysterious**. In fact, she's very boring.
h I know somebody who's very wealthy, but you wouldn't know it because he's so **unpretentious**.
i I've got a friend who's really **selfish** – probably because her parents spoiled her when she was a child.

**Can you identify with any of the sentences above? Discuss with your partner.**

## PRONUNCIATION

1 2.16 **Mark the stress on each of the adjectives in the box. Then listen and check.**

compatible flexible friendly generous happy lively mature sad sensitive weak

2 **Make the adjectives in Exercise 1 into nouns by adding the suffixes *ity* or *ness*. Use your dictionary if necessary.**

2.17 **Listen, check, and repeat.**

3 **What is the effect on the word stress when you change the adjective into a noun ending in *ity*?**

https://friendshipmatters.com

# How Do We Make Friends?

*Friendships are an important part of our lives. Some researchers even say that having friends improves our health and helps us to live longer. Researchers at the University of Chicago ran an experiment to understand the dynamics at play when people meet for the first time. Which personality traits do we notice in others, and which traits do we find likable? To answer these questions, the researchers observed ten young people at a casual get-together. They had never met each other before. Below are extracts from their interviews with the researchers.*

## Max

This was my first time at Arlene's annual barbecue. It was a lot of fun. I met Maria, who I really got along with. She is **down-to-earth** and interesting. I didn't chat much with Phillip. He was quite **stand-offish** and we didn't seem to have a lot in common.

## Farah

I really enjoyed the party. I met so many new people here. I spent the most time with Ally. She is really cool and so **open-minded**. I probably spoke the least with Victor. He was a bit boring to be honest.

## Victor

This is my second time attending this barbecue and both times I have met such interesting people. This year I hit it off with Max, maybe because he is quite **mature** and has an interesting take on things. Betty was in our little group, but I didn't talk to her much. She seemed a bit **sensitive** about some of the topics.

## Betty

I was kind of overwhelmed with how many people there were at the party. I attended one four years ago, and it was a much smaller group of people back then. This year I met Fernando who was in our little circle. I found him quite **enigmatic**. On the other hand, I found Farah to be quite boring.

## Phillip

I've had such a great time at the party, partly because I met Ally there. She was great fun, and we spoke all afternoon. We will definitely keep in touch. I didn't get on so well with Fernando. I thought he was really **self-centered**.

## Maria

This has been the best party all summer. I met so many wonderful people. One of my favorites was Max. He opened up a lot during our conversation, and I get the feeling that he is **trustworthy**. I also met Reena, who was one of the more **laid-back** people at the party.

## Martin

I don't usually go to barbecues because I am a vegetarian, but I am happy I went to this one. I spent a lot of time talking with Reena. She is cool, a vegetarian like me, but she doesn't take herself too seriously, like most vegetarians. On the other hand, I didn't click with Betty. There is no personal reason for this; she just isn't someone I would hang around with.

## Reena

I had an amazing time at the barbecue. I met Martin, who I really liked. He's **sensible** and doesn't try to dominate the conversation. He's a good listener. Fernando was the person I got on least with. He really likes the sound of his own voice!

## Fernando

This was my third time at this annual party, but I don't think it really compared to previous years. The people there weren't really my crowd, although I did get along well with Betty. She was really engaging and had a lot of interesting things to say. I didn't really get on with Max. I thought he was very **uptight**.

## Ally

I was so happy to be invited. I had heard about this annual barbecue and all the great people who attend. I met Maria there, and we hit it off immediately. She is bubbly and a lot of fun. However, I don't think I even spoke to Martin, so I can't really say too much about him. I'm sure he's a nice guy, but I just didn't get a chance to talk to him.

## LISTENING & SPEAKING

1 **Before you listen to the radio show, read the sayings (1-5). Work with a partner and discuss questions *a* and *b* below.**

1 Like attracts like.
2 A leopard can't change its spots.
3 All that glitters is not gold.
4 What goes around, comes around.
5 Be careful what you wish for ...

a What do you think the sayings mean?
b Do you have any similar sayings in your language?

2 2.18 **Listen to a radio show about the "law of attraction." According to Dr. Hudson, how is the "law of attraction" similar to a genie?**

3 **Listen again. For questions (1-7), choose the best option: *a*, *b*, or *c*.**

1 How many copies of *The Secret* have been viewed?
   a Two million.
   b One and a half million.
   c One million.
2 How old is the theory behind the "law of attraction?"
   a It has been around for ages.
   b It's a new phenomenon.
   c It has appeared in recent times.
3 How does Dr. Hudson explain the "law of attraction?"
   a Positive thinking is less stressful than negative thinking.
   b Positive thinking and negative thinking both exist in the universe.
   c Positive thinking attracts good things. Negative thinking attracts bad things.
4 What everyday problem does Dr. Hudson claim can be solved by positive thinking?
   a Finding a parking space at a grocery store.
   b Finding a grocery store with no other shoppers.
   c Finding your way to a grocery store.
5 Where does Dr. Hudson suggest you should start visualizing your parking space?
   a In the grocery store.
   b On the way to the grocery store.
   c In the grocery store parking lot.
6 What is a potential criticism of the "law of attraction," according to the presenter?
   a It might encourage people to buy really expensive houses.
   b It might make people more materialistic and greedy.
   c It might make people believe in genies.
7 Why does Dr. Hudson say it's important to think big?
   a Because it's better than being mediocre.
   b Because there's no point in asking for something small.
   c Because it will help improve things in the world.

**Do you believe in the "law of attraction?" Why? / Why not? Tell your partner.**

## GRAMMAR

**Unreal conditional structures**

**Imagine** you were rich.
**Suppose** you had millions.
**Assuming** you were to make a will, who would you leave your money to?

**1 Complete the questions with *would* or *were*.**

- **a** If you _____ able to change three things in your life, what _____ they be?
- **b** Suppose somebody _____ to give you a check for any amount you liked - how much _____ you ask for and what _____ you do with it?
- **c** Imagine a genie _____ to grant you any wish you wanted - what _____ you wish for?
- **d** Supposing you could go on a date with anyone in the world, who _____ it be?
- **e** Assuming money _____ no object, what _____ be your ideal evening out?
- **f** If you _____ to have a movie made of your life, which actor _____ you choose to play the part of you and why?

**Work with a partner. Underline the words you can use instead of *if*.**

**Think about your answers. Ask your partner. How similar are your ideas?**

**2 Work with your partner. Complete the questions with your own ideas.**

- **a** Imagine you could change places with a celebrity for a day - _____ ?
- **b** Suppose you could afford to have any car in the world - _____ ?
- **c** Imagine you were the President of your country - _____ ?
- **d** Suppose you could live anywhere in the world - _____ ?
- **e** Assuming your English were perfect, _____ ?
- **f** Supposing you could change your name, _____ ?

**Use your questions to interview other people in the class.**

**3** **Grammar Extra 8, Part 2** page 146. Read the explanations and do Exercise 2.

## SPEAKING: ANECDOTE

**You are going to tell your partner about the most positive (or negative) person you know.**

- Ask yourself the questions below.
- Think about *what* to say and *how* to say it.
- Tell your partner about the person.

- **a** Who is this person? A teacher? A boss? A member of your family? ...
- **b** What's his/her name and how old is he/she?
- **c** When and how did you meet him/her?
- **d** How did you get to know him/her?
- **e** What examples of his/her positive (or negative) nature can you give?
- **f** What do you think makes this person so positive (or negative)?
- **g** How does his/her positive (or negative) outlook affect you?
- **h** How often do you see this person?
- **i** When was the last time you saw him/her?
- **j** How positive (or negative) do you think *you* are?

## LANGUAGE FOR LIFE

**1** 2.19 **Read and listen to the conversation. Underline eight phrases that are different from the conversation on the recording.**

**Laura:** Hey, Phil, how are you doing?
**Phil:** Oh, hi, Laura – not too bad, thanks. How are you?
**Laura:** Oh, really busy as usual. I'm on my way to my third meeting today. How's Mandy?
**Phil:** Oh, we broke up three months ago. She's on vacation with her new boyfriend.
**Laura:** Oh, no – trust me to say something to make you feel worse. I'm really sorry.
**Phil:** No, it's OK. I need to talk about it.
**Laura:** Who's her new boyfriend?
**Phil:** You wouldn't know him. He's not from around here.
**Laura:** How did she meet him?
**Phil:** Through work, I think. He's one of those people who seems to be involved in a lot of things. He owns several companies, including the one Mandy was working for.
**Laura:** Oh, Phil, I don't know what to say.
**Phil:** Yeah – it's hard. I mean, we were supposed to be going on vacation together in a couple of weeks.
**Laura:** So, what are you going to do?
**Phil:** I don't know – I haven't decided yet. It was really expensive, so I might go anyway, but I might not feel like it when the time comes. I don't know. I'll just have to see how I feel at the time.
**Laura:** Look Phil, I'm afraid I have to run – but if you need someone to talk to, you know where to find me.
**Phil:** Thanks, Laura – I'll be fine.

**2 Work with a partner. Match the useful phrases (a–h) with the phrases you have underlined in Exercise 1.**

**a** put my foot in my mouth
**b** play it by ear
**c** a shoulder to cry on
**d** get it off my chest
**e** up to my eyes in work
**f** this neck of the woods
**g** made up my mind yet
**h** cost an arm and a leg

**Listen again and check.**

**Use at least three of the useful phrases to write example sentences about yourself or people you know. Tell your partner about them.**

**3 Work with your partner. You are going to write a conversation that includes some different expressions.**

brain eye foot hand head leg nose tongue

- Use a dictionary and find six expressions based on the body parts in the box.
- Write a conversation using the expressions you have found.
- Practice your conversation and perform it for the rest of the class.

### LIFE SKILLS: Effective Communication

**Layout of Reports and Essays**

Our personal presentation is important. To a certain degree, first impressions are important. In the same way, our written work must also be well presented.

**1** 2.20 **Listen to a consultant giving advice on how to improve the layout of documents. Complete the list below with advice from the podcast.**

1 *The text is aligned to the left.*
2
3
4
5
6

**2 Use the information from the podcast to rewrite or type the document below with more appropriate formatting.**

**Heading 1.** Use this paragraph to practice how you would create a professional looking report. Your report would be longer than a couple of paragraphs, so this is just a sample for you to work with. Where possible, use tables, charts, and illustrations to get your message across clearly. The layout of your document is as important as the content, so pay close attention to the details.

**Sub-heading.** The advice above can be applied to school reports, essays, and corporate documents.

MACMILLAN LIFE SKILLS

# 8 Vocabulary Extra

## METAPHOR

**1 Match each sentence (a-f) with an adjective or phrase from the box to describe the person's emotions.**

angry busy happy losing your temper nervous sad

a She's on top of the world.
b He feels really down about it.
c She often gets hot under the collar.
d He's snowed under with work.
e She's very strung out about it.
f He totally blew his top.

**2 Underline the word or phrase in sentences (a-f) in Exercise 1 which illustrates each of these common metaphors. Using the dictionary boxes, find other examples that illustrate each metaphor.**

1 being angry = being hot or on fire, e.g. *flared up*
2 losing your temper = exploding, e.g. ______
3 being busy = being covered or surrounded, e.g. ______
4 being happy = being high up, e.g. ______
5 being sad = being low down, e.g. ______
6 being nervous = being pulled or tied, e.g. ______

**3 Decide which emotion from Exercise 1 can be described using these words.**

a drowning / swamped / inundated / buried
b tense / strained / taut / uptight
c burning / heated / blazing / boil
d lifted / rise / over / high
e blow up / outburst / go ballistic / erupt
f low / depths / sink / dump

**Find example sentences from the dictionary metaphor boxes to understand how the words are used. Choose one phrase for each metaphor that you would like to learn.**

**4 Underline the correct alternative to complete these statements.**

a The current economic outlook is very **gloomy** / **foggy**.
b If you're good at time management, you never get **rained** / **inundated** with work.
c Everybody needs to **let** / **put** their hair down once in a while.
d People should cheer **up** / **away** a bit; the future is **shining** / **bright**!

**Work with a partner. Check your answers in the metaphor boxes. Find out if your partner agrees or disagrees with the statements.**

**5 Work with your partner. Ask each other these questions.**

When was the last time you ...

a lost your cool?
b blew your top?
c were up to your ears in work?
d were in seventh heaven?
e were feeling blue?
f let your hair down?

**6 Check your own dictionary. How does it show information about metaphor?**

### Metaphor

Feeling happy and hopeful is like being **high up** or like **moving upward**. Feeling sad and unhappy is like being **low down** or like **falling**.

*The news* **lifted** *her spirits.* ♦ *Things are looking* **up**. ♦ *Cheer* **up**! ♦ *My spirits* **rose** *when I got her letter.* ♦ *I've been* **walking/floating on air** *ever since.* ♦ *She's* **on top of the world/on cloud nine.** ♦ *I was in* **seventh heaven.** ♦ *I feel really* **down/low** *about it all.* ♦ *He's in very* **low** *spirits.* ♦ *He's in the* **depths** *of despair.* ♦ *My heart* **sank** *when I saw him.* ♦ *They looked very* **down in the mouth/down in the dumps.**

Happiness and hope are like **bright light** or **bright colors**. Sadness and lack of hope are like **darkness** or **dark colors**.

*The future looks very* **bright/rosy.** ♦ *She* **brightened** *up when she heard the news.* ♦ *His face* **lit up** *when he saw them.* ♦ *They had* **shining** *eyes and* **beaming/dazzling** *smiles.* ♦ *The bride looked* **radiant.** ♦ *You have to look for* **the light at the end of the tunnel.** ♦ *He was in a* **black** *mood.* ♦ *I was feeling* **blue.** ♦ *There's no point in having these* **dark** *thoughts.* ♦ *His face* **darkened.** ♦ *They led a* **gray** *empty existence.* ♦ *I'm afraid the outlook is very* **gloomy/bleak/dismal.** ♦ *The news cast a* **shadow** *over the evening.*

### Metaphor

Being very busy at work is like being **covered with things** or **surrounded by** something such as water or the ground, so that you cannot move easily.

*They keep* **piling** *more work* **on** *me.* ♦ *I'm* **up to** *my* **eyes/ears/eyeballs/neck** *in work.* ♦ *I'm* **drowning** *in paperwork.* ♦ *I have got a lot of work to* **wade through.** ♦ *I'm* **snowed under** *with work.* ♦ *I don't have time to* **turn around.** ♦ *We're absolutely* **swamped** *at the moment.* ♦ *We've been* **inundated** *with phone calls.* ♦ *They* **buried/immersed** *themselves in their work.*

→ RESPONSIBILITY

### Metaphor

Being angry is like being **hot** or **on fire**.

*She* **burned** *with indignation.* ♦ *He has a* **fiery** *temper.* ♦ *Jack was a* **hot-tempered** *young man.* ♦ *Their parents were having a* **heated argument/debate** *about where to go.* ♦ *She often* **flares up** *over nothing.* ♦ *It made my blood* **boil.** ♦ *I* **lost** *my* **cool.** ♦ *Alison was getting very* **hot under the collar.**

Losing your temper is like an **explosion**.

*When she told him, he nearly* **exploded.** ♦ *He* **blew up** *at her.* ♦ *Steve* **couldn't contain** *his anger any longer.* ♦ *It was an* **explosive** *situation.* ♦ *I'm sorry I* **blew** *my* **top.** ♦ *There was another angry* **outburst** *from Chris.* ♦ *She'll* **blow a fuse/a gasket** *if she finds out.* ♦ *Bob* **went ballistic** *when he saw what they had done.* ♦ *A major row* **erupted** *at the meeting.*

→ CRITICIZE

### Metaphor

When you feel nervous, it is like being **pulled**, **tied**, or **stretched tightly**. When you relax, it is like becoming loose again.

*I was feeling a little* **tense.** ♦ *I find running is a good way to release* **tension.** ♦ *Her voice was high and* **strained.** ♦ *There's no need to get so* **wound-up** *about it.* ♦ *I've been really* **strung out** *lately.* ♦ *She's so* **highly-strung**, *she needs very sensitive handling.* ♦ *I felt* **taut** *and tense with nerves.* ♦ *I don't know why he gets so* **uptight** *about things.* ♦ *Her stomach seemed to be* **tying itself in knots.** ♦ *You should try to* **loosen up** *a little.* ♦ *It's good to* **unwind** *at the end of the day.* ♦ *Just* **let go** *of all your worries.* ♦ *I told her to* **hang loose** *and stop worrying.* ♦ *It's a place where people can* **let their hair down.**

→ FEELING

From the *Macmillan English Dictionary (American and British editions)*

# 9 Genius

## READING & VOCABULARY

**1** **Work with a partner. Who do you consider to be a genius? Try to name somebody (dead or alive, from your country or elsewhere) for each of these categories.**

- architecture
- art
- literature
- math
- movies
- music
- science and technology
- sports
- theater

**SANTIAGO CALATRAVA** is one of the most respected architects and designers of the 20th century. His designs include bridges, buildings, and train stations around the world. Perhaps his most famous collection of works are the buildings he designed for the City of Arts and Sciences in Valencia, Spain.

**2** **Look at the picture on page 93 of the City of Arts and Sciences in Valencia, Spain. Which of the words in the box could you use to describe it? Use your dictionary if necessary.**

> contemporary eccentric hideous important metallic 19th Century post-industrial post-modern run-down semi-derelict shiny space-age sprawling tough urban

**Read the article on page 93 and check your ideas. Classify the words in the box as follows.**

**a** Words to describe the City of Arts and Sciences (Check (✓) them)
**b** Words to describe the city of Valencia (Circle them)
**c** Words to describe the area around the City of Arts and Sciences (Underline them)

**3** **Work with your partner. Explain the connections (a–f) from memory.**

**a** Santiago Calatrava + art
**b** The City of Arts and Sciences + nature
**c** The government of Valencia + the creation of the City of Arts and Sciences
**d** The movie *Tomorrowland* + the City of Arts and Sciences
**e** Santiago Calatrava + the Turning Torso
**f** The Turia River + the City of Arts and Sciences

**Read the article again and check your ideas.**

**4** **Replace the underlined words and phrases in the sentences (a–g) with words and phrases from the article.**

**a** The City of Arts and Sciences is a large leisure and entertainment complex in Valencia, Spain.
**b** Five of the complex's six buildings were designed by the famous architect Santiago Calatrava.
**c** The Turia River, which once ran through the city of Valencia, used to practically divide the city into two.
**d** One of the interesting things about the complex is that it merges natural and man-made features into its design.
**e** Calatrava is responsible for the design of many highly recognizable buildings, bridges, and other structures around the world.
**f** He is one of a handful of architects who has produced a great number of works of art.
**g** Despite his fame, his work also causes a lot of disagreement.

**Work with your partner. Adapt each sentence to describe your own city or a city you know well.**

- **Grammar:** Past modals of deduction. *look, seem, appear*
- **Vocabulary:** Describing places. Time expressions. Collocations. Word families
- **Language for Life:** Explaining how something works

# Architecture as Art

It is no exaggeration when they say that the City of Arts and Sciences looks like something out of a science fiction movie. This unique, futuristic museum complex was primarily designed by renowned architect, artist, and structural engineer Santiago Calatrava. It was featured in Disney's 2015 film '*Tomorrowland*,' starring George Clooney, with some scenes actually shot on location in Valencia, Spain. The film's towering urban landscape took its inspiration from Calatrava's inventive designs, which were used as the blueprint for the fictional city.

Located on the eastern Mediterranean coast, Valencia is the third largest city in Spain and the birthplace of Santiago Calatrava. The city's architecture is an exercise in contrasts, with an eclectic mix of the old and the new. There are medieval castles and breath-taking, modernist structures like those that make up the expansive 35-hectare City of Arts and Sciences. An interesting fact about this stunning complex is that it sits upon the dry bed of what was the Turia River, a wide, raging river which once bisected the city. Because of its unique location, the City of Arts and Sciences integrates natural and man-made landscape features into its design. Calatrava would probably consider this to be a perfect combination of nature, art, and architecture in one place.

Calatrava embarked upon the design of the City of Arts and Sciences to realize the Valencian government's vision to create, from an underdeveloped area, a museum of national significance. Another goal of the government was to link the city center to the Mediterranean coast. True to his style, each of the five structures he conceived for this complex incorporates sculpture and movement or some organic component as important elements of the design. Calatrava is known for his iconic structures which dot cities around the world, and whose sculptural forms often resemble living organisms. Such is the case of the Prince Felipe Science Museum, which reminds us of the skeleton of a whale. In fact, many times he uses observation of the human body as the base element of design. The Turning Torso in Sweden, for example, clearly gives this impression, both in name and execution.

Calatrava's designs and inspiration perhaps stem from his view of the integration of his art with all aspects of life, rather than stand-alone functional buildings or structures. In a 2009 interview, he stated that "Architecture is more than just buildings. It gives a sense of the heritage of a particular time … it is a time capsule." He has expressed views on a wide range of topics, from economics, city planning, and infrastructure to spirituality and man's divinity. Growing up, Calatrava was exposed to art from an early age, visiting important museums in Madrid with his father. By the age of eight, he was enrolled in art school and has remained connected with art and design ever since, studying in different parts of Europe. The length and depth of his involvement with art probably account for the kind of thinking which goes into his work.

Although prolific and in steady demand across the world, Calatrava's work is controversial. Some of his work has been criticized on the grounds of the tendency for massive cost overruns and delays as well as problems related to functionality. However, his talent for neo-futurist design is undeniable. The City of Arts and Sciences, among other works across the world, stands as a physical testament to both the architectural genius of this artist as well as to the controversy that rages around his work.

**Glossary**

**blueprint** noun [C]: plan or model

**raging** adjective: moving with great natural force

**resemble** verb [T]: to be similar to

**(a) testament to something** idiomatic expression: proof and evidence

## LISTENING & VOCABULARY

**1** **Work with a partner. Look at the photograph, picture, and map showing Stonehenge and guess the correct answers (*a*, *b*, or *c*) to the questions (1-6).**

1 How long has Stonehenge been standing?
   **a** 5,000 years. **b** 50,000 years. **c** 5,500 years.
2 How were the stones laid out originally?
   **a** In a line. **b** As a square. **c** As a circle.
3 What makes the bluestones turn blue?
   **a** The sun. **b** The rain. **c** The cold.
4 How were the Sarsen stones transported?
   **a** They were carried. **b** They were pushed. **c** They were dragged.
5 How far were the bluestones transported?
   **a** 20 miles. **b** 250 miles. **c** 215 miles.
6 Why was Stonehenge built?
   **a** It's a mystery. **b** It's a secret. **c** It's a work of art.

▶ 2.21 **Listen to an architect and an archaeologist talking about Stonehenge in a radio show. Check your ideas and underline the correct answers.**

**2** **Find two synonyms in the box for each underlined word or phrase in sentences (a-e). Use your dictionary if necessary.**

| alluring drew drizzling enchanting endures enigmatic inspired intriguing just a mere spitting survives |
|---|

**a** "... The sky is overcast and it's raining lightly."
**b** "... it's been standing there for 5,000 years - and it continues to exist."
**c** "... it remains such a mysterious and captivating place."
**d** "... the inner circle is made up of bluestones, and they weigh only four tons each."
**e** "... Something compelled them to bring all these materials here."

**Listen again and check (✓) the word from the box that was actually used in the radio show.**

**What is the oldest building that you have ever visited? Tell your partner about it.**

## GRAMMAR

1 ▶ 2.22 **Listen to five visitors answering the question, "What do you think Stonehenge was built for?" Underline whether they are "almost certain" or "uncertain" about the theories (a–e) they suggest.**

**Past modals of deduction**

It **must have** taken ages.
They **may/might/could have used** slaves.
It **couldn't have** been easy.

**a** It was a kind of temple, a religious place. **almost certain / uncertain**
**b** It wasn't only a calendar. **almost certain / uncertain**
**c** It was a place where important ceremonies took place. **almost certain / uncertain**
**d** It was a landing site for spacecraft from other planets. **almost certain / uncertain**
**e** It was a healing place. **almost certain / uncertain**

**Use *couldn't*, *could*, *may*, *might*, or *must* to rewrite the sentences (1–3).**

1 I'm almost certain it happened. → It _____
2 I'm almost certain it didn't happen. → It _____
3 I'm uncertain whether it happened or not. → It _____ / It _____ / It _____

2 **Complete the second sentence so that it has a similar meaning to the first sentence. Use between two and five words, including the word given in bold.**

**a** It's possible that the stones for Stonehenge were moved by a system of levers.
**might**
The stones for Stonehenge _____ by a system of levers.
**b** It is almost certain that the material to build the Sphinx of Giza was transported down the Nile.
**must**
The material to build the Sphinx of Giza _____ down the Nile.
**c** The construction of the Great Pyramid of Giza probably involved up to 50,000 workers.
**could**
The construction of the Great Pyramid of Giza _____ up to 50,000 workers.
**d** Perhaps the Nazca Lines in Peru were a map of underground water supplies.
**may**
The Nazca Lines in Peru _____ a map of underground water supplies.
**e** The Easter Island statues obviously didn't come from outer space.
**couldn't**
The Easter Island statues _____ from outer space.
**f** Machu Picchu was almost definitely built as a fortress against powerful enemies.
**been**
Machu Picchu _____ as a fortress against powerful enemies.

**What other theories do you know about the origin of these (or other) ancient ruins? Which do you think are the most / least likely? Tell a partner.**

3 **Grammar Extra 9, Part 1** page 148. Read the explanations and do Exercise 1.

## SPEAKING: ANECDOTE

**You are going to tell your partner about your favorite historic place (building, monument, or ruin).**

- Ask yourself the questions below.
- Think about *what* to say and *how* to say it.
- Tell your partner about the place.

**a** What kind of place is it and what is it called?
**b** Where is it located?
**c** What does it look like?
**d** What are the surroundings like?
**e** How old is it?
**f** What is it used for now?
**g** When did you first see it?
**h** What do you like most about it?

## LISTENING & GRAMMAR

1 **Work with a partner. Look at the two paintings by Almeida Júnior and discuss what you think the story might be behind each painting.**

2.23 **Listen to a museum guide's descriptions and compare your ideas.**

*The Guitar Player* (1899)
Almeida Júnior (1850-1899).
Media: oil, canvas.
Dimensions: 141 x 172 cm.
Location: Pinacoteca do Estado de São Paulo, São Paulo, SP, Brazil.

*Longing* (1899)
Almeida Júnior (1850-1899).
Media: oil, canvas.
Dimensions: 197 x 101 cm.
Location: Pinacoteca do Estado de São Paulo, São Paulo, SP, Brazil.

2 **Match the sentence beginnings with the sentence endings from the museum guide's decriptions. Then match the sentences with the paintings.**

a She looks like — 1 a bit nostalgic.
b She looks — 2 if she has suffocated feelings.
c She looks as — 3 a widow.

***look, seem, appear***

**look/seem** + adjective
**look like** + noun
**look/seem as if/though** + verb phrase
**seem/appear** + to be

3 **Listen again and read the Audioscript on page 152. Find sentences that include examples of the different verb structures for *look*, *seem*, and *appear*.**

4 **Grammar Extra 9, Part 2** page 148. Read the explanations and do Exercise 2.

5 **What is your memory like? Look at the two paintings again for thirty seconds. Then go to the Additional material on page 136 and answer as many questions as you can.**

## READING & VOCABULARY

**1 Read the following summary of Frida Kahlo's life. With a partner, discuss any aspect of her life that calls your attention.**

# Frida Kahlo

Frida Kahlo was born in Coyocán, Mexico in 1907. When she was six, she contracted polio and spent nine months confined to her room. As a result, her right leg was very thin. From then on, she always concealed her right leg.

When she was eighteen, she was seriously injured in an accident between a streetcar and a bus: a metal handrail pierced her body. Over the years, she underwent thirty-two major operations and suffered enormous pain for the rest of her life.

It was while she was convalescing from the streetcar accident that she took up painting.

She married a famous muralist, Diego Rivera, when she was twenty-two. He was forty-two and had been married twice before. She told a journalist, "When I was seventeen (subtracting three years from her age) Diego began to fall in love with me. My father didn't like him … they said it was like an elephant marrying a dove."

Soon after she met Rivera, Kahlo began to dress in traditional Mexican clothes. In particular, she chose the regional costumes of the Tehuana women of southern Mexico, partly to please Rivera, and partly to conceal her thin leg and scars from her terrible accident. Yet it was also a political statement in support of her Mexican heritage.

In January 1939, she travelled to Paris where she met Picasso. The Louvre purchased one of her self-portraits.

Frida and Diego had a stormy relationship. In fact, in April, on her return to Mexico, Frida and Diego began divorce proceedings. Frida was devastated, and for a while she stopped wearing the traditional Mexican dresses that Diego loved so much. Ironically, she painted some of her most powerful works during her separation from Diego. The couple remarried in December 1940.

When asked why she painted herself so often, she replied, "Because I am so often alone." Frida Kahlo passed away in 1954.

Although Frida Kahlo did achieve some success while she was alive, with exhibitions in New York, Paris, and her native Mexico, it was her husband Diego Rivera who was the more famous of the two. He had received commissions in various cities across the United States and had an exhibition at the MoMa in New York.

The opposite is now true, as the name Frida Kahlo probably generates more interest and recognition nowadays. A sort of Frida Kahlo revival started in the 1970s with the "rediscovery" of her art by art historians and grew even more in the 1990s with interest from various communities, such as the Chicano movement. She was brought into mainstream with the launch of the successful biopic Frida in 2002, played by Salma Hayek, a Mexican actress who had fought for many years to bring Frida's story to the big screen. Explaining her fascination for Frida, Salma said, "She was a fighter. Many things could have diminished her spirit, but she wasn't crushed by anything."

**2 Look at some possible alternatives to the time expressions underlined in the text. In each case one is correct and has a similar meaning to the original. The other one is incorrect – cross it out.**

- **a** At the age of six / ~~With six years~~ (lines 1-2)
- **b** After that / At that moment (line 4)
- **c** During the years / During her life (line 7)
- **d** during her convalescence / throughout her convalescence (line 10)
- **e** earlier / previously (line 14)
- **f** as soon as she returned / by her return (line 27)
- **g** while she was separating / while she was separated (line 31)

**3 Think about a famous person you know something about (an artist, a musician, a politician, …). You are going to write a few lines about their life.**

- Do not reveal their identity. Use *he* or *she*.
- Use at least three of the time expressions from Exercise 2.
- Read your partner's sentences and guess who they are describing.

## SPEAKING & LISTENING

**1 Work in groups. Look at the pictures of six products (a–f) that have been invented over the last five hundred years. Discuss in what order you think they were invented and guess a date for each one.**

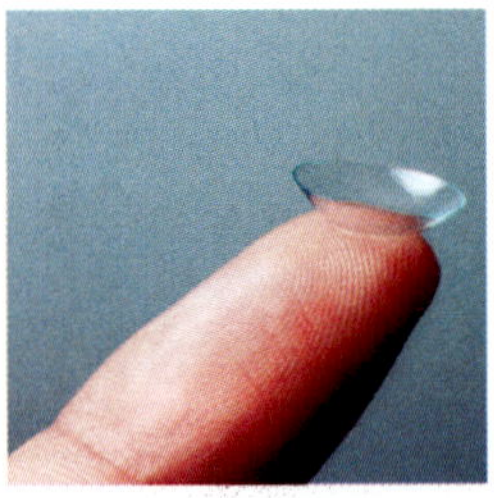

**a** contact lens

**b** toilet

**c** zipper

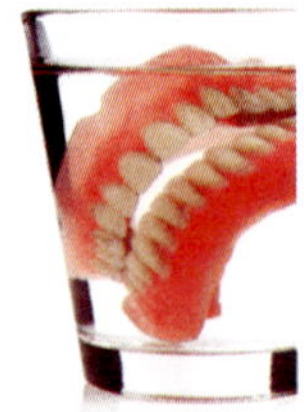

**d** false teeth

**e** razor

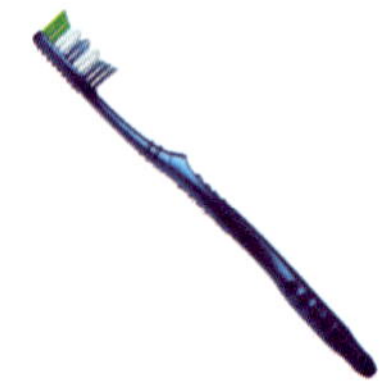

**f** toothbrush

**Go to page 137 to check your answers. Now discuss the questions.**

- Which of the above inventions is the most / least important for society?
- Which of the above inventions could you / couldn't you live without?
- What do you consider to be the three most important inventions of all time?

**2** 2.24 **Listen to an interview with British inventor Trevor Baylis talking about his clockwork radio. Put the questions in the order in which they are asked.**

**a** How many radios are produced each month?
**b** How easy was it to find a backer and set up production?
**c** What advice would you give to someone who had a good idea?
**d** What gave you the idea for the clockwork radio?
**e** How long did it take you to design a prototype?
**f** How long was it then before the production of the radios started?

**TREVOR BAYLIS'S** passion is inventing – especially products that might help people with physical disabilities. In 1993, he invented the clockwork radio.

**3 Match Trevor Baylis's responses (1–6) with the questions (a–f) in Exercise 2.**

**1** "... Don't go down the pub and tell everyone about it."
**2** "... it would have taken me two to three months, I guess ..."
**3** "... I'm sure they must be doing 200,000 a month."
**4** "... I was actually watching a program about the spread of AIDS in Africa ..."
**5** "... Well, the important thing was funding."
**6** "... I was given a chance through the BBC World Service to meet up with the guys from the BBC *Tomorrow's World* program ..."

**Listen again and check your answers.**

**4 Work with a partner. What do you remember about the story of Trevor Baylis and the clockwork radio? Complete the summary with appropriate words.**

# Dream **Invention**

One evening in 1993, Trevor Baylis was watching a program on television about the AIDS (1) **epidemic** in Africa. The program explained that the only way to stop the (2) s______ of AIDS was to educate people about the disease. However, broadcasting the information was extremely difficult. Most people didn't have a radio, as there was no (3) e______ , and batteries were too expensive. At this point Trevor Baylis dozed off and had a (4) d______ . He had dreamed up the concept of the clockwork radio.

It took him just two to three months to develop a (5) p______ and decide that his idea could really work. He filed for a (6) p______ , and then the problems began. He wanted to find a backer for his idea, but every British company he contacted turned him down. However, his unexpected TV appearance on the BBC program, *Tomorrow's World*, changed everything. Trevor Baylis was approached by a South African businessman, and soon money was found to (7) s______ up a company with a factory based in Cape Town. The company was called Baygen, which stands for Baylis Generators. Today, 200,000 radios are made in Africa each month.

According to Trevor Baylis, you do not need to be a genius to be an inventor. His advice to anybody who has a good idea – keep the idea to (8) y______ until you've filed a patent, and never give up.

**5 What do you think of the clockwork radio? Which electrical appliance would you miss most if you lived in an area of the world where there was no electricity?**

## VOCABULARY & PRONUNCIATION

**1 Look at the collocations from the Trevor Baylis interview. Underline the verb in parentheses which best collocates with the noun to give a similar meaning. Use your dictionary if necessary.**

- **a** form a company (set up / do)
- **b** do some experiments (make / carry out)
- **c** have an idea (find / come up with)
- **d** file for a patent (apply for / look for)
- **e** start production (begin / make)
- **f** design a prototype (develop / do)
- **g** do a search (conduct / make)

**2 Work with a partner. Arrange the "stages of production" in Exercise 1 in the most logical order.**

**3 Complete the table with word families and underline the stressed syllable in each word. Use a dictionary if necessary. Practice saying the words.**

| | Noun (subject) | Noun (person) | Adjective | + example collocations |
|---|---|---|---|---|
| **a** | biology | | | weapons |
| **b** | | chemist | | reactions / weapons |
| **c** | | | economic | growth / research |
| **d** | genetics | | | engineering |
| **e** | | mathematician | | equations / research |
| **f** | science | | | advances / research |
| **g** | | technologist | | advances / research |

2.25 **Listen and repeat the words in the table.**

**4 Complete these sentences taken from newspaper reports. Use appropriate adjective-noun collocations from the table in Exercise 3.**

His thesis was full of numbers and complex (1) ______ which made the document impossible for a layperson to read.

(2) ______ has discovered that many types of seaweed are rich in a variety of vitamins and essential minerals which are good for your health.

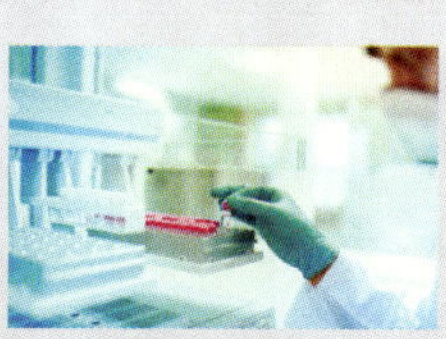

For a long time, many had been skeptical about (3) ______ because of past bad press. Now, the benefits are self-evident: disease prevention, pharmaceutical advancement, agricultural output, and many more.

The low (4) ______, projected at only 2 to 3% for the coming year, is a concern among specialists.

The UN will continue to perform strict (5) ______ inspections as a part of its broader program against weapons of mass destruction.

(6) ______ in computer hardware have made wondrous devices, such as smartphones, an everyday reality.

Recent research showed that ozone-depleting (7) ______ in the atmosphere increased after Mount Pinatubo's eruption.

**5 Use your dictionary. Find at least one more noun collocate for each adjective in the table in Exercise 3. Choose five new collocations to learn and write an example sentence for each one.**

## LANGUAGE FOR LIFE

**1** 2.26 **Listen to a conversation between two friends. Brigit is going to stay at Alice's house while Alice is away. Match each object (a-f) with its function (1-6).**

| | |
|---|---|
| **a** a small key | **1** for turning the TV on and off |
| **b** a dial | **2** for turning the coffee machine on |
| **c** a silver remote control | **3** for opening the front door |
| **d** a black remote control | **4** for turning the stove fan on |
| **e** a red button | **5** for changing channels |
| **f** a switch | **6** for controlling the thermostat |

Alice

**What surprise does Brigit get at the end of the conversation?**

**2 Complete the useful phrases from the conversation by adding the word *it* in the correct position in each sentence.**

- **a** You need to turn twice counterclockwise. *You need to turn it twice counterclockwise.*
- **b** You turn until it clicks.
- **c** Make sure you turn down again.
- **d** You use the silver remote control to turn on and off.
- **e** Press the red button above the stove to turn on.
- **f** Plug in at the wall.
- **g** Put water into the thing above.

Brigit

**What does *it* refer to in each case?**

**Listen again and check.**

**3 Read Alice's description of how to use the coffee machine. Compare her spoken instructions with the written instructions. Underline the written (or formal) equivalents of the highlighted words and phrases.**

| Spoken instructions | Written instructions |
|---|---|
| You put a filter into the filter holder and put the coffee into the filter. | Insert a filter into the filter holder. Place the coffee in the filter. |
| Put water into the thing above it, and make sure the lid's on tight. | Pour water into the water tank. Ensure that the lid is secure. |
| Then put a cup under the place where the coffee comes out. | Place a cup under the spout. |
| The machine will warm the water up to the right temperature, so you just have to wait a few seconds. When the cup's full, take it out and your coffee's ready. | The machine will heat the water to the correct temperature. When the cup is full, remove it immediately and your coffee is ready to drink. |

**4 Think about a machine or a gadget in your house. Explain how to use it to your partner using spoken instructions.**

### LIFE SKILLS: Self Awareness

Knowing Yourself Better

**1** 2.27 **Listen to the definition of a genius. Is it similar to your concept of a genius?**

**2** 2.28 **Listen to Uzo's profile. Do you think she is a genius? Justify your answer.**

**3 Write down what you are good at and how can you use your skill to help others or make someone's life better.**

MACMILLAN LIFE SKILLS

# 9 Writing Extra

## NARRATIVE

**1 Read about the invention of the 3M Post-it® note. Complete the text with time expressions from the box.**

a few months earlier
Each Sunday
In 1977
One Sunday
The following day

(1) ______ , Art Fry was a product designer with the huge 3M Corporation in the USA. (2) ______ , as a member of his local church choir, he would check which hymns he was to sing during the service and mark them with pieces of paper in his hymn book. Inevitably, just as a hymn was about to start, the paper would drop out, and Fry would have a frantic search for the right page. (3) ______ he was listening to the sermon when his mind began to wander. He remembered that (4) ______ , a research colleague had made a glue which had been discarded when it proved to have poor sticking power. (5) ______ he managed to obtain some of this failed glue and started making his bookmarks with it. Post-its are now a billion-dollar business.

**2 Read about the invention of the microwave oven. Underline the most appropriate verb structures to complete the description.**

In 1946, Dr. Percy LeBaron Spencer (1) **worked** / **was working** on a radar-based research project when he (2) **felt** / **was feeling** something sticky in his pocket. It turned out to be a melted peanut bar. Spencer guessed that it (3) **had been affected** / **was affected** by high frequency radio emissions from the magnetron – a key component in radar. He (4) **heard** / **had heard** stories of partially cooked birds being found at the base of early radar installations but had, until now, dismissed them. Intrigued, he sent a boy out to buy a packet of popcorn. When he placed it close to the magnetron, the popcorn exploded. By the end of that year, the first prototype microwave oven (5) **was installed** / **had been installed** in a Boston restaurant.

**3 You are going to write the story of another smart innovation, the social-networking site Facebook®. Complete the sentences below by expanding the notes provided. Pay particular attention to tenses.**

Mark Zuckerberg founded Facebook while studying psychology at Harvard University.
He had already developed ... including ...
In February 2004, ...
Within 24 hours, ... and after one month ...
The site became "Facebook" in August 2005 when ...
Previously, the site was only available to college students, but since September 2006 ...
In 2008, four years after three Harvard classmates ...
...

[Notes – the story of Facebook]

Mark Zuckerberg

- Mark Zuckerberg – founder of Facebook.
- Studied psychology at Harvard University.
- Developed a number of social-networking sites for fellow students, e.g. Facemash – a site for rating people's attractiveness.
- February 2004 – launched "The Facebook."
- In one day, 1,200 students signed up.
- Half the student population of Harvard set up profiles in the first month.
- August 2005 – Zuckerberg purchased the name "facebook.com" for $200,000.
- September 2006 – Facebook became available to anyone over thirteen.
- Three of Zuckerberg's classmates accused him of stealing the idea for Facebook. Four years later, Zuckerberg settled out of court.
- October 2010 - The movie 'The Social Network,' a fictionalized account of how Facebook began, is released.
- April 2012 - Facebook purchases Instagram for $1 billion.
- October 2012 - Facebook reaches one billion active monthly users worldwide.
- February 2014 - Facebook announces its purchase of WhatsApp for $19 billion.
- As of June 30, 2017, Facebook has 2.01 billion monthly active users.
- The average time spent on Facebook per visit is 20 minutes.
- Zuckerberg is now one of the youngest billionaires in the world.

# Review C

Grammar Extra pages 146-149

## GRAMMAR

**1 Underline the correct alternative.**

**Kate:** Excuse me. Could you give me some information? Your airline just (1) **announced us** / **announced** that all your flights are canceled today.

**Man:** I'm afraid that's true, but I can (2) **assure you** / **assure** that we will find you another flight as soon as possible.

**Kate:** So can you (3) **confirm me** / **confirm** that we will fly today?

**Man:** I must (4) **admit you** / **admit** I can't make any promises. However, I will (5) **inform you** / **inform** as soon as we have any further information.

**Kate:** Well, could you at least (6) **explain us** / **explain** why this has happened?

**Man:** I'm sorry. I (7) **suggest you** / **suggest** that you take a seat and wait for our next announcement, which is due soon.

**2 Complete the text with the words in the box.**

| allowed didn't had need should should |
|---|

Recently I traveled from Chicago to New York on business. I didn't (1) _____ to fly but foolishly I did! First, I (2) _____ to take off most of my clothes at security. Then I wasn't (3) _____ to use my cell phone during the flight. After an uncomfortable three hours, it took another hour to get out of the airport, only to learn my meeting had been canceled. I know I (4) _____ have to fly back the same day. I know I (5) _____ have stayed the night to see more of New York, but I just wanted to go home! Unfortunately, the return trip was even worse. I (6) _____ have taken the train! It would have been quicker and easier.

**3 Complete the sentences with *a/an* or *the*, or leave it blank where an article is not necessary.**

a I wish I had _____ curly hair.
b I've never owned _____ expensive car.
c I'd love to spend a week cruising on _____ Amazon.

**4 Complete each sentence so that it means the same as the one above it.**

a We expect that the rate of inflation will rise sharply.
The rate of inflation ...
b People think the President will resign soon.
It ...
c Scientists say that the world's climate will become more extreme.
It ...
d They think vast oil reserves exist under the Arctic ice cap.
Vast oil reserves ...

**5 Write the questions in the correct order.**

a won / you / $10 million, / If / all / keep / you / it / would / ?
b could / someone famous, / Supposing / be / it / who / you / be / would / ?
c what / able to do / you / dream job, / do / would / you / Imagine / your / were / ?
d would / time / like / new skill / no object / to learn / were / you / what / Assuming / ?

**Answer the questions and compare with a partner.**

**6 Write sentences for each of the situations using *might have, must have,* or *couldn't have*.**

a Amy isn't here yet and it's 9:30.
b Will has a terrible headache this morning.
c Daniela didn't answer her doorbell.
d Kenji's arm is in a cast.

**7 Complete the statements with the words in the box. Change the form if necessary.**

| as if ~~look~~ look like seem though to be |
|---|

a My best friend always **looks** worried.
b My mother _____ a model when she was young.
c I never feel as _____ I have enough time.
d When I was young, my father always _____ to be busy.
e It looks _____ tomorrow is going to be sunny.
f My teacher never seems _____ happy with my homework.

**Which sentences are true for you? Discuss with your partner.**

## VOCABULARY

**1 Add suffixes *ful*, *ish*, or *less* to make adjectives.**

**a** bull_____ **d** fool_____ **g** self_____
**b** cheer_____ **e** home_____ **h** stress_____
**c** end_____ **f** relent_____ **i** tear_____

**2 Put each adjective in the box into the correct column.**

adequate adventurous appropriate capable decisive divided honest legal legible literate logical loyal mature moral obedient patient polite rational relevant resistible responsible satisfied usual willing

| dis- | il- | im- |
|---|---|---|
| _____ | _____ | _____ |
| _____ | _____ | _____ |
| _____ | _____ | _____ |
| _____ | _____ | _____ |

| in- | ir- | un- |
|---|---|---|
| _____ | _____ | _____ |
| _____ | _____ | _____ |
| _____ | _____ | _____ |
| _____ | _____ | _____ |

**3 Complete the text with facial features.**

It is believed that to qualify as "beautiful" you have to have a big (1) m_____ , full (2) l_____ , and high (3) c_____ . Other desirable qualities are smooth (4) s_____ , white (5) t_____ , big, sparkling (6) e_____ , and (7) d_____ in the cheeks. Surprisingly, women appear to prefer a softer face on a man, rather than the classic "square (8) j_____ " look.

**Discuss with your partner which features you think make a person attractive.**

**4 Match each adjective (a–k) with its synonym (1–11).**

| | | | |
|---|---|---|---|
| **a** | down-to-earth | **1** | unfriendly |
| **b** | enigmatic | **2** | unpretentious |
| **c** | laid-back | **3** | selfish |
| **d** | mature | **4** | caring |
| **e** | open-minded | **5** | mysterious |
| **f** | self-centered | **6** | tense |
| **g** | sensible | **7** | level-headed |
| **h** | sensitive | **8** | relaxed |
| **i** | stand-offish | **9** | dependable |
| **j** | uptight | **10** | experienced / grown-up |
| **k** | trustworthy | **11** | tolerant |

**Choose three adjectives to describe yourself. Compare with your partner.**

**5 Complete the text with the words in the box.**

After As Barely During Soon When While

Audrey Hepburn was born in Belgium in 1929. (1) _____ she was ten, war broke out. (2) _____ the war, she lived with her mother in the Netherlands. (3) _____ the war she went to London and started acting. (4) _____ she was filming in France, she met the novelist Colette, who insisted she play the role Gigi in her Broadway play. (5) _____ after she finished on Broadway, she starred in her first movie, *Roman Holiday*, with Gregory Peck. (6) _____ soon as the movie came out, she was nominated for (and later won) an Oscar. She went on to enjoy a distinguished career. (7) _____ four months after being diagnosed with colon cancer, in 1992, Audrey Hepburn was dead. She was only sixty-three.

## PRONUNCIATION

**1 Look at some words from Units 7–9. Say the words and add them to the table.**

~~attractive~~ company cosmetics drizzle encourage genuine lively meander qualities science traveler urban

| A: □▫ | B: ▫□▫ | C: □▫▫ |
|---|---|---|
| | attractive | |

**2 <u>Underline</u> the stressed syllable.**

▶ 2.29 **Listen, check, and repeat.**

# 10 Sell

## SPEAKING & VOCABULARY

1 **Work with a partner. Look at "Know your Logos!" Identify the brand in each case and circle the correct version of each logo. Check your answers on page 137.**

2 **Discuss the questions.**

**a** Which of these brands are popular in your country?
**b** How many more logos can you draw? See if your partner can identify them.

3 **Look at these different ways of saying *look* and *see*. Put them in the correct category and discuss the differences in meaning with your partner.**

~~glance~~ make out gaze notice stare spot catch sight of eye

| Look | See |
|---|---|
| glance | |

- **Grammar:** Relative clauses. Emphasis (cleft sentences)
- **Vocabulary:** *look at* and *see*. Sales and marketing collocations. Spoken discourse markers
- **Language for Life:** Using emotive language

**4** **Underline the appropriate verb phrases to complete this description.**

https://fashionaddicted.com

I'm addicted to fashion! My dream is to one day become a fashion designer, but for now I still have a day job. That doesn't mean I can't practice – I spend hours **(1) glancing at / gazing at** pictures in fashion magazines, and then I try to recreate my favorite looks. I can't walk past a clothing store without **(2) eyeing / spotting** all the different styles, and I'm inspired by all kinds of clothes from different cultures. I can't stand people who only look at the brand and don't care about the quality. Expensive isn't always better, you know! For example, if you show me two handbags, I can always **(3) spot / catch sight of** the one made with cheap materials, even if it has a fancy brand name. In the end, it's all about quality. I have to admit though, I do always **(4) stare at / glance at** well-dressed people in the street – I can't look away. As for my own style, I think it's important to feel good and to be confident in the way you look. Most of my friends wear casual clothes, so when I go out people **(5) stare at / gaze at me** because I like to dress up and wear original items. But I don't care – it doesn't bother me if I get **(6) noticed / made out**, and I know that as soon as people **(7) stare at / catch sight of** me, they'll get a sense of my personality. Isn't that what fashion is really all about?

**How would you describe your own attitude towards clothing and brands? Tell your partner.**

## LISTENING & VOCABULARY

**1** **You are going to listen to these two people giving their opinions about children and advertising. Guess which person is likely to have made each statement (a–f).**

**a** "... children are being brainwashed by all the advertising that goes on around them."
**b** "Brands give children a sense of identity and help them fit in with a peer group."
**c** "... it's time the government put a stop to all this aggressive TV advertising."
**d** "Companies donate free computers, and in exchange, they can advertise their brands on book covers and posters. I think it's fantastic - the kids benefit, and the companies get brand loyalty from a very early age."
**e** "I'd love to be a child today. They really know what they want ..."
**f** "I don't think all this choice is liberating for children - it just means that they're encouraged to be materialistic ..."

Joe Smedley, marketing executive

Sally McIlveen, school principal

2.30-2.31 **Listen and check your answers. Work with a partner. Do you agree or disagree with the statements?**

**2** **Work with your partner. Student A look at page 137, Student B look at page 139.**

## READING & VOCABULARY

1 **Look at the title of the magazine article and the pictures on page 107. Discuss possible answers to these questions:**

- **a** What do you think 'cord cutter' means?
- **b** What do you think the article will be about?

**Read the first paragraph of *Cutting the Cord* and check your answers. Then read the rest of the article and match the three people being interviewed (a-c) with their opinions (1-3).**

| | |
|---|---|
| **a** Ramesh | **1** focused on one area where advertisements are very valuable |
| **b** Corinne | **2** optimistic about future opportunities despite popular opinion |
| **c** Bailey | **3** interested in the evolution of online advertising |

2 **Read the text again and answer the questions.**

- **a** How has the way that people avoid ads changed?
- **b** Why does Ramesh say that 'traditional advertising is slowing down'?
- **c** What three ways do Ramesh and Corinne describe to stop people from skipping ads?
- **d** Why is sports programming becoming increasingly valuable?
- **e** What is the danger of paying for expensive ads during a sporting event?
- **f** What does Bailey mean when she says that 'traditional TV and ads are like the dinosaurs at this point'?
- **g** What are the advantages of 'targeted ads'?
- **h** What evidence does the author give that we will continue to see ads?

3 **Look at the words and phrases highlighted in the article. Discuss their possible meaning with your partner. Then complete the glossary at the bottom of the article.**

4 **Work in groups. Go to the Additional material on page 137.**

## GRAMMAR

1 **Look at the sentences that begin on lines 5, 20, and 36 in the article on page 107. Underline the relative clauses in each sentence. Then choose the description that best defines the function of each relative clause.**

1. It comments on the whole of the main clause (*non-defining*).
2. It identifies something in the main clause (*defining*).
3. It gives extra information about something in the main clause (*non-defining*).

**What punctuation is used to show that a relative clause is *non-defining*?**

> **Relative clauses**
>
> I watched an action movie, **which is unusual for me**.
>
> I watched the action movie **that you suggested**.
>
> The movie, **which stars Dwayne Johnson**, is excellent.

2 **Work with your partner. Look at the sentence pairs (a-h). Decide which is the most suitable follow-up (*1* or *2*) for each sentence.**

| Main sentence | Follow-up sentence |
|---|---|
| **a** She offered me some candy that was very strange. | **1** They were red and blue. |
| **b** She offered me some candy, which was very strange. | **2** She knows I don't eat sugar. |
| **c** He's dating Julie, who I can't stand. | **1** He should be going out with me! |
| **d** He's dating Julie, which I can't stand. | **2** She's such a gossip. |
| **e** She bought me an expensive tie that I didn't like. | **1** Why waste money on ties? |
| **f** She bought me an expensive tie, which I didn't like. | **2** It was an awful orange color. |
| **g** My brother who lives in Rio is a model. | **1** My other brother is an accountant. |
| **h** My brother, who lives in Rio, is a model. | **2** He absolutely loves his job. |

3 **Look again at the main sentences in Exercise 2 and the type of relative clauses in Exercise 1. Answer the questions.**

- **a** What type of relative clause does each main sentence contain: 1, 2, or 3?
- **b** Which relative pronoun (*who*, *which*, and *that*) cannot be used with non-defining relative clauses?
- **c** Which relative pronoun is always used to introduce a comment on the whole main clause?

4 **Grammar Extra 10, Part 1** page 148. Read the explanations and do Exercises 1 and 2.

# CUTTING THE CORD

*Ads are annoying. You know it, I know it, everyone knows it. It's no surprise then that most people try to avoid watching them whenever possible. Whereas in the old days this meant actually changing the channel, most of the time now we can just skip right past the ads on TV or close a pop-up window in our browser. In fact, there is even a name for the current generation who have given up on cable TV: 'cord cutters', people who have stopped paying for cable and just watch everything online. Now, traditional media is scrambling to stay relevant to advertisers and their all-important dollars. To find out more about this shifting media landscape, we interviewed three advertising experts in different fields to see what they thought about this phenomenon.*

## Ramesh – TV network executive

*I know what everyone is saying these days about the fall of network TV. It's true, there are a number of challenges facing us. In 2017 alone there were 22.2 million cord cutters in the US, so it's clear that traditional advertising is slowing down. With that said, I do think people are overlooking all the new opportunities that we're seeing nowadays.*

*Although it's difficult to measure, we believe that actually more people might be watching TV these days than ever before, which is encouraging – they're just visiting our online platforms instead of turning on the TV. And yes, it's easier to skip ads online, but that's why we've shifted our focus. Instead of long commercials, we are now including shorter spots that aren't so intrusive. Also, advertisers can now sponsor segments. This means that they are paying to introduce a part of your favorite show, an online clip, or some other online content.*

*Admittedly, it's not easy to know how to please both advertisers and consumers, but with enough creativity I think we can be as strong as ever. And of course, we have to remember not to cater just to millennials – older generations watch TV too!*

## Corinne – Media buyer

*Well, one thing that has changed is the relative value of ad time with different kinds of programs. Even a few years ago, you could rely on big network shows, which aired every week, to have huge viewing numbers all year round. Now, the most reliable way to predict big numbers is with live events. Sport, especially, is something that everyone wants to watch at the same time, and over 99% of sports are viewed live. It's no wonder that the College Football National Championship game in 2015 was the most watched broadcast in cable TV history.*

*It's still a risk since people are more likely to tune out if the game is a blowout with one team winning by a huge amount, but in general, this is a trend I'd expect to keep seeing – increasingly expensive ads for the big events like the Super Bowl. Another prediction I'd make is that networks will get really creative during the games themselves, for example by putting an ad and the game on at the same time with split screen. Then people won't have a choice but to watch!*

## Bailey – Online technology journalist

*Yeah, traditional TV and ads are like the dinosaurs at this point, even if they don't know it yet. Soon no one will be paying for cable, instead just relying on internet viewing options. What does this mean for advertising? My guess is that there will be more ads than before but different. Instead of long ads for the general public, companies will get better and better at finding ways of inserting targeted ads, specifically designed for their online audiences. Say you're watching a cooking show, well then you probably will see ads mostly related to food, home, etc. rather than video games for teenagers. This will also allow companies to take more risks and create branded, interactive content – ads that actually look like programs and let the viewer interact in some way. I'm not sure exactly what all this will look like, but I'm excited to find out!*

*So there you have it, traditional ads may be on the decline, but there's no escape from ads in general, even if you cut every cord in sight. In fact, Google estimates that we are exposed to 3000–5000 ads per day in one form or another! It looks like there are still plenty of opportunities for advertisers to convince us that what we need is what they're selling …*

### Glossary

**a** ______ noun [C]: a computer program that allows you to look at the Internet

**b** ______ verb [T]: to fail to notice or do something

**c** ______ verb [I]: to hurry or try very hard to get something

**d** ______ adjective: becoming involved in something in a way that is not welcome

**e** ______ noun [C/U]: a reduction in the amount or quality of something

**f** ______ noun [C]: a way of showing two or more pictures on one screen

**g** ______ phrasal verb [I/T]: to stop paying attention

**h** ______ verb [T]: to broadcast a program on television

**i** ______ noun [C]: something that is very impressive or surprising

**j** ______ verb [T]: to put something into something else

**k** ______ verb [I]: to try to satisfy a need or demand

## LISTENING & SPEAKING

**1 Discuss the following questions with a partner.**

- Who are the most photographed celebrities in your country?
- Which magazines devote themselves to celebrity news and gossip?
- What do you think are the pros and cons of being constantly in the public eye?

**2** ▶ 2.32 **Listen to a radio show discussing truth and accuracy in the tabloids. Who do you sympathize with most: the celebrity or the editor?**

**Work with your partner. Use the words in the box to explain why the actress is unhappy.**

co-star breakfast hotel morning good friend divorce

**3 Read the sentences below taken from the interview. Who said each sentence: the presenter (P), the celebrity (C), or the magazine editor (E)?**

**a** The popular press has been criticized yet again, this time for their apparent lack of respect for truth and accuracy.
**b** ... before you were famous, you were urging us to write articles about you.
**c** Take last week – your magazine wrote this story about me and my co-star, who, by the way, happens to be married to a very good friend of mine.
**d** I am sick of the popular press making up stories just so that they can put sensational headlines across the front page.
**e** I think we need to address the cause of the problem.
**f** If a magazine prints something shocking or embarrassing about a famous person, they'll almost certainly deny it.

Shelley Russell

Jim Falmer

**Replace the highlighted words with the words that were actually used in the interview. Choose from the words in the box. Listen again and check your answers.**

begging 're bound to disregard features incidentally root scandalous splash under fire

**4 Use the words in the box to complete the phrases said by the speakers in the radio discussion in Exercise 2.**

but but finish here is is is question saying was

**a** Sorry, ______ ...
**b** If you would just let me ______ ...
**c** But the thing ______ ...
**d** Anyway, to get back to what I was ______ ...
**e** The point I'm trying to make here ______ ...
**f** What you didn't say ______ ...
**g** If I could just come in ______ ...
**h** If you would let me answer the ______ ...
**i** The problem ______ ...
**j** I'm sorry to interrupt you, ______ ...

**Look at the Audioscript on page 152 and check your answers.**

**5 Use the following table to categorize the phrases according to their function.**

| Interrupting | Responding to an interruption | Introducing a point |
|---|---|---|
| Sorry, but ... | If you would just let me finish ... | But the thing is ... |

**6 Work in small groups. Think of points for and against each statement. Discuss the statements and take turns agreeing or disagreeing.**

**a** For celebrities, any publicity is good publicity, the more sensational the better.
**b** It is a magazine editor's job to increase circulation, not to worry about accuracy.
**c** The public has a right to read articles about the private lives of famous people.

## GRAMMAR

1 **Work with a partner. Sentences *A* and *B* are two ways of saying the same thing. How does the emphasis change in sentence *B*?**

A Yes, but you didn't say what the inaccuracies were …
B Yes, but what you didn't say was what the inaccuracies were …

**Which sentence did Shelley Russell use in the radio show on page 108?**

**Emphasis (cleft sentences)**

I don't understand why I'm always poor.
**What / The thing I don't understand is** why I'm always poor.

Money doesn't make you happy. Friendship does.
**It isn't money that** makes you happy, it's friendship.

2 **Change the emphasis of these sentences using the sentence beginnings provided.**

**a** I don't understand why I never seem to have any money.
*What I don't understand is …*
**b** I like weekends because I can go shopping with my friends.
*The thing I like about weekends is …*
**c** People who only talk about money really annoy me.
*What really annoys me is …*
**d** I really feel like going to the movies tonight.
*What I really feel like doing tonight is …*
**e** I hate the winter because it gets dark so early.
*The thing …*
**f** I'd really like to live and work abroad in the future.
*What …*

**How many of the sentences are true for you?**

3 **Work with your partner. Which one of the statements about celebrities is true?**

**a** Barack Obama was the Democratic candidate in the 2016 US Elections.
**b** Benedict Cumberbatch replaced Pierce Brosnan as James Bond.
**c** Katie Holmes used to be married to Tom Cruise.
**d** Stephenie Meyer wrote the *Harry Potter* series.
**e** Brad Pitt plays Captain Jack Sparrow in *Pirates of the Caribbean*.
**f** Shakira is married to Javier Bardem.

Penélope Cruz

**Use the information in the box and correct all the false statements, beginning with *It isn't … / It wasn't …***

J.K. Rowling | Penélope Cruz | Daniel Craig | Johnny Depp | Hillary Clinton

It wasn't Barack Obama who was the Democratic candidate, it was …

4 **Grammar Extra 10, Part 2** page 148. Read the explanations and do Exercises 3 and 4.

## PRONUNCIATION

1 **Practice saying the following sentences with the appropriate emphasis.**

- Underline the stressed words.
- Mark with // where there is a slight pause.

**a** What I love about Peter is his great sense of humor.
What I love about Peter // is his great sense of humor.
**b** The thing I can't stand about this country is the weather.
**c** What I really hate about my job is having to work on weekends.
**d** What I find annoying about politicians is that they never give a straight answer.
**e** The thing I find most difficult about English is the spelling.
**f** What I would really like to do is to take a year off.

2.33 **Listen, check, and repeat.**

2 **Work with your partner. Use the sentence beginnings in Exercise 1 to express your feelings about your family, your friends, your job, etc.**

## READING & VOCABULARY

1 **Work with a partner. You are going to read an article about the role of advertising in the *Iron Man* movies.**

- **a** Say what kind of movies they are and who the usual audience is.
- **b** Name some of the actors (or the characters) who are in *Iron Man*.
- **c** Name some of the cars, products, or brands that have appeared in *Iron Man* movies.

**Read the article on page 111, ignoring the blanks. How many of your ideas are mentioned?**

2 **Six sentences have been removed from the article on page 111. Choose from the sentences (a-g) the one which fits each blank (1-6). There is one extra sentence which you do not need to use.**

- **a** However, if they're watching the movie and see their favorite star drinking a Dr Pepper, well what could be more effective than that?
- **b** In *Die Another Day*, twenty different companies paid $70 million between them for the privilege of having their products included in the movie.
- **c** Well, it looks like product placement is losing some of its momentum.
- **d** A quick glance at the box office statistics show staggering numbers: $585 million in ticket sales for the original *Iron Man*, $621 million for *Iron Man 2*, and an incredible $2.4 billion for *Iron Man 3*!
- **e** Well, it doesn't seem like product placement is going to slow down anytime soon.
- **f** Maybe the companies should just make the movies themselves - how does Audi Man sound?
- **g** Perhaps more honestly, Audi has also publicly acknowledged that the success of their R8 is in part due to the film series.

3 **Look at the words and numbers below. Quickly find them in the text and write what they refer to.**

621 million <u>Iron Man 2 box office total</u>

Yili ____________________

1964 ____________________

Pepper Potts ____________________

70 million ____________________

R8 ____________________

Robert Downey Jr. ____________________

BMW ____________________

4 **Apart from Iron Man, think of three famous fictional movie characters. Which one is your favorite? Tell your partner.**

# PRODUCT PLACEMENT MAN

Even if you've never seen any of the *Iron Man* movies, you probably still recognize the star: Robert Downey Jr. and his iconic metallic red and gold suit. In fact, at this point it's almost unavoidable. With marketing budgets reaching over $100 million per movie, and world-wide distribution and advertising, the presence of Iron Man is ubiquitous. And that's before we even consider the number of people who have visited the theater to watch one of the *Iron Man* films. **[1]**

No wonder then, with so many eyeballs glued to the screen, that multinational companies are jumping at the chance to attach themselves to this franchise. Yes, there are TV ads, billboards, and merchandise, but in this day and age, the real prize for any company is product placement. After all, when people (and especially kids) are able to skip ads, change channels, and avoid traditional marketing, it becomes harder and harder to catch and keep their attention. **[2]**

Right from the start, the *Iron Man* franchise has taken full advantage of its captive audience, selling screen time, especially to car and food companies. In terms of vehicles, Audi is the brand of choice; not only does the main character, Tony Stark, drive an Audi R8, his assistant Pepper Potts, played by Gwyneth Paltrow, drives an Audi too. Of course, Audi says this is because Tony Stark's 'drive for innovation represents the constant quest for progress', but you don't need to be much of a cynic to question this statement. **[3]**

Even more blatant is the food and drink on display in the movies. After talking about how much he wants an American burger, Tony Stark can be seen with a Burger King wrapper while he gives a press conference. However, there is one example of product placement in *Iron Man* that is even more surreal. It turns out that the version of *Iron Man 3* released in China was four minutes longer than anywhere else. The reason? There were scenes added with Chinese actors drinking Yili, a milk drink, purely for product placement reasons.

Of course, product placement in the cinema is nothing new, as a look back at other older action films will attest to. Take for example the classic Bond movies in which 007, James Bond, famously drove an Aston Martin in 1964's *Goldfinger*. In the five decades since, product placement has become as common in the Bond movies as car chases and technological gadgets. **[4]**

So what does the future hold for Iron Man and his many products? **[5]** To be sure, there has been some criticism from parents, movie critics, and consumer groups like Campaign for a Commercial Free Childhood. But if the audience keeps approving of these movies by opening up their wallets, then you can be sure that companies will keep paying for the privilege of squeezing in their products. Even within the automobile industry, various big name players have already aligned themselves with other Hollywood franchises – Dodge are heavily invested in the *Transformers* franchise (the transformers turn into Dodge vehicles), and BMW is the car of choice for Tom Cruise in the *Mission Impossible* movies. **[6]**

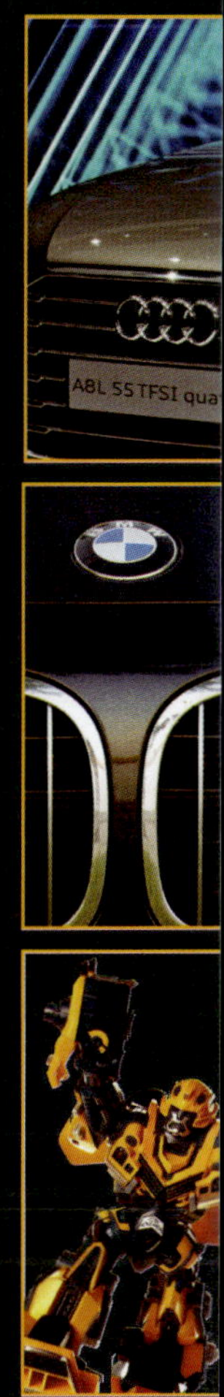

### Glossary

**ubiquitous** adjective: present everywhere

**jump at the chance** phrase: take an opportunity in a very enthusiastic way

**product placement** noun [U]: use of a company's product in a movie as a way of advertising it

**cynic** noun [C]: someone who believes that people are not sincere or honest

**blatant** adjective: done in an obvious way that shows you are not embarrassed or ashamed

**align with** verb [T]: to give your support publicly to a group

## SPEAKING: ANECDOTE

**You are going to tell your partner about a blockbuster movie you have seen.**

- Ask yourself the questions below.
- Think about *what* to say and *how* to say it.
- Tell your partner about the movie.

**a** What was the name of the movie?
**b** Who was in it and who directed it?
**c** When and where did you see it?
**d** Who did you see it with?
**e** What did you know about the movie before you saw it?
**f** What did you particularly like or dislike about the movie?
**g** Were there any characters you could identify with?
**h** Were there any characters who annoyed you?
**i** What was the best/worst part of the movie?
**j** Would you go and see another movie by the same director?

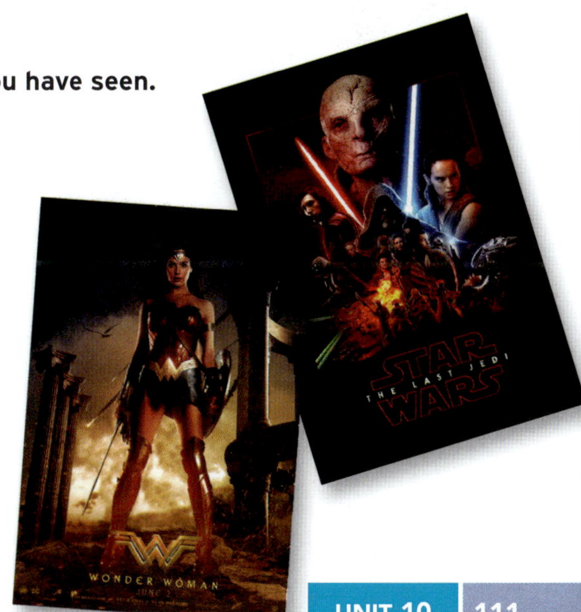

## LANGUAGE FOR LIFE

**1** ▶ 2.34 **Listen to six people describing how they feel about a movie they are just about to see. Which movie (*a*, *b*, *c*, or *d*) is it?**

a

b

c

d

**2** **<u>Underline</u> the word or phrase each person used to describe their feelings.**

1. "**Pretty** / **Totally** / **Extremely** nervous, actually."
2. "Yeah, **distinctly** / **utterly** / **a little** uneasy, I must admit."
3. "I'm looking forward to being **scared** / **nervous** / **bored** to death."
4. "To be **scared** / **afraid** / **bored** stiff - hopefully."
5. "I feel **completely** / **terribly** / **pretty** apprehensive."
6. "I expect it to be **absolutely** / **quite** / **very** terrifying!"

**Listen again and check.**

**Look at the two other options in the useful phrases above. ~~Cross out~~ the option that doesn't form a common collocation and check (✓) the option that does. Use your dictionary if necessary.**

1 "<u>Pretty</u> / ~~Totally~~ / Extremely ✓ nervous, actually."

**3** **Work with a partner. Look at the adjectives in the box and decide which ones fit sentence frame *A* and which ones fit sentence frame *B*.**

amazing awesome awful boring disappointing entertaining extraordinary funny good interesting ridiculous spectacular

**A** (*gradable adjectives*): The movie was very, extremely ____ .
**B** (*absolute adjectives*): The movie was absolutely ____ .

**4** ▶ 2.35 **Listen to the six people from Exercise 1 being interviewed after the movie. What was the general reaction?**

### LIFE SKILLS: Communication

Persuading Others

**It is not only salespeople who need to sell. Whether you are at a job interview, giving a presentation, or applying for a scholarship, being *persuasive* is an important skill. By being persuasive, you can sell things, ideas, or even yourself.**

**1** ▶ 2.36 **Listen to Eric explain to some investors why they should invest in his shoe company. Check (✓) the boxes of the things he does to be persuasive.**

☐ speaks very quickly to try to squeeze in more information
☐ asks questions to involve the listener
☐ gives examples and evidence
☐ commands the listener to do what he says
☐ uses descriptive words to add more detail
☐ says why other opinions are stupid
☐ shows the logic of what he is saying
☐ describes what the benefits would be
☐ uses lots of terminology that is difficult to understand
☐ gives the listener an emotional reason to care

**Useful language: persuading**

*Just imagine ...*
*Don't you think that ... ?*
*If you know that ... then ...*
*Let me ask you ...*
*I'm sure that ...*
*I truly believe that ...*

**2** **Work with a partner. Choose an item in the classroom or an item that you have with you, e.g. a pencil, a water bottle, etc. Your partner will try to sell this item to you, and he/she will choose an item for you to sell. Before you speak, think about ...**

- the positive qualities of the item
- why your partner needs it
- what descriptive words you will use to talk about it
- what language from the *Useful Language* box you can use

**Listen to your partner. Would you buy the item from them? Why / Why not?**

MACMILLAN LIFE SKILLS

# 10 Vocabulary Extra

## COLLOCATIONS

**1 Work with a partner. Words which often go together are called *collocations*. Read the text and identify the collocations with the key words in bold. Some words may have more than one collocate, e.g. *extremely important* and *important aspect*.**

> Recognizing and using collocations is an extremely **important** aspect of learning a language. Learners soon **realize** that particular words regularly and naturally combine with each other. However, deciding which words go with which can **cause** problems. Occasionally, difficulties **arise** when the wrong word is used. Fortunately, good dictionaries provide useful **information** to help learners make informed **decisions**. This page offers some practical **suggestions**.

**Find at least one collocation for each of the following grammatical categories.**

- **a** adverb + adjective: *extremely important*
- **b** adjective + noun: *important aspect*
- **c** verb + noun (as object): ______
- **d** noun (as subject) + verb: ______
- **e** adverb + verb: ______

**Check your ideas in the dictionary extracts. Add any more collocations that you find to the categories above.**

**2 Using appropriate alternative collocations, rewrite the text in Exercise 1 so that the meaning stays approximately the same.**

*Recognizing and using collocations is a particularly important part of learning ...*

**3 Look at the dictionary extracts for *problem* and *decision*. Divide the verb collocates for each noun into two "meaning" groups.**

**a** problem
- have — *encounter*
- solve — *address*

**b** decision
- make — *arrive at*
- reject — *overrule*

**Words frequently used with suggestion**

| | | |
|---|---|---|
| *adjectives* | alternative, constructive, helpful, positive, practical, sensible, tentative | 1 |
| *verbs* | adopt, make, offer, oppose, reject, submit, volunteer, welcome | 1 |

**Words frequently used with realize**

| | | |
|---|---|---|
| *adverbs* | belatedly, gradually, instantly, quickly, soon, suddenly | 1 |

**Words frequently used with problem**

| | | |
|---|---|---|
| *adjectives* | big, fundamental, important, insoluble, intractable, major, pressing, real, serious | 1 |
| *verbs* | address, alleviate, cause, compound, create, encounter, exacerbate, experience, face, overcome, pose, resolve, solve, tackle | 1 |

**Words frequently used with important**

| | | |
|---|---|---|
| *adverbs* | crucially, extremely, most, particularly, terribly, vitally | 1 |
| *nouns* | aspect, element, factor, feature, issue, part, point | 1 |

**Words frequently used with cause**

| | | |
|---|---|---|
| *nouns* | alarm, concern, confusion, controversy, damage, distress, embarrassment, harm, problems, suffering, trouble | |

**Words frequently used with arise**

| | | |
|---|---|---|
| *nouns* | difficulty, issue, matter, need, opportunity, problem, question, situation | 1 |

**Words frequently used with issue**

| | | |
|---|---|---|
| *adjectives* | contentious, controversial, divisive, important, key, major, pressing, sensitive, thorny, unresolved | 1 |
| *verbs* | address, cloud, complicate, confront, confuse, consider, dodge, duck, evade, examine, explore, fudge, raise, tackle | 1 |

**Words frequently used with information**

| | | |
|---|---|---|
| *adjectives* | accurate, additional, confidential, detailed, further, inside, relevant, useful | 1 |
| *verbs* | collect, elicit, extract, gather, get, obtain, receive, retrieve | 1 |

**Words frequently used with decision**

| | | |
|---|---|---|
| *adjectives* | controversial, difficult, final, informed, momentous, strategic, tough, unanimous | 1 |
| *verbs* | arrive at, come to, make, overrule, overturn, quash, reach, reconsider, rescind, reverse, take | 1 |

From the *Macmillan English Dictionary (American and British editions)*

**Choose two verb collocates for each noun that are new to you. Look them up in your dictionary. Write a definition and an example sentence for each one.**

**4 Look at the adjectives frequently used with *information* and *decision*. Find one or two alternative ways of expressing each of the following.**

**INFORMATION**

- **a** correct information *accurate information*
- **b** extra or more information
- **c** secret information
- **d** useful information

**DECISION**

- **a** a difficult decision
- **b** a historic decision
- **c** a decision based on facts
- **d** a decision where everybody agreed
- **e** a decision as part of a plan
- **f** a decision where not everybody agreed

**5 Work with your partner. Look at the collocation boxes for *issue* and *problem*. In each case, arrange the verb collocates and the adjective collocates in different groups according to similarities in meaning.**

**6 Check your own dictionary. How does it show information about collocations?**

# 11 Student

## VOCABULARY & READING

**1 Work with a partner and complete the tasks.**

- **a** Write a list of qualities that make a good teacher.
- **b** Compare your lists and agree on a class list of the three most important qualities.
- **c** Follow the same procedure to compile a list of qualities that make a good student.

**2 Match the two halves of these expressions to make some questions about education.**

- **a** How easy is it to **get a**
- **b** Have you ever **taken a class**
- **c** What qualifications do you need if you want to **go**
- **d** What kinds of things do you think it is best to **learn**
- **e** What time of day did you find it hardest to **pay**
- **f** How do you **apply to**
- **g** In which school subjects did you always use to **get**
- **h** When was the last time you **failed a**

1. **in** a foreign language?
2. **low grades**?
3. **attention** in class?
4. **on to higher education**?
5. **class**?
6. **by heart**?
7. **college**?
8. **bank loan** to pay your college fees?

**Think about the questions. Then ask your partner and compare your answers.**

**3 Read the article on page 115 in which the author reflects on being a student and teachers who made a mark. Answer the questions.**

- **a** What adjectives would the author probably use to describe himself?
- **b** Why did he dislike his math teacher?
- **c** Which celebrity's teachers were right about their student?

**How do you think your teachers would describe you?**

**Read the article again and underline the expressions in bold from Exercise 2 that are used. Which expressions are *not* used in the article?**

**4 Find expressions in the article which mean the same as the underlined structures. Complete the sentences.**

It is inevitable that he will make an impact. → He _____ .

It is improbable that he will go anywhere. → He _____ .

It is not expected that he will have trouble. → He _____ .

**5 Complete these predictions about education in the USA using the words in parentheses. Do you think these things will happen in your country? When?**

- **a** Classrooms *are expected* to get less crowded as the birth rate decreases. (expected)
- **b** More eighteen-year-olds _____ take a break between high school and college. (likely)
- **c** It _____ that classroom teachers will ever be replaced by computers. (highly unlikely)
- **d** Standards of spelling and grammar _____ get worse due to new technologies. (likely)
- **e** Students _____ rely more on websites than on books to do their homework. (bound)

**Work with your partner. Write down three predictions about the future of education in your country. Find out if other students agree.**

- **Grammar:** Future forms. Future time clauses
- **Vocabulary:** Education. *is likely to / is expected to.* Exaggeration. Colloquial expressions
- **Language for Life:** Using appropriate language in a job interview

# *Confessions of a* **Bad** *Student*

I was not the most dedicated student, as the reports from my former teachers will attest. I didn't get bad grades, and I never failed a class, but there was always an understanding that I could do better. An early teacher wrote, "We don't expect Jay to have trouble handling advanced classes, but he needs to show more discipline." I think I frustrated my teachers by not living up to my potential.

It is a mystery why Mr. Holly, my 12th grade English teacher, had so much faith in me. He convinced me to take an advanced placement English class, encouraged me to try out for the school play, and entrusted me with organizing the book room. I think he believed in me more than I believed in myself. Here's what Mr. Holly wrote about me: "Jay has tremendous energy, but needs guidance. If he can harness that energy in productive pursuits, he is bound to make an impact, whatever he chooses to do."

On the other hand, Mr. Ingram, my 10th grade math teacher, inspired in me a life-long dislike for math. I can still hear the sarcasm in his voice. "No homework again? What a surprise!" In his defense, I probably did deserve at least some of his snide remarks. All in all, I think I turned out better than he thought I would. In a school report, Mr. Ingram wrote, "Jay is unlikely to go anywhere if he doesn't stop playing around and get serious."

But I'm not alone! For example, Einstein's teacher declared that, "He will never amount to anything." John Lennon's teacher opined, "Hopeless. Rather a clown in class. He is just wasting other pupils' time. Certainly, on the road to failure." About David Bowie, a high school teacher wrote, "David is a quiet student who needs to stop playing with his motorcycles and learn that music will not make him a livable wage."

As a former terrible student, and current successful teacher, looking back at my school days, I can't help but think about things I would do differently if I had the chance. I'm not sure my teenage self would listen, but it's worth a shot. Pay attention, Jay.

First of all, listen, really listen to Mr. Ingram and see if there's something behind the sarcasm. You may not like the way he's saying it, but he probably wants the best for you. Whatever you do, don't let a bad experience with a teacher turn you off a subject completely. Mr. Ingram and math are two different things. Why slam the door on whole fields of knowledge?

More importantly, pay attention to the people who are betting on you, and ask yourself why. At 17 we can be blind to our own qualities and underestimate ourselves. What qualities does Mr. Holly see in you, and what can you do to cultivate them?

Finally, don't forget to say thank you. Thank you, Mr. Holly!

## PRONUNCIATION

1 2.37 **Listen and repeat these common abbreviations. Check (✓) the ones that you pronounce as words (acronyms). Underline the stressed letter for the ones you pronounce as individual letters.**

| | | | | |
|---|---|---|---|---|
| **1** AIDS | **3** FAQ | **5** NATO | **7** PhD | **9** UNICEF |
| **2** BS | **4** MBA | **6** OPEC | **8** PIN | **10** IRS |

2 **Work with a partner. How many of the abbreviations in Exercise 1 do you know? What do the letters stand for? Which abbreviations are to do with education?**

2.38 **Listen and check your ideas. What are the equivalent abbreviations in your language?**

## SPEAKING: ANECDOTE

**You are going to tell your partner about your favorite (or least favorite) teacher at school.**

- Ask yourself the questions below.
- Think about *what* to say and *how* to say it.
- Tell your partner about the teacher.

**a** What was the teacher's name?
**b** What did he/she look like?
**c** What kind of clothes did he/she use to wear?
**d** Was he/she strict or easy-going?
**e** What subject did he/she teach?
**f** Were you good at that subject?
**g** Where did you sit in the classroom?
**h** What kinds of things did you use to do in class?
**i** What characteristics did you most like (or dislike) about the teacher?
**j** What did your classmates think about him/her?
**k** When was the last time you saw him/her?

## LISTENING & VOCABULARY

1 **Work in small groups. Decide at what age you think young people should …**

- make their own decisions.
- be financially independent.
- leave home.

2 2.39 **Listen to Mr. and Mrs. Benitez talking about their eighteen-year-old daughter, Serena. Which of the following sentences best summarizes their feelings?**

Mr. and Mrs. Benitez

**a** They want Serena to go to college, but they're worried about the cost.
**b** They think Serena should graduate from college before she tries to become a rock star.
**c** They think that it would be a waste of time for Serena to go to college.

3 **Underline the correct alternative in each of these extracts from the interview in Exercise 2.**

**a** "Now she figures she's going to **do** / **make** it in the music world."
**b** "… once she gets a **taste** / **feel** of freedom, she'll find it harder to go back to college."
**c** "At least if it doesn't work out, she'll have a qualification **behind** / **under** her."
**d** "We're just hoping that she'll get it out of her **body** / **system** …"
**e** "… and then come to her **thoughts** / **senses** and go back to her studies."
**f** "… we can't afford to pay for her to live in Los Angeles, so it's **up** / **over** to her to make it work."

**Listen again and check your answers.**

4 **Work with a partner. Complete the following statements with an appropriate expression from Exercise 3. Change *her* to *you* / *your* as necessary.**

Serena

**a** If you want to travel, it's best to _____ before you start a career.
**b** Once young people have had _____ , it's hard for them to live with their parents again.
**c** The more qualifications you have _____ , the better your chances are of getting a good job.
**d** You don't need talent to _____ as a singer: just good looks and a good manager.
**e** Whether or not you succeed in life is _____ . Nobody else can help.

**Decide whether you agree or disagree with the statements. Would your parents have the same opinion?**

## READING & GRAMMAR

**1 Work with your partner. Read a conversation between an interviewer (*I*) and Serena (*S*) in which Serena talks about her future. Think carefully about the context and underline the most appropriate future forms.**

**I:** You're graduating from high school soon, aren't you?

**S:** Yes, (1) **exams start** / **exams'll start** next week, but I'm not too worried about the results, because when I'm done with school (2) **I'm concentrating** / **I'm going to concentrate** on my music career. I'm the lead singer in a band, and I don't need any qualifications to do that. I see my future very clearly – it's obvious that I've got what it takes to be successful. (3) **I'm going to be** / **I'm being** incredibly famous and fabulously rich.

**I:** So you've already got a contract then?

**S:** No, not yet. Actually, we don't have a manager yet, but the minute I've taken my last exam, (4) **I'm finding** / **I'm going to find** a really good one.

**I:** So, do you intend to continue living at home?

**S:** No way. (5) **I'll have moved** / **I'm moving** to Los Angeles as soon as I graduate. LA's where it all happens in the music industry.

**I:** Do you think (6) **you'll be able** / **you're able** to live off your music right from the start?

**S:** Well, if we don't make it right away, (7) **we're having to** / **we might have to** get part-time jobs for a few months or something. I know (8) **it's being** / **it's going to be** hard at first, but I bet you, by this time next year, (9) **we're having** / **we'll have had** a single in the charts.

**I:** And where do you see yourself five years from now?

**S:** In five years (10) **I'm staying** / **I'll be staying** in the best hotels and won't be able to walk down the street without being recognized. In fact, (11) **I'll give** / **I'm giving** you my autograph now if you like – (12) **it'll be** / **it's being** worth a fortune in a few years!

**2** 2.40 **Listen and check your answers. Have your parents ever been against something you wanted to do? Tell your partner.**

## GRAMMAR

**1 Work with a partner. Complete the table of different future forms. Use examples from the conversation with Serena on page 117 to illustrate each use.**

| Form | Use | Example |
|---|---|---|
| **a** *will ('ll)* + infinitive | 1 for prediction<br>2 to make an offer | 1 _____<br>2 *I'll give you my autograph now if you like.* |
| **b** *might* + infinitive | for possibility | _____ |
| **c** _____ | 1 to talk about your intentions<br>2 to base a prediction on present evidence | 1 _____<br>2 *I'm going to be incredibly famous.* |
| **d** Present progressive | for plans and arrangements | _____ |
| **e** _____ | for fixed future events | *My exams start next week.* |
| **f** Future progressive | to talk about something happening around a certain time in the future | _____ |
| **g** _____ | to talk about something completed by a certain time in the future | *By this time next year, we'll have had a single in the charts.* |

### Future forms and future time clauses

I **start** / I'**ll start** / I **might start** / I'**m going to start** / I'**m starting** / I'**ll be starting** / I'**ll have started** tomorrow.

I'll do it **if I have** time.
I'll do it **when I've finished** this.
I won't do it **unless I'm feeling** OK.

**2 Look at the sentences (a-c). In each sentence underline the main clause, put the subordinate clause in parentheses, and circle the conjunction. Then answer questions (1-3) below.**

... (*when* I graduate), *I'm going to concentrate on my music career.*

**a** ... the minute I've taken my last exam, I'm going to find a really good one. (lines 13-15)
**b** ... I'm moving to Los Angeles as soon as I graduate. (lines 17-18)
**c** ... if we don't make it right away, we might have to get part-time jobs ... (lines 23-25)
**1** In which clause (main or subordinate) can you use a future form?
**2** What verb forms can you use after a conjunction?
**3** When do you use a comma to separate the two clauses?

**3 Complete the sentences about the future with an appropriate form of the verbs in parentheses.**

**a** If I (fail) _____ my exams, my parents (kill) _____ me.
**b** I (grow) _____ a beard as soon as I (graduate) _____ from school.
**c** I (never read) _____ another poem once I (take) _____ my literature exam.
**d** You (like) _____ the new teacher once you (get) _____ used to her.
**e** He (not come out) _____ until he (do) _____ his homework.
**f** When I (finish) _____ my business course, I (set up) _____ my own business.

**4 Complete the sentences in any way that is true for you.**

**a** Once this class has finished, ...
**b** The moment I get home today, ...
**c** When I have enough money, ...
**d** As soon as I have some free time, ...
**e** When I'm next on vacation, ...
**f** This time next year, ...
**g** In five years, ...
**h** By the time I retire, ...

**Compare your sentences with your partner.**

**5** **Grammar Extra 11** page 150. Read the explanations and do Exercise 1 and 2.

## READING & VOCABULARY

**1 Work in groups and discuss the questions.**

- **a** Is it common in your country for students to do outdoor sports during their summer vacation?
- **b** What do you think are the advantages and disadvantages of camping?
- **c** What are the best places to go for outdoor and radical sports? What outdoor sports have you tried? Which ones would you like to try?

**2 Read a story about a friend and outdoor enthusiast.**

https://www.outdoorsports.com

# Wild Times, Wild Stories

I've known my best friend Kenny since we were in middle school. We both love the outdoors and have been on some epic camping trips together. As soon as the semester ends, we hit the trails. When we graduate, we're planning to do the Appalachian Trail, a 2,200-mile hike from Georgia to Maine. Nothing like cooking up a nice dinner after a long day hiking and telling stories or going over the day's adventures. On our last hike, Kenny was telling me about his recent close shave with a grizzly bear.

Now there's something you've got to know about Kenny; whatever he tells you, you've got to take it with a grain of salt as he is known to embellish things. A simple hike through the woods becomes a life-or-death ordeal. That 50-foot cliff he jumped off is more like twenty feet. And all of his girlfriends, of course, are models. It's not a big deal, all his friends know not to believe 100% of anything he says.

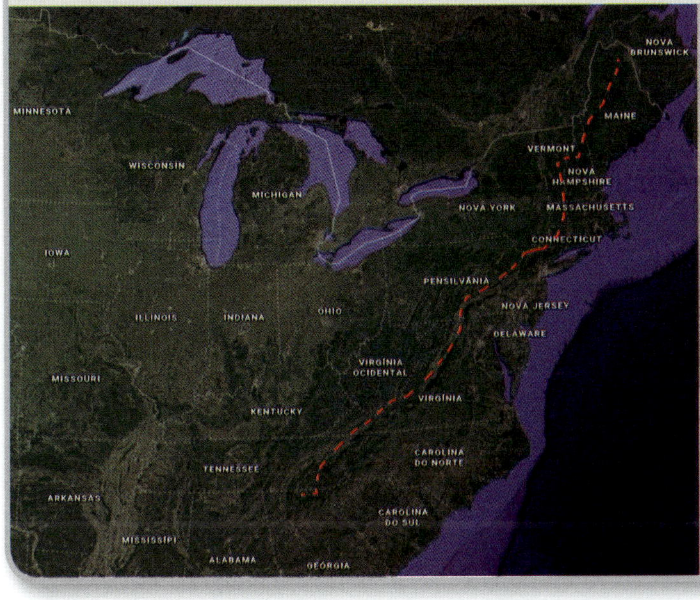

**3 Find words and expressions in the text that mean ...**

- **a** a dangerous situation which almost ended in injury.
- **b** to be suspicious of something someone tells you.
- **c** to make a story more interesting by adding details which may be untrue.
- **d** a painful, horrible, or traumatic experience.
- **e** a steep precipice or rock face.

## READING

1 **My friend Kenny loves to solo hike during the summer vacation. He recalls a hike that did not turn out so well. Read the two versions of his backpacking story. Which do you prefer and why?**

https://nottobelieve100percent.com

### VERSION 1

"I was trekking through some sparse woods in a remote area when I got a little lost. I ran into a wild dog that barked at me and gave me a bit of a scare. I walked about 15 miles over some hilly terrain and had to cross a stream and some wet patches. It was almost dark when I finally found my way out. The whole experience was rather tiring. I was dirty from the hike when I finally got home, which my brother found rather amusing."

### VERSION 2

"I was trekking through in an impenetrable forest in the middle of nowhere when I got hopelessly lost. I was attacked by a rabid wild dog that snarled and snapped at me, scaring me half to death. I tramped probably 25 miles over some mountainous terrain and had to cross raging rapids and a veritable swamp. It was pitch black when I finally found my way out. The whole experience was an exhausting brush with death. I was filthy and mud-splattered when I finally got home, which my brother thought was hysterical."

2 **Have you ever been in a situation that did not turn out well? Tell your partner.**

## VOCABULARY

**1 Read version 2 of Kenny's story again on page 120. Was the wild dog really rabid? Find nine more examples of language that has been exaggerated. Use your dictionary if necessary.**

*sparse → impenetrable* *in a remote area → in the middle of nowhere*

**2 Work with a partner. Read two versions of Kenny's second story. Combine elements from each version to rewrite the story as dramatically as possible.**

**VERSION 1**

"Last year I almost died when I contracted a severe stomach infection. I made the mistake of drinking water without treating it first. Almost instantly, I was near the end of my hike when I started feeling weak. My stomach felt terrible, and I was sick all the time. I barely made it back. When I got to town, I went to the hospital, where they gave me medication. It took me almost a year to recover."

**VERSION 2**

"Last year I had a pretty bad time of it when I contracted a nasty parasite. I made the huge newbie mistake of drinking water without treating it. A week later, with miles and miles to go in my hike, I started to feel like I was going to die. My stomach was bubbling and boiling, and I vomited incessantly. I barely crawled into town, and they raced me to the hospital, where they pumped me full of meds. It took me about a month to feel better."

2.41 **Listen and check your ideas.**

**3 Match each of the informal exaggerated expressions (a-j) from column *A* with its meaning (1-10) in column *B*.**

| A | B |
|---|---|
| a I was in seventh heaven. | 1 I thought it was really exciting. |
| b I was at death's door. | 2 I thought it was beautiful. |
| c I burst into tears. | 3 I was very happy. |
| d I was scared stiff. | 4 I started crying. |
| e It was mind-blowing. | 5 I was very tired. |
| f I was at the end of my rope. | 6 I was very worried. |
| g It took my breath away. | 7 I was desperate. |
| h I was on my last legs. | 8 I was very thirsty. |
| i I was dying for a drink. | 9 I felt very sick. |
| j I was going out of my mind. | 10 I was very frightened. |

**Choose three of the expressions from column *A* and use them in sentences describing the last time you felt like this.**

*The first time I saw Buenos Aires, it took my breath away. I thought it was the most beautiful place I'd ever seen.*

## SPEAKING

**1 Work with your partner. Imagine that you recently came back from an exciting and eventful vacation including a traumatic six-hour boat trip. Prepare a story from the notes below. Make it as dramatic as possible and add some details of your own.**

| Story ideas | Useful linkers |
|---|---|
| It was a small fishing boat - | To begin with, ... |
| There were a lot of people on the boat - | Then ... |
| The sea was calm when we left the harbor - | Later, ... |
| The sky turned black - | Suddenly, ... |
| A storm blew up - | Eventually, ... |
| We noticed there were no lifejackets or radio in the fishing boat - | To my horror, ... |
| The waves were big - | The worst thing was ... |
| We thought we were going to die - | It turned out that ... |
| I cried and then I fainted - | In the end, ... |

**2 Tell your story to another pair of students in the class.**

## LANGUAGE FOR LIFE

**1 Work with a partner. You're going to listen to Sam being interviewed for a job. Put the interview questions (a–g) in the most logical order according to your ideas.**

- **a** Do you have any questions you'd like to ask us?
- **b** What would you say your weaknesses are?
- **c** In your opinion, what are your greatest strengths?
- **d** What would you like to be doing five years from now?
- **e** Tell us a little about yourself.
- **f** Why do you think you'd be right for a position in this company?
- **g** What are your long-term objectives?

2.42 **Listen and check. Do you think Sam will get the job?**

**2 Look at the advice about how to do well in a job interview. In what ways do you think Sam could have improved his interview skills?**

### HOW TO DO WELL IN A job interview

- Don't ramble! Answer questions concisely and stick to the point.
- Try to sound confident but admit your weaknesses or lack of experience in certain areas.
- Show enthusiasm and interest in the job.
- Do your homework before the interview: find out as much as you can about the company and think about the kinds of questions you may be asked.
- Prepare your answers.

**3 Match the model answers (1–7) with the questions (a–g) in Exercise 1.**

1. **I would say my greatest weakness has been** my lack of proper planning in the past. However, since I've come to recognize that weakness, **I've taken steps** to correct it.
2. **I graduated from** college last year and then spent four months traveling in South America. Now, **I'm ready** to embark on my career, and **I'm very interested in** working for a company like yours.
3. I'm highly motivated and conscientious. I'm a team player, but **I can work** equally well my own.
4. **I've always been interested in** working in the media. **I think I'm well-suited** to this kind of work because I work well under pressure. I don't have much experience yet, but anything I don't know, **I'm willing to** learn.
5. Ideally, **I'd like to be** managing my own team.
6. **I'd like to know a little about** the training opportunities in this job.
7. **I'd like to gain some experience in** this field for a few years and then decide which area I want to specialize in.

2.43 **Listen to Layla being interviewed and check your answers. Which of the highlighted useful phrases could be used in other interview contexts?**

**4 Work with your partner. Choose one of the jobs in the box or your own idea, and write an interview. Use some of the highlighted useful phrases in Exercise 3. Practice your interview.**

bank clerk fitness trainer flight attendant teacher interior designer realtor

### LIFE SKILLS: Getting Organized

Getting a Handle on Your Email

**It's Monday morning and you just fired up your computer. You open up your email and see that number in parentheses: (117)! There's a little of everything in there: personal, work-related, spam, and subscribed emails. Here are some practical tips for getting a handle on your inbox:**

- Avoid multi-tasking and interruptions by setting up specific times to look at your email.
- Unsubscribe to newsletters and advertising you're not interested in anymore.
- Use the two-minute rule. When you receive an email ask yourself, "Can I read and respond to this in two minutes?" If so, do it! This will help empty your inbox.
- Set up a filing system for your emails and use it.

**By following these simple tips, you'll be down to Inbox (0) in no time!**

- **Now, it's your turn. In groups, discuss strategies for streamlining your other online habits. Write an introduction to an advice column with a list of 3 tips for improving on one of the following, then share your tips with the class.**
  - Messaging
  - Social media
  - Bookmarks

MACMILLAN LIFE SKILLS

## RÉSUMÉ AND APPLICATION EMAIL

**1 Arrange the following tips for writing a résumé under the headings *DO* and *DON'T*.**

a be honest.
b mention your bad points or failures.
c try to be amusing.
d use a clear layout.
e use bold and italic for headings.
f include dates.
g check for spelling and typing errors.
h use family or friends as references.

**2 Read Brad Arnoldson's résumé. Apply the tips from Exercise 1 and identify where he has gone wrong.**

**3 Work with a partner. Look at Brad's "Employment" and "Skills." Think about ways in which he could express this information in a more formal and positive way.**

~~Worked in an office.~~ *Office assistant.*

*Improved my computer skills.*

**Now look at page 138 for an improved version of Brad's résumé and compare your own ideas.**

**4 Read Brad's application email. Some parts of the email are acceptable, and some parts are completely inappropriate. ~~Cross out~~ all the parts which you think are inappropriate in order to produce a good email.**

**5 Write your own résumé and email of application for a job as a summer camp counselor.**

**RESUME**

3120 N. Vine St
Victoria, TX 77901
Telephone: 360-428-4296
Cell Phone: 360-555-4296
email SuperSam@hotmail.com
DOB 8/12/2000

**Brad Arnoldson**

**EDUCASION**
Graduated Victoria High School 2.9 GPA – June 2017

**EMPLOYMENT**
- Worked in an office
- Did some babysitting
- Washed dishes in a Mexican beach resort
- Backpacked around Mexico and Guatemala and did some fruit picking
- Worked in my mother's store

**SKILLS**
- I can use a compUter
- I can speak pretty poor Spanish
- Drivers licence failed three times. Hope to try again

**PERSONNEL INTERESTS**
- Donating blood – 14 pints so far
- Music

*References:*
*Mrs. Betty Arnoldson*
*3120 N. Vine St.*
*Victoria, TX 77901*
*360-428-4296*

**NEW MESSAGE**
**To:** robbie.newsome@lakechippewacamp.com
**From:** SuperSam@hotmail.com
**Subject:** Summer Job

**DO NOT DELETE!!!!!**
Dear Sir or Madam or Ms:
I am writing to apply for the position of summer camp counselor advertised on your website this week. As you can see from my attached résumé, I do not have a great deal of work experience and no experience whatsoever as a camp counselor. However, what I lack in experience I am willing to make up for in enthusiasm and hard work.
Since I graduated from high school in June last year, I have been in continual employment. First of all, I worked as a sales clerk, where I learned a lot about the retail industry. But it was my mother's store and we fought all the time, so I quit. After that, I worked at a beach resort in Mexico, where I enjoyed working as part of a team and improved my spoken Spanish. I quit because the pay was awful and I never had time to go scuba diving.
Through the variety of positions I have held, I have learned important interpersonal skills, improved my knowledge of Spanish, and have gained extensive computing skills. I feel the job you are offering will enable me to put these skills into practice.
As I'm unemployed right now, I can be available for an interview at your convenience.
I look forward to hearing from you.
Sincerely,

*Brad Arnoldson*

**3120 N. Vine St.**
**Victoria, TX 77901**
**SuperSam@hotmail.com**
**Home: 360-428-4296**
**Cell: 360-555-4296**

# 12 Home

## READING & VOCABULARY

**1 Work with a partner. How do you imagine your dream house? Look at the pictures below.**

My dream house ...

- is eco-friendly.
- is light and bright.
- is quiet.
- is in the middle of nowhere.
- has a terrace.
- has bedrooms with en suites.
- is on the coast.
- has amazing views.

**Look at the pictures on pages 126 and 127 of two unique houses. Which features above do you expect each house to have? Read the article and check your ideas.**

**2 Which house would you prefer to live in? Discuss your reasons with your partner.**

**3 Work with a partner. Try to complete each collocation with a suitable word. Then check your ideas by finding the collocations in the article on pages 126 and 127.**

**a** What is the cost of _____ in your city?
**b** Don't you just love the fresh _____ out here in the country?
**c** What are some examples of fossil _____?
**d** Do you know who lives next _____?
**e** What can cause your surroundings to be pitch _____?

**Discuss the answers to the questions.**

- **Grammar:** Participle clauses. Nouns and quantity expressions
- **Vocabulary:** Houses. Collocations. Furnishings. Breakfast food
- **Language for Life:** Ways of saying *hello* and *goodbye*

## GRAMMAR

**1 Complete the table with the two appropriate sentences from the article on pages 126 and 127.**

| | |
|---|---|
| **Two separate sentences** | We found the perfect houseboat. It was designed by a local boat builder. There is a growing group of people. They are working towards having a simpler life. |
| **A single sentence with a relative clause** | We found the perfect houseboat which was designed by a local boat builder. There is a growing group of people who are working towards having a simpler life. |
| **A single sentence with a participle clause** | 1) _____ 2) _____ |

**2 Rewrite each of the following as one sentence using the participle in parentheses.**

**a** My apartment building is modern. It was built in the 1990s. (built)
My apartment building, built in the 1990s, is modern.

**b** My own apartment is very light and airy. It is located on the top floor. (located)

**c** Every morning I am woken up by the sun. It streams through my window. (streaming)

**d** My bedroom is full of souvenirs. They have been collected on my travels. (collected)

**e** The neighbors are very friendly. They live across from us. (living)

**Are any of these sentences true for you?**

**Participle clauses**

The people **living next door** moved in last month. (Defining clause: no commas needed.)

The house, **redecorated throughout**, took ages to sell. (Non-defining clause: commas needed.)

**3** **Grammar Extra 12, Part 1** page 150. Read the explanations and do Exercise 1.

# THE HOUSEBOAT

Tom and Kelly Fishburn live in a houseboat with their two children, Penelope, 7, and Carlos, 4.

Tom: "There was a time in my childhood when my family lived on a houseboat, and those were the happiest years of my life. Even though my wife and I lived in an apartment for the first few years of our marriage, I had always longed for that free-spirited way of life. I wanted my own children to have the same wonderful experiences that I had living on the water. We started talking to people from houseboat communities around our area and looking around for a houseboat to buy. Then, luckily, we found one designed by a local boat builder.

Living on the houseboat gives us free access to nature and outdoor activities. Swimming, kayaking, fishing, collecting insects, and bird watching wouldn't be available to us if we lived in the suburbs. I find it incredibly exciting and a much healthier lifestyle for my family.

Additionally, now that we have our own houseboat, our cost of living is half of what it used to be, and we are saving a considerable amount of energy and money.

We downsized from a spacious two-bedroom apartment to a 770 sq ft houseboat but we adjusted fairly quickly. People often ask us how we manage living in such a small space. I tell them it makes for a close-knit family and regularly forces us outdoors into the fresh air. We sacrifice our privacy but the trade-off is economy and a much happier, healthier lifestyle."

# THE TREEHOUSE

A retired couple, William and Mary Bousson, live in a treehouse and operate a 'treesort' consisting of four individual, self-contained treehouses that they rent out.

William: "Business is very good. We are always fully booked as our treehouses are in high demand. I think they are popular because many people find living in a tree curious and they are willing to give it a try for a week. Our customers find that there is a real sense of serenity when you are high up in a tree.

The other reason the treesort is in demand is its appeal to those who love the outdoors and camping as well as to those who are looking for an eco-friendly, sustainable way of living. Our treehouses, made from recycled materials, are powered by solar energy; therefore we avoid using any type of fossil fuels. Almost all of our appliances are energy-efficient so we live quite frugally.

Advancements in treehouse design and construction have come a long way. In the past, treehouses were not expected to last more than a few years but now they can last over 30 years. They are also cheaper to build and maintain than traditional houses.

Our treehouse is a bit isolated. Our nearest neighbor is a few kilometers away, so we can't just go next door and borrow a cup of sugar. This also means that at night, when all the lights are off, it gets pitch dark, because there are no street lights or houses with lights nearby. The best part of living in a treehouse is being close to nature. We feel like we have extended our lives by moving into this natural environment away from the pollution and stress of city life. Now, there is a growing trend of people working towards having a simpler life like ours."

### Glossary

**downsize** verb [T/I]: to reduce in size

**a close-knit family** adjective: a family whose members are close to and supportive of each other

**trade-off** noun [C]: a compromise a balance achieved between two seemingly incompatible features

**frugal** adjective: economical, so that less money or food is wasted

## VOCABULARY

1 **Work with a partner. List each item in the box under an appropriate heading to show where you would expect to find it. Use your dictionary if necessary.**

> candlesticks coat hooks dish towels a doormat a dustpan and brush
> a fireplace an ironing board a mantelpiece ornaments a sink
> patterned wallpaper a shaving outlet a shower curtain a towel rail a tumble dryer

| In the kitchen | In the bathroom | In the living room | In the hallway |
|---|---|---|---|
| | | | |

2 **With which part of a room would you associate these groups of items? Choose from: *a window, a wall, a door,* or *the floor*.**

**a** wall-to-wall carpets, parquet, rugs, tiles
**b** blinds, drapes, double-glazing, shutters, a sill
**c** outlets, light switches, radiators, shelves
**d** a bell, a bolt, a knocker, a latch, a mailbox

**Check (✓) all the items in Exercises 1 and 2 that you have in your own home.**

## SPEAKING & LISTENING

1 **Work with your partner. Compare the two pictures and discuss these questions.**

**a** What kind of people do you think each of these rooms belongs to?
**b** What kind of house do you think each room is part of?
**c** Which room do you like best and why?

2 **You're going to listen to a psychologist talking about what each room says about the people who live there. Before you listen, match each of his interpretations (a–f) with the room you think it applies to.**

**a** This is obviously a family room.
**b** I imagine that, like many families nowadays, both partners pitch in with housework in the evenings and on weekends.
**c** There's plenty of evidence to suggest that this is a successful, career-oriented person.
**d** This person wants to be ready to pack their bags and leave at short notice.
**e** I think the people who live here are sociable young professionals who enjoy entertaining.
**f** I think this is somebody who doesn't actually spend much time at home.

▶ 2.44-2.45 **Listen and check your ideas. Do you agree with the psychologist's comments? Go to page 138 to find out if the people who live there agree.**

## GRAMMAR

**1 Work with a partner. Complete the extracts from the room descriptions on page 128 with *There is* or *There are*.**

a _____ several cushions.
b _____ very few clues.
c _____ hardly any personal objects.
d _____ plenty of evidence.
e _____ n't really enough furniture.

**Arrange the highlighted quantifiers in a logical order from "none" to "a lot more than necessary."**

**2 Work with your partner. Look at the sentence beginnings (a–d). Decide which is the most suitable ending (*1* or *2*) for each sentence.**

a My father speaks **a little** English — 1 so he probably won't understand you.
b My father speaks **little** English — 2 so he'll probably understand you.
c **A few** people can understand him, — 1 which he finds encouraging.
d **Few** people can understand him, — 2 which he finds discouraging.

**Which quantifiers in bold mean: a) *some*; b) *not much*; c) *not many*?**

### Nouns and quantity expressions

**Countable nouns**
Use: *none, not any, few, a few, several, some, many, a lot, loads, plenty*

**Uncountable nouns**
Use: *none, not any, little, a little, some, much, a lot, loads, plenty*

*not enough* = less than you need
*too much/many* = more than you need

**3 Complete the sentences so that they are true for you. Compare with your partner.**

a I try to find a little time each day for ...
b There are few people I know who ...
c If I met the President of the USA, I'd ask him a few questions about ...
d This year, I've had very little ...
e I have very little patience with people who ...

**4 Underline the correct verb form for these statements.**

a There **isn't** / **aren't** nearly enough nightlife.
b There**'s** / **are** loads of traffic.
c There**'s** / **are** very few tourists.
d There**'s** / **are** no underground system.
e There**'s** / **are** plenty of job opportunities for young people.
f There**'s** / **are** plenty of space to park in the city.

**Change the statements as necessary to describe your hometown or city. Add two more statements and then compare your answers with your partner.**

**5** **Grammar Extra 12, Part 2** page 150. Read the explanations and do Exercise 2 and 3.

## SPEAKING: ANECDOTE

**You are going to tell your partner about your favorite room.**

- Ask yourself the questions below.
- Think about *what* to say and *how* to say it.
- Tell your partner about the room.

a Which is your favorite room?
b What do you use it for?
c What size and shape is it?
d How is it decorated?
e What kind of furniture does it contain?
f What kind of floor does it have?
g What do the windows look out on to?
h How much time each day do you spend in it?
i What's the best thing about the room?
j What – if anything – would you like to change about it?

## READING & SPEAKING

1 **You're going to read an extract from *Sons and Lovers* by D.H. Lawrence on page 131. First, look at the picture of the kitchen and write three adjectives to describe it and three adjectives to describe the life of the people who might live there. Then compare with a partner.**

2 **Read the extract to find out if your ideas were correct. Then answer the questions.**

**a** What time does Morel get up, and what time does he go to work?
**b** What does he have for breakfast, and what does he have for lunch?
**c** How does he feel about having breakfast alone?

3 **Put Morel's morning routine in the correct order. Then read the extract again and check your answers.**

[1] He got out of bed.
[ ] He took his wife a cup of tea.
[ ] He boiled the kettle.
[ ] He put on his pants.
[ ] He ate his breakfast.
[ ] He made his lunch.
[ ] He put on his work shirt.
[ ] He read yesterday's newspaper.
[ ] He blocked out the draft under the door.

4 **Work in small groups. Based on the extract, discuss the questions about Morel and his relationship with his wife.**

**a** What kind of man do you think Morel is?
**b** What kind of lifestyle do you think he and his family have?
**c** Do you think Morel and his wife have a happy relationship? Why? / Why not?

**Go to page 139 to read a summary of *Sons and Lovers* and check your ideas. Were you surprised by any of the information?**

## LISTENING & VOCABULARY

1 **How do people in the class start the day? Ask questions to find someone who ...**

- slept more than eight hours last night.
- slept with the drapes or blinds open.
- woke up naturally, without an alarm clock.
- can remember what they dreamed about.
- had something cooked for breakfast.
- spent more than twenty minutes eating breakfast.

2 **Work with your partner. The food and drink in the box is a mixture of breakfast items from around the world. Answer the questions.**

**a** Is there anything in the box that you or your family normally have for breakfast?
**b** Is there anything you would find difficult to eat for breakfast?

bacon bread rolls cereal cheese coffee cold meat eggs green tea ham grilled fish jelly miso soup orange juice omelet pancakes pickled vegetables rice seaweed tea toast

3 2.46-2.48 **The food and drink in Exercise 2 are some breakfast items from the USA, Germany, and Japan. Which items do you think belong to a typical breakfast from which country? Listen and check.**

Lizanne, USA

Nicola, Germany

Michiko, Japan

4 **What's your perfect breakfast? Tell your partner.**

# A MINER'S BREAKFAST

He always made his own breakfast. Being a man who rose early and had plenty of time he did not, as some miners do, drag his wife out of bed at six o'clock. At five, sometimes earlier, he woke, got straight out of bed, and went downstairs. When she could not sleep, his wife lay waiting for this time as for a period of peace. The only real rest seemed to be when he was out of the house.

He went downstairs in his shirt and then struggled into his pit-trousers, which were left on the hearth to warm all night. There was always a fire, because Mrs Morel raked. And the first sound in the house was the bang, bang of the poker against the raker, as Morel smashed the remainder of the coal to make the kettle, which was filled and left on the hob, finally boil. His cup and knife and fork, all he wanted except just the food, was laid ready on the table on a newspaper. Then he got his breakfast, made the tea, packed the bottom of the doors with rugs to shut out the draught, piled a big fire, and sat down to an hour of joy. He toasted his bacon on a fork and caught the drops of fat on his bread; then he put the rasher on his thick slice of bread, and cut off chunks with a clasp-knife. Then, in solitude, he ate and drank, often sitting, in cold weather, on a little stool with his back to the warm chimney-piece, his food on the fender, his cup on the hearth. And then he read the last night's newspaper – what of it he could – spelling it over laboriously. He preferred to keep the blinds down and candle lit, even when it was daylight; it was the habit of the mine.

At a quarter to six he rose, cut two thick slices of bread-and-butter, and put them in the white calico snap-bag. He filled his tin bottle with tea. Cold tea without milk or sugar was the drink he preferred for the pit. Then he pulled off his shirt, and put on his pit-singlet, a vest of thick flannel cut low round the neck, and with short sleeves like a chemise.

Then he went upstairs to his wife with a cup of tea because she was ill, and because it occurred to him.

*Sons and Lovers, 1913*

**Glossary**

**pit-trousers** noun [C]: pants worn in the mine

**hearth** noun [C]: the floor of a fireplace

**rake** verb [T/I]: to use a tool to separate pieces of burning coal

**hob** noun [C]: the top part of a stove that you put pans on

**draught** noun [C]: *British* a draft

**rasher** noun [C]: a thin flat piece of bacon or ham

**chimney-piece** noun [C]: mantelpiece

**fender** noun [C]: a low frame around a fireplace

**calico** noun [U]: heavy white cloth made of cotton

**pit-singlet** noun [C]: a shirt worn in the mine

## LANGUAGE FOR LIFE

**1 Ann is saying goodbye to Bob after an evening at his house. Read the conversation and complete the "goodbye" expressions using the words in the box.**

> already better Call for good have to inviting Love
> regards safely so Take too will you yourself

**Ann:** I'd (1) _____ be going.
**Bob:** It was (2) _____ to see you.
**Ann:** Thank you for (3) _____ me.
**Bob:** Thanks (4) _____ coming.
**Ann:** Well, (5) _____ long.
**Bob:** Give my (6) _____ to your family.
**Ann:** I (7) _____ .
**Bob:** (8) _____ me.
**Ann:** OK. I really (9) _____ be going.
**Bob:** (10) _____ care.
**Ann:** See (11) _____ .
**Bob:** Drive (12) _____ .
**Ann:** (13) _____ you.
**Bob:** Me (14) _____ .
**Ann:** Take care of (15) _____ .
**Bob:** Missing you (16) _____ !

2.49 **Listen and check.**

**2 Work with a partner. Match each phrase (a-j) with an appropriate response (1-10). Which exchanges are ways of saying hello and which are ways of saying goodbye?**

- **a** Imagine seeing you here!
- **b** You have to come and stay again soon.
- **c** Good to see you again! You haven't changed a bit.
- **d** Have a safe trip!
- **e** Long time no see!
- **f** What have you been up to?
- **g** Thank you for everything.
- **h** Hi, how are you doing?
- **i** We've got to get together again soon.
- **j** Keep in touch.

1. Not much. The usual.
2. I will.
3. Oh, I come here all the time.
4. Yes, it must be over a year.
5. Absolutely, that would be great.
6. Thanks. I'll call when I get there.
7. Neither have you. As beautiful as ever.
8. Fine, thanks. How about you?
9. You're most welcome.
10. I'd love to.

2.50 **Listen, check, and repeat the useful phrases.**

### LIFE SKILLS: Influencing Others

Dealing with Different Opinions

**"It were not best that we should all think alike."**

**Mark Twain**

**1** 2.51 **Listen to some suggestions from a psychologist on positive attitudes to adopt and suitable expressions to use when dealing with different opinions or ideas.**

**2 What would you do in the following situations?**

| Situation | What attitude would you adopt? | What would you say? |
|---|---|---|
| Your colleague thinks you should hire an outside contractor for a job. That way, it would be easier to manage the project. You think the work should be done in-house because the material is too sensitive to be handled by anyone outside the company. | | |
| Your friend loves onions on her pizza but you hate them. You don't object to any other ingredient. The pizza place can make customized orders, such as ingredients on only half the pizza. | | |
| You haven't seen your friends for a long time. They want to meet up to go bowling. You don't mind bowling, but you'd rather go dancing. | | |

MACMILLAN LIFE SKILLS

# 12 Vocabulary Extra

## GET IT RIGHT

Based on evidence from the *Louvain International Corpus of Learner English*, the following exercises address some of the most common and persistent learner errors at this level. Test your knowledge and then check your answers in the dictionary extracts.

**1** FALSE FRIENDS **Complete the statements with *actual / actually* or *current / currently*.**

a The _____ economic situation is not very good.
b Homeowners are _____ paying very high rates of interest.
c The official number of unemployed is two million. However the _____ number is probably much higher.
d The _____ government talks a lot but _____ has no idea what to do.
e Saying you'll do something and _____ doing it are two very different things.

**Do you agree or disagree with the statements?**

**2** VERB PATTERNS **Which verb or verb phrase doesn't belong? Test your ideas by using sentence frames *A* and *B*.**

afford / avoid / help / risk / spend time / suggest

**A** He couldn't _____ to do it. **B** He couldn't _____ doing it.

**3** VERB + PREPOSITION **Underline the correct alternative.**

a I agree **my parents / with my parents** about most things.
b I don't approve **children / of children** wearing make-up.
c I don't like discussing **about politics / politics**.
d I sometimes enter **into competitions / competitions** but I never win.
e I use my credit card to pay **products / for products** I buy online.

**Which sentences are true for you?**

**4** COUNTABILITY **Are the nouns in the box usually countable or uncountable?**

advice behavior evidence information knowledge news progress proof research work

**Which of the nouns in the box can replace *advice* in the sentence "Advice is important"?**

**5** NOUN + PREPOSITION **What is the common error in these sentences from the *Louvain International Corpus of Learner English*?**

a ✗ The experiment has not led to the expected decrease of crime.
b ✗ Women in those times were totally dependent of their husbands.
c ✗ There is a big difference of grammar between Japanese and English.
d ✗ Is gun ownership connected with the increase of violent crime?
e ✗ The main reason of poverty is unemployment.
f ✗ The role of the government is to find a solution of this problem.

**Correct each sentence with *for*, *in*, *on*, or *to*.**

**6 Check your own dictionary. Identify six errors that you sometimes make and find example sentences that show the correct usage.**

**Get it right**

Don't confuse **actual** with **current** or **present**. **Actual** is not used for referring to things that are happening now or that exist now. Use **current** or **present** to express these ideas:

✗ *The ~~actual law~~ obliges every young man to do military service.*
✔ *The current law obliges every young man to do military service.*
✔ *The present law obliges every young man to do military service.*
✗ *They have to work together to improve ~~the actual situation~~.*
✔ *They have to work together to improve the current situation.*
✔ *They have to work together to improve the present situation.*

**Actual** is used for referring to what is really true or exact:

*The report cites 554 AIDS cases, with 2,600 persons infected with HIV. But officials concede that the **actual number** may be closer to 8,000.*

**Get it right**

**afford** is never followed by a verb in the **-ing** form. Use an infinitive.
**avoid** is never used with an infinitive. It is followed by a verb in the **-ing** form.
**help:** The **-ing** form is only used with **help** in the fixed expression **can't help doing something**.
**risk** is never followed by an infinitive. Use the pattern **risk doing something**.
**spend:** When you use **spend** with another verb use the **-ing** form of the verb, not the infinitive.
**suggest:** When **suggest** means "to offer an idea or a plan," it is never followed by an infinitive. Use the pattern **suggest doing something**.

**Get it right**

**agree:** When you want to say that you approve of something or think it is the right thing to do, use the pattern "**agree with something**" (not "agree something").
**approve:** When **approve** means "to have a positive feeling towards something or someone," it is followed by **of**, not by a direct object.
**discuss** is never used with the preposition **about**. It is simply followed by a direct object.
**enter** is usually a transitive verb, and it takes a direct object. It is not used with the prepositions **into** or **in**.
**pay** is never followed by a direct object that refers to the thing you are buying. We **pay for** a product or a service.

**Get it right**

**advice** is an uncountable noun
**behavior** is usually an uncountable noun
**evidence** is an uncountable noun
**information** is an uncountable noun
**knowledge** is an uncountable noun
**news** is an uncountable noun
**progress** is an uncountable noun
**proof:** When **proof** means "information that proves something," it is almost always an uncountable noun.
**research** is an uncountable noun
**work:** In most of its meanings, **work** is an uncountable noun.

**Get it right**

**decrease:** Don't use **decrease of** when you want to talk about what is decreasing. Use **decrease in**.
**dependent:** The usual preposition to use with **dependent** is **on**, not **of**.
**difference:** When you are talking about a way in which two people or things are different, use the pattern **a difference in something** (not "difference of" or "difference about").
**increase:** Don't use **increase of** when you want to say what is increasing. Use **increase in**.
**reason:** After **reason**, use the preposition **for**, not **of**.
**solution:** The usual preposition to use with **solution** is **to**, not **of**.

*From the Macmillan English Dictionary (American and British editions)*

# Review D

▶ Grammar Extra **pages 148-151**

## GRAMMAR

**1 Complete the sentences with *which* or *who*.**

- **a** This is Sandra, _____ is studying art.
- **b** He calls her "sweetiepie," _____ I can't stand.
- **c** My sister, _____ lives in Boston, is a lawyer.
- **d** Oh, look. It's that strange man _____ came into the store yesterday.
- **e** They gave me a brown sweater, _____ is absolutely awful.

**2 Write the sentences in the correct order. The first and last words of each sentence are given.**

- **a** **What** annoys / really / at / talk / me / is / who / the / people **theater**.
- **b** **What** sense / I / like / Connie / is / her / of / about **humor**.
- **c** **What** eating / and / feel / like / tonight / is / steak / I **fries**.
- **d** **The** I / summer / thing / can't / about / stand / the / is **mosquitoes**.
- **e** **What** like / really / to / do / is / watch / I'd **TV**.

**3 Underline the correct alternative.**

Right now, I'm working in an office, but I've always wanted to be a doctor. A few months ago, I applied for a place at medical school, and, guess what? I (1) **'ll have** / **'m having** an interview next Tuesday. I feel very nervous about it! It (2) **isn't going to be** / **isn't being** an easy interview. It's a very good school, and I (3) **won't get** / **might not** get a place. I (4) **'m not going to tell** / **don't tell** anyone at work about the interview, in case I don't get in. Another thing I'm worried about is that I might not be able to earn enough money to go back to full-time education. My parents have said they (5) **'re helping** / **'ll help** me, but they can't really afford to give me very much. I know I (6) **'m having to support** / **'ll have to support** myself while I'm studying. The semester (7) **starts** / **will start** next September. And, if all goes well with the interview, by September I (8) **'m going to leave** / **'ll have left** my office job, and I (9) **'ll be starting** / **'ll start** medical school. Wish me luck!

**4 Complete the conversation between May and Jim with the correct form of the verbs in parentheses.**

**M:** Could you do some photocopying for me today?
**J:** Of course. I'm just sorting the mail, but I'll do the copying as soon as I (1 finish) *'ve finished*.
**M:** Thanks. And when you (2 do) _____ the photocopying, could you take these invoices to the accounts department?
**J:** OK. I'll do that once I (3 organize) _____ the papers for the conference tomorrow.
**M:** But I really need you to (4 do) _____ it now.
**J:** Well, Mrs. Blunt said I shouldn't do anything until I (5 do) _____ the papers.
**M:** But if these invoices don't go to accounts, they (6 not be) _____ paid.
**J:** Well, if I (7 not get) _____ these papers done, Mrs. Blunt (8 be) _____ furious!
**M:** But the invoices are urgent.
**J:** Everything (9 be) _____ always urgent here!
**M:** Are you OK, Jim? You seem stressed.
**J:** Yes, I am stressed. The minute Mrs. Blunt comes back, I (10 tell) _____ her I quit.

**5 Complete each sentence so that it means the same as the two sentences above it.**

- **a** My house was built one hundred years ago. It's situated in the middle of the town.
  *My house, situated in the middle of the town, was built one hundred years ago.*
- **b** These ornaments are very valuable. They were given to me by my grandmother.
  These ornaments, ...
- **c** The cat had kittens last year. She's sitting on the windowsill.
  The cat ...
- **d** Those children are my brothers and sisters. They are playing volleyball.
  Those children ...
- **e** The people are really nice. They live around here.
  The people ...

## VOCABULARY

**1 Complete the sentences with the correct form of the words in the box.**

> catch sight   gaze   make out
> notice   spot   ~~stare~~

**a** Stop *staring* at people. It's rude.
**b** On vacation we spent many evenings on the balcony, _____ at the stars in the sky.
**c** I just _____ of myself in that store window. Why didn't you tell me I had chocolate on my chin?
**d** Despite the big crowd, we managed to _____ Brad Pitt going into the hotel.
**e** Through her binoculars, Penny could just _____ the island in the distance.
**f** Did you _____ that ad in the store window? It said, "Kittens for sale."

**2 <u>Underline</u> the correct words.**

Today, Adam Grant is one of the country's most successful businessmen, but he was not always a success. He had a troubled childhood, and was brought up in an orphanage. Moreover, he was dyslexic at school and found reading a problem. Because of that it was an effort for him to (1) **make** / **pay** attention in class, and he often (2) **got** / **had** bad grades at school. For most students like Adam, (3) **applying** / **going on** to higher education was highly unlikely. It was generally expected that he would (4) **miss** / **fail** all his classes and leave school at sixteen. But, luckily, Adam had a teacher, Ms. Phelps, who realized that he showed great talent in science. Ms. Phelps helped Adam with his reading and encouraged him to think about college, an idea that Adam had never considered before. At the age of eighteen, Adam (5) **applied for** / **passed** and succeeded in getting into Stanford University and (6) **studied** / **followed** mechanical engineering. He also (7) **passed** / **won** a scholarship to pay for his studies.

**3 Complete the sentences with the correct form of the expressions in the box.**

> at death's door
> at the end of (your) rope
> dying for a drink
> in seventh heaven
> on (your) last legs
> ~~take (your) breath away~~

**a** I loved their performance last night. It *took my breath away.*
**b** They were _____ about their lottery win.
**c** I've really had enough of the twins' behavior. I'm _____ .
**d** Is that car going to get us to Miami? It looks as if it's _____ .
**e** Justin was _____ when he got malaria on his trip.
**f** Let's stop here and buy some water. I'm _____ .

## PRONUNCIATION

**1 Look at some words from Units 10–12. Say the words and add them to the table.**

> ~~absolutely~~   advertise   disappointing
> education   epitomize   evidence
> experience   nostalgically   ornament
> relationship   understanding   thoroughly

| A: □▫▫ | B: ▫▫□▫ | C: ▫□▫▫ |
|---|---|---|
| | *abso<u>lu</u>tely* | |

**2 <u>Underline</u> the stressed syllable in each word.**

▶ 2.52 **Listen, check, and repeat.**

# Additional Material

## Unit 1 Grammar (page 11)

**Follow these instructions to play Auxiliaries Bingo. You will need to use the sentences you wrote in Exercise 2 on page 11.**

### Instructions

**a** Copy the Bingo card onto a separate piece of paper.
**b** Take turns reading out one of your sentences from Exercise 2. If your partner can answer with a response on the Bingo card, cross out the square. If what you say is not true for your partner, wait for your turn to try another sentence.
**c** The winner is the first person to cross out all the squares on the card.

| | | |
|---|---|---|
| So was I. | Neither do I. | So have I. |
| So would I. | Neither am I. | So did I. |
| Neither have I. | So am I. | Neither can I. |

## Unit 4 Listening & Vocabulary (page 45)

**Work with a partner. Make sentences beginning *Find someone who …* by matching each verb with an appropriate noun phrase.**

Find someone who …

burns off does feels gets goes goes for has cancelled is stuck wears works out

+

a brisk walk on weekends a gym membership calories by cycling to work inside all day Lycra gear at the gym out of shape plenty of fresh air running team sports at the gym

**Find someone in the class who does (or has done) each of these activities.**

## Unit 4 Language for Life & Pronunciation (page 48)

**Student A**

**Work with Student B. Take turns describing your problems. When you hear your partner's problem, react sympathetically or unsympathetically and then give some advice.**

- You don't want to go out because you have a huge pimple on your nose - you ate too much chocolate yesterday.
- You think you caught a cold - you can't stop sneezing.
- Your back is killing you. You did four hours at the gym yesterday.
- You have trouble remembering people's names.
- Your teeth hurt when you eat something cold.

## Unit 9 Listening & Grammar (page 96)

**Test your memory. Answer these questions about the two paintings on page 96. Then look back and check your answers. Which painting did you remember best?**

*The Guitar Player*, **1899**

**a** Describe the woman's clothes.
**b** What is the man wearing?
**c** What is the man holding?
**d** There's something in the woman's hands - what is it?
**e** What color is the man's shirt?

*Longing*, **1899**

**a** Describe the woman's face.
**b** What is she wearing?
**c** What is she holding in her left hand?
**d** What kind of room is it?
**e** What's hanging at the top of the painting?

## Unit 9 Speaking & Listening (page 98)

**Answers**

**Listed in the order in which they were invented**

**f** The toothbrush – the first mention of a toothbrush with bristles at right angles to the handle is in a Chinese encyclopedia of 1498.

**b** The water closet toilet – Queen Elizabeth I was delighted to add this new "throne" to her collection when her godson Sir John Harrington invented it in 1596.

**d** False teeth – before French pharmacist Alexis Duchateau perfected a set of porcelain dentures in 1770, it was common practice to use "dead men's teeth" – particularly plentiful after the frequent wars at the time.

**a** Contact lenses – the first workable pair were produced in 1887 by F.E. Muller, a glassblower from Wiesbaden in Germany.

**e** The razor – US citizen King Camp Gillette first had the idea of creating a new kind of razor with cheap disposable blades in 1895. He founded the Gillette Safety Razor Company in 1901, and the business was a huge success.

**c** The zipper – there were several attempts at this before the Swedish engineer Gideon Sundback finally got the zipper to work in 1913. It was later claimed that by replacing the buttons on pants the new device would eliminate any risk of embarrassment. Sadly ...

## Unit 10 Speaking & Vocabulary (page 104)

**Answers**

**1 b** Starbucks **2 b** Nike **3 a** Apple **4 c** Adidas **5 c** McDonald's

## Unit 10 Listening & Vocabulary (page 105)

**Student A**

**You are going to complete some lists of common noun collocations often used to talk about sales and marketing. Complete each list with a word from the box. Use your dictionary if necessary. Then check your answers with Student B.**

advertising bank cash consumer finance price purchase

**a** ______ choice / confidence / goods / groups / products / spending
**b** ______ cut / index / list / rise / tag / war
**c** ______ agency / campaign / executive / industry / revenue / space

Student B answers:
**a** sales
**b** brand
**c** market

**Choose six useful collocations from the lists and write an example sentence for each one.**

## Unit 10 Reading & Vocabulary (page 106)

**Work in groups and discuss the questions.**

**a** Where do you usually see advertisements? What do you do when you see an ad on TV? Are there any advertisements that you have found interesting? Why / Why not?

**b** If you were making an advertisement for a new car, how would you do it? Consider the following questions.

- Who would the advertisement be aimed at?
- What mood would the ad have? (funny, serious, dramatic, etc.)

**Compare your ideas with other groups.**

## Unit 11 Writing Extra (page 123)

**The correct version of the résumé**

# RÉSUMÉ

### PERSONAL DETAILS

| | |
|---|---|
| **Name** | Brad Arnoldson |
| **Address** | 3120 N. Vine St., Victoria, Texas 77901 |
| **Telephone** | 360-428-4296 |
| **Email** | brad.arnoldson@hotmail.com |

### EDUCATION

| | |
|---|---|
| **June 2007** | 2003–2007 Victoria High School |

### EMPLOYMENT

| | |
|---|---|
| **Jan to March 2009** | Office assistant. Improved my computer skills |
| **Sept to Dec 2008** | Babysitting. Gained experience in working with children |
| **April to Sept 2008** | Fruit picking in Mexico and Guatemala. Improved my language skills |
| **Jan to March 2008** | Worked in a hotel. Gained experience of Mexican tourism industry |
| **July to Dec 2007** | Sales clerk. Gained experience of the retail industry |

### SKILLS

| | |
|---|---|
| **Computer skills** | Proficient in Word, Excel, MS Access, internet, and email |
| **Languages** | Working knowledge of Spanish |
| **Driver's license** | Taking lessons; test booked for next month |

**INTERESTS** Sports, music, tourism, and foreign travel

**REFERENCES** Available on request

## Unit 12 Speaking & Listening (page 128)

**Room 1: Paula, homemaker**

"Some of what he said is true. We are a family, and this is the room where we spend a lot of our time. But one thing he got wrong was that I don't actually work right now. The children are still small, so I'm at home with them. I don't really like housework very much, but I like to keep the place clean, so that's why it does tend to be neat most of the time."

**Room 2: Colin, documentary maker**

"He got some things right about me. I do work in the media but not in advertising. I work for a movie company that makes travel documentaries, so obviously I travel a lot. He was right about that. I'm hardly ever at home. And that's why my apartment's so neat. But I'm more sociable than he thinks! I entertain a lot, but usually abroad, so I tend to do most of my socializing in restaurants. I am single, but if I find the right person, commitment wouldn't be a problem."

## Unit 12 Reading & Speaking (page 130)

# *SONS AND LOVERS* BY D.H. LAWRENCE

MOREL

Walter Morel is the head of the family. A miner, he was once a humorous, lively man, but over time he has become a cruel, selfish alcoholic. His family, especially Mrs. Morel, despises him.

He is not interested in the arts or even in his work, which for him is just a source of income. He is a man who lives for whatever pleasures he can find in eating, drinking, and his bed. At first a warm and passionate man, he later becomes rough and brutal to his family and fights with them verbally and physically.

THE MARRIAGE

Gertrude Morel is from a good family. She is unhappily married to Walter, and she redirects her affection to her sons, her only passion in life. She wishes she weren't the wife of a miner. An intellectual, she feels that society has limited her opportunities, another reason why she lives through her sons.

It is hard to imagine how quiet, sensitive Gertrude may have been attracted to Walter in the first place, but Lawrence set out to show how opposites attract, as well as repulse. The relationship is a disaster; Walter is irresponsible with his family and drinks his wages away.

Another feature of the oppositions explored here is how contradictory human nature is. Morel is usually heartless and detached, but he sometimes shows flashes of concern and love for his family.

This passage is taken from the second chapter of the book, and Gertrude is about to give birth to her third child. She is 31 years old and has been married for eight years.

BACKGROUND

This novel is largely autobiographical and was sparked by the death of Lawrence's mother. Here, he re-examines his childhood and his relationship with his mother. The roots of *Sons and Lovers* are clearly located in Lawrence's life. His childhood coal-mining town of Eastwood becomes Bestwood, and Walter Morel was modeled on Lawrence's hard-drinking, irresponsible father, Arthur, who was also a miner.

## Unit 4 Language for Life & Pronunciation (page 48)

**Student B**

**Work with Student A. Take turns describing your problems. When you hear your partner's problem, react sympathetically or unsympathetically and then give some advice.**

- You have a terrible earache.
- You feel sick. You ate too much.
- You keep getting migraines.
- Your feet are killing you. You've been wearing a pair of new shoes all day.
- Your wrist is swollen - you tripped over and fell on it.

## Unit 10 Listening & Vocabulary (page 105)

**Student B**

**You are going to complete some lists of common noun collocations often used to talk about sales and marketing. Complete each list with a word from the box. Use your dictionary if necessary. Then check your answers with Student A.**

benefit brand credit corporation deposit market sales

**a** ______ conference / figures / force / rep / targets / team
**b** ______ awareness / identity / image / loyalty / name
**c** ______ forces / leader / price / research / sector / value

Student A answers:
**a** consumer
**b** price
**c** advertising

**Choose six useful collocations from the lists and write an example sentence for each one.**

# Grammar Extra

## Unit 1 Verb structures. Auxiliaries

### Part 1: Verb structures

#### Present verb structures

You use the simple present to talk about habits and routines or things that are always true. *I usually **go** to bed around midnight. / The sun **rises** in the east.*

You use the present progressive to talk about activities that are in progress now, or to describe changing situations. ***I'm learning** Japanese as well as English. / The Earth **is getting** warmer.*

You use the present perfect to talk about present situations which started in the past and are continuing now, or which happened at an indefinite time in the past. *I**'ve been taking** English classes since last year. / We**'ve seen** Madonna in concert nine times!*

**See page 144 for more on the present perfect simple and progressive.**

#### Past verb structures

You usually use the past progressive in contrast with the simple past to talk about activities that were in progress when something happened. *He was **living** in Detroit when he **met** her.*

You use the past perfect to show that one past event happened before another past event. *The movie **had started** when I arrived.*

**See page 142 for more on the past perfect simple and progressive.**

You can use both *would* and *used to* to refer to regular or repeated past actions. *When she lived with us, she **used to** get up at six o'clock and **would** always have coffee for breakfast.* You can also use *used to* – but not *would* – to refer to past states or situations. *I **used to** have a motorcycle, but I sold it.*

▶ **Now do Exercise 1.**

### Part 2: Auxiliaries

#### *so / neither*

The auxiliary verbs *be*, *have*, and *do* are used to form different verb structures. They are also used with *so* and *neither* in tag questions, and in short answers. You use so to mean "also" in the structure *So* + auxiliary + subject. *"I'm Mexican." "So am I."*

You use *neither* to mean "also not" in the same structure.

*"I can't swim." "Neither can my brother."*

Both *so* and *neither* are used to show agreement between speakers. Note what happens when there is disagreement between speakers. *"I'm Chilean." "I'm not."* (NOT "~~**I'm not Chilean**~~.") / *"He doesn't have a car." "She does."* (NOT "~~She's~~.")

#### Tag questions

You usually use a negative tag question with a positive statement, and a positive tag question with a negative statement. *You're Chilean (+), aren't you (-)? / You're not Chilean (-), are you (+)?*

You use *they* to refer to *somebody, anybody/everybody*, and *nobody*. ***Somebody** must have seen her, mustn't **they**?*

You use a positive tag question after *never*, *hardly*, *little*. *He **never** gives up, **does he**?*

You can use *will/would* or *can/can't/could* after imperatives. ***Get** me some milk from the store, **would** you?*

Other cases: ***Let's** go out for dinner, **shall** we? / **There**'s no time left, is **there**? / **Nothing** can go wrong, can **it**?*

▶ **Now do Exercises 2 and 3.**

## Unit 2 Verb patterns (1)

#### verb + *to*-infinitive

These verbs *don't* typically take an object before the *to*-infinitive: *aim, arrange, attempt, can't afford, decide, hope, intend, manage, offer, plan, refuse, seem, tend, try.*

*She **manages to stay** in shape.*

#### verb + object + *to*-infinitive

**a** These verbs *sometimes* take an object before the *to*-infinitive: *expect, help, want.*

*I **wanted her to go out** with me, but she said she was busy.*

**b** These verbs *usually* take an object before the *to*-infinitive: *allow, encourage, force, remind, teach, urge, warn (not).*

*My father **taught me to swim** when I was five.*

#### verb + gerund

You use the *gerund* after these verbs: *avoid, can't stand, don't mind, enjoy, finish, keep, miss, spend/waste time.*

*I **can't stand being** the center of attention.*

#### verb + object + gerund

These verbs sometimes take an object before the *gerund: avoid, don't mind, dread.*

*I **dreaded** my parents finding out.*

#### verb + object + infinitive without *to*

*Make* and *let* take an object before the infinitive without *to*. *They **let me have** my own beliefs.*

▶ **Now do Exercises 1 and 2.**

## Unit 1 Exercises

1 <u>Underline</u> **the most appropriate verb structure.**

a **I'm remembering** / **remember** where I was when I **was hearing** / **heard** about Princess Diana's death.
b Over the years, **I've seen** / **saw** the footage of J.F. Kennedy's assassination many times.
c **I've watched** / **watched** the news about 9/11 live on TV.
d **I'm thinking** / **think** that Bill Clinton **was** / **has been** a good president.
e I **used to** / **would** love flying, but airport security checks **have changed** / **had changed** how I feel about it now.
f The recent global recession **was affecting** / **affected** me personally.
g I **never enjoyed** / **'d never enjoyed** the Olympic Games until I**'ve seen** / **saw** the last one.

**Are any of the sentences true for you?**

2 **Write one response to show agreement and one response to show disagreement.**

a I've been to the USA. *So have I.* / *I haven't.*
b I'm from South America. ________ / ________
c I don't like coffee. ________ / ________
d I was born in Canada. ________ / ________
e I've never been to New York. ________ / ________
f I watched TV last night. ________ / ________
g I can't swim. ________ / ________
h I wouldn't want to be famous. ________ / ________

**Check (✔) the statements that are true for you and compare with a partner.**

3 **Complete the statements with a tag question.**

a You're Mexican, *aren't you?*
b It's a beautiful day, ________?
c She can't swim, ________?
d We don't have much time, ________?
e He must be cold, ________?
f They haven't been to the US before, ________?
g Let's play a game of tennis, ________?
h Answer the phone, ________?

## Unit 2 Exercises

1 <u>Underline</u> **the correct form of the verb.**

Steve and I decided (1) **to get** / **getting** married when we were eighteen. Our parents warned us not (2) **to rush** / **rushing** into anything. I don't think any of them wanted us (3) **to go** / **going** through with it. But, to their credit, they helped us (4) **to buy** / **buying** our house, and they didn't mind (5) **to take** / **taking** care of our children when they came along. Even though I dreaded my mother-in-law (6) **to come** / **coming** over, I must say she was fantastic. So now we feel that whatever our kids want (7) **to do** / **doing**, we're ready to let them (8) **make** / **to make** their own mistakes.

2 **Complete the sentences with the correct form of the verbs in parentheses.**

a My mother taught me (cook) ________ .
b I can't stand (live) ________ at home, but I can't afford (move) ________ out.
c I enjoy (go) ________ shopping, as long as it's for clothes.
d I've always wanted (have) ________ a large family of my own.
e My father always made me (obey) ________ his rules, while my mom always let me (do) ________ what I wanted, as long as I avoided (get) ________ into trouble.

**Which sentences are true for you? Discuss with a partner.**

## Unit 3 Reported speech. Unreal conditionals

### Part 1: Reported speech

Reporting speech means using your own words to report what somebody has said. You usually use the verbs *say (that)* or *tell (someone that)* and *ask (someone if / whether)* for questions.

#### Tenses

There is usually a "back-shift" of tense. Simple present, present progressive, and present perfect change to simple past, past progressive, and past perfect. Simple past and past progressive change to past perfect simple and past perfect progressive. Modal verbs *can* and *will* change to *could* and *would*. Some forms don't need to change: a verb already in the past perfect remains in the past perfect; modal verbs *could, might,* and *would* remain in the same form.

#### Word order in reported questions

The word order in reported questions is the same as in statements (subject + verb). You don't use *do/does/did*. For *yes/no* questions you use *if* or *whether*.

"Do you have enough money?" → *She asked me **if** / **whether** I had enough money.*

#### Pronouns

Pronouns and possessive adjectives may change. Direct speech: *"**I** like **your** ideas."*

Report 1: ***My** boss told **me** that **she** liked **my** ideas.*

Report 2: ***His** boss told **him** that **she** liked **his** ideas.*

#### Time references

Here are some common changes from direct speech to reported speech when referring to time: a few weeks ago → a few weeks earlier; now → then; today → that day; tomorrow → the following day; this week → that week; next week → the following week. *"I'll see you **tomorrow**."* → *He said he'd see me **the following day**.*

▶ **Now do Exercise 1.**

### Part 2: Unreal conditionals

These sentences consist of an *if*-clause and a main clause and are used to refer to unreal situations in the present or past.

#### *if*-clause

The *if*-clause expresses the condition. To show that a situation is imaginary, the tense backshifts (present → past; past → past perfect).

| Real situation | | Imaginary situation |
|---|---|---|
| *I'**m** not rich.* | → | *If I **was**/**were** rich, ...* |
| *I **spent** too much money.* | → | *If I **hadn't spent** so much money, ...* |

#### Main clause

The main clause expresses the outcome of the condition, and can either refer to the present (1) *would/n't* + infinitive without *to*, or the past (2) *would/n't* + *have* + past participle.

| *if*-clause | | Main clause |
|---|---|---|
| *If I hadn't wasted all my money,* | → | *I **wouldn't be** poor now. (1)*<br>*I **wouldn't have lost** my house. (2)* |

▶ **Now do Exercises 2 and 3.**

## Unit 4 Narrative tenses. Future progressive and future perfect

### Part 1: Narrative tenses

#### Simple past and past progressive

The simple past is usually used to fix events in the past. You can use it to describe the main events of a story. Most verbs are regular and end in *-d/-ed/-ied*, although the most common ones are often irregular. There is a fuller list of irregular verbs on page 175.

The past progressive is often used in contrast with the simple past. You can use it to describe an activity in progress when the main events of the story happened.

*When they **looked** back, the polar bear **was running** after them.*

#### Past perfect: simple and progressive

The past perfect can be used when you want to refer to an event (simple) or activity in progress (progressive) which clearly took place before the time of the main events of the story. *When they made their first stop, they **had been traveling** for twelve hours. / He was just twenty-three and **had never been** on a polar expedition.*

▶ **Now do Exercise 1.**

### Part 2: Future progressive and future perfect

You use the future progressive to talk about an action that will be in progress at a certain time in the future. *Don't call at 8:00 - we'**ll be having** dinner.*

You use the future perfect to talk about an action that will be completed before a certain time in the future. *I'**ll have finished** work by 5:30.*

▶ **Now do Exercise 2.**

## Unit 3 Exercises

1 **Complete each reporting sentence.**

- **a** "I was just thinking about you!" He said *that he was just thinking about me.*
- **b** "We went to Paris a few days ago." She told us ...
- **c** "When I get my bonus, I'm going to spend it wisely." He said ...
- **d** "How do you manage to live on so little money?" He asked us ...
- **e** "What will happen to us tomorrow?" She asked him ...
- **f** "I think your work is excellent." My manager told me ...
- **g** "Can we afford a vacation this year?" I asked her ...

2 **Make unreal conditional questions using the verb in parentheses.**

- **a** I can't speak English fluently. (do)
  *If you could speak English fluently, what would you do?*
- **b** I didn't win the lottery. (buy)
- **c** I'm not rich. (go)
- **d** I can't afford an expensive car. (choose)
- **e** I arrived on time this morning. (happen)
- **f** I'm not the president of my country. (change)
- **g** It rained yesterday. (do)
- **h** I had to work last weekend. (go)

3 **Write full answers to the questions in Exercise 2. Compare with a partner.**

- **a** *If I could speak English fluently, I'd become a teacher.*

## Unit 4 Exercises

1 **Underline the correct form of the verb.**

Canadian explorer Jamie Clarke (1) **was climbing** / **climbed** Mount Everest when he (2) **was having** / **had** the idea to cross the Arabian desert. Two years later, Jamie and two friends, three Bedouin guides, and twelve camels (3) **were setting off** / **set off** from Salalah in Oman on their desert crossing. They (4) **were following** / **had been following** the route British explorer Wilfred Thesiger (5) **took** / **had taken** fifty years earlier. Before starting their journey, Thesiger (6) **was advising** / **had advised** them to take good care of their camels. It (7) **was** / **has been** good advice because without the camels, they wouldn't have survived. They (8) **were wearing** / **wore** the traditional clothes of the Bedouin and (9) **were eating** / **ate** bread and meat. They (10) **have never experienced** / **had never experienced** such temperatures: by day 49°C, dropping to around 8°C by night. Thirty-nine days later, they (11) **have arrived** / **arrived** in Abu Dhabi. They (12) **were traveling** / **had traveled** 1,000 km in that time. Throughout his travels he (13) **was keeping** / **had been keeping** a diary and a year after his return from Arabia, he (14) **wrote** / **written** *Everest to Arabia*, an account of the challenges he (15) **has faced** / **had faced** on his two epic journeys.

2 **Complete the sentences to make them true for you. Use future progressive (action in progress) or future perfect (completed action).**

- **a** This time next week, I'll ... (in progress)
  *be lying on a beach.*
- **b** By the end of the week, I'll ... (completed)
- **c** At 1:00 p.m. on Sunday, I'll ... (in progress)
- **d** Two years from now, I'll ... (completed)
- **e** At 10:00 a.m. the day after tomorrow, I'll ... (in progress)
- **f** Five years from now, I'll ... (completed)
- **g** At 8:00 p.m. this evening, I'll ... (in progress)
- **h** In ten years, I'll ... (completed)

**Compare your answers with a partner.**

## Unit 5 Present and past habits. Verb patterns (2)

### Part 1: Present and past habits

***will / would***

To talk about habitual behavior which is characteristic and predictable, you can use *will* for the present and *would* for the past.

*He**'ll get up** at seven o'clock and he **won't talk** to anyone until he's finished his breakfast. / I**'d walk** home every day unless it was raining.*

*Will* and *would* are almost always contracted (*'ll, 'd*). The full forms can make you sound angry. *She **will insist** on opening all the windows.*

***used to***

You can use *used to* to talk about past habits or past states or situations.

*I **used to have** a pet rabbit called "Dingbat." / I **used to come** home from school every day at five o'clock.*

*I **didn't use to enjoy** sports.*

▶ **Now do Exercise 1.**

### Part 2: Verb patterns (2)

A small group of verbs can be followed by both the *to*-infinitive and the gerund, each with a change in meaning.

**1 *try***

With the *to*-infinitive the action of the verb is not completed successfully. *I **tried to make** her understand my feelings, but she wouldn't listen.*

With the gerund the action of the verb is completed successfully, but it doesn't have the desired effect. *I **tried leaving** her messages, but she never replied.*

**2 *stop***

With the *to*-infinitive you are giving the reason for stopping. *She **stopped to tell** me about her boyfriend when I saw her at the mall.*

With the gerund you are saying that an activity has stopped. *She **stopped talking** to him after they broke up.*

**3 *remember, (never/not) forget***

With the *to*-infinitive you are referring to actions somebody is/was supposed to do. *I **remembered to buy** her a birthday card. But I **forgot to mail** it.*

With the gerund you refer to definite events - things that people actually did. *I **remember meeting** her in a bar.* (= I met her and now I remember this meeting.) / *I'll never **forget kissing** her for the first time.*

Note: It's uncommon to use the affirmative of *forget* + gerund (~~*He forgot meeting Bob.*~~). "*Don't remember*" is more usual (*He **didn't remember meeting*** Bob.).

▶ **Now do Exercise 2.**

## Unit 6 Present perfect: simple and progressive. Passives review

### Part 1: Present perfect: simple and progressive

The present perfect always shows a connection between the past and the present. It describes actions or processes that have happened (*finished*) or have been happening (*unfinished*) in time "up-to-now."

The simple form usually describes *finished* actions. You don't say *when* they happened. *I**'ve been** to Rome.*

The progressive form usually describes *unfinished* actions or processes. You normally say *how long* for. *I**'ve been going** to Florida since I was a child.*

⚠ Verbs describing single actions are unusual in the progressive form. *I've had two cups of coffee already* (NOT ~~*I've been having two cups of coffee already*~~).

⚠ Verbs describing states are very rarely used in the progressive form. *I**'ve known** her for years* (NOT ~~*I've been knowing her for years*~~).

▶ **Now do Exercises 1 and 2.**

### Part 2: Passives review

In passive sentences the object of the active verb becomes the subject of the passive verb.

| **subject** | **active verb** | **object** |
|---|---|---|
| Somebody | ate | my sandwich! |

| **subject** | **passive verb** |
|---|---|
| My sandwich | was eaten! |

| **subject** | **active verb** | **object** |
|---|---|---|
| The police | are holding | two men. |

| **subject** | **passive verb** | ***by* + agent** |
|---|---|---|
| Two men | are being held | by the police. |

In passive sentences the "doer" of the action - known as the "agent" - is either not mentioned at all, or mentioned at the end of the sentence after *by*.

▶ **Now do Exercise 3.**

## Unit 5 Exercises

**1 Rewrite the sentences describing habits and states using *will*, *would*, and *used to*. Use contractions (*'ll*, *'d*) where possible.**

- **a** My father insists on smoking in the car. I hate it!
  My father will insist on smoking in the car. I hate it!
- **b** My family and I lived in a large house.
- **c** During the school vacations I spent all my time with my friends.
- **d** I didn't have dark hair when I was young.
- **e** During the week I don't go to bed until after midnight.
- **f** At school I took a lucky charm into my exams.
- **g** My girlfriend talks for hours on the phone. It drives me crazy!

**Which sentences are true for you? Compare with a partner.**

**2 Complete the conversation with an appropriate form of the verbs in parentheses.**

**A:** Did you know that Emily and Sam are breaking up? I'm not surprised. Emily is not an easy person. I tried (1) (get along with) ________ her but I couldn't.

**B:** What about Sam? He never stops (2) (flirt) ________ with other women. I'll never forget (3) (see) ________ him dancing with Alice at the Christmas party. It was outrageous!

**A:** I just remember them (4) (argue) ________ all the time. It's very sad. They wanted the marriage to work. They even tried (5) (have) ________ counseling.

**B:** Anyway, are you ready? Don't forget (6) (bring) ________ the keys and the camera.

**A:** Fine, oh, and we need to stop (7) (get) ________ some gas. And I have to remember (8) (buy) ________ a card. I think it's going to be a really nice wedding. Don't you?

**B:** Yeah. Let's hope that Emily's brother is luckier in love than she has been.

## Unit 6 Exercises

**1 Write sentences using the simple or progressive form of the present perfect.**

- **a** I /learn/ English/ for six years.
  I've been learning English for six years.
- **b** I /know/ my best friend since I was a child.
- **c** I'm exhausted. I /work/ hard all day.
- **d** I /not see/ my parents for ages.
- **e** I'm tired. I /not feel/ well lately.
- **f** I /not done/ any housework for weeks.
- **g** I /sit/ here for more than an hour.
- **h** I /think/of changing my job lately.

**Check (✓) the sentences which are true for you. Compare with a partner.**

**2 Complete the sentences with *for* or *since*.**

- **a** I've been in this town ________ **2001**.
- **b** I haven't eaten ________ **two hours**.
- **c** I've been studying English ________ **I was a child**.
- **d** I haven't had a break ________ **three hours**.
- **e** I haven't seen my friend **Tom** ________ **the beginning of the month**.
- **f** It's been **sunny** here ________ **more than two weeks**.
- **g** I've been feeling **great** ________ **last Sunday**.

**Replace the words in bold with information which makes the sentences true for you. Compare your new sentences with a partner.**

**3 Write passive sentences. Use *by* + agent if you need to mention the "doer" of the action.**

- **a** My brother made that chair.
- **b** Someone introduced us yesterday.
- **c** They could recycle more than 80% of our waste.
- **d** Someone is processing your application now.
- **e** Alexander Graham Bell invented the telephone.
- **f** Around 400 million people speak English as a first language.
- **g** The police have arrested a man in connection with the robbery.
- **h** They will make an announcement later on in the week.

## Unit 7 Past modals. Articles

### Part 1: Past modals

In addition to the eight "pure modal verbs" (*can, could, may, might, will, would, should, must*), there are some phrases which express similar functions, and so are classed as "semi-modals": *be allowed to, have to, need to*, and *ought to*.

| Function | Affirmative | Negative | Structure |
|---|---|---|---|
| Expressing permission | *was/were allowed to*<br>*could* | *wasn't/weren't allowed to*<br>*couldn't* | + infinitive (without *to*)<br>(*go / do*, etc.) |
| Expressing necessity | *had to*<br>*needed to* | *didn't have to*<br>*didn't need to* | |
| Talking about the "right course of action." | *should have*<br>*ought to have* | *shouldn't have*<br>*ought not to have* | + past participle<br>(*gone* / done, etc.) |

▶ **Now do Exercise 1.**

### Part 2: Articles

**No article**

You don't use articles with proper nouns such as places, people, and companies.

***Ian Smith** is from **Toronto**. He works at **IBM**.*

Exceptions are when the article is part of a name (***The USA***, ***The BBC***, ***The Beatles***).

As the indefinite article means "one," you don't use it with plurals or uncountable nouns. *He had lots of **ideas**, but not much **money**.*

**Indefinite article *a/an*: introducing**

You use *a/an* when you first mention new people, places, or objects. *There was **a tourist** from the USA.*

**Definite article *the*: referring or identifying**

You can use *the* when referring back to a person or thing that has already been introduced. ***The** tourist took a picture of a fisherman.* (We have already been introduced to *the* "tourist.")

You can also use *the* when the person or thing is shared knowledge. ***The sun** shone brightly as he looked out at **the ocean**.* (It's obvious which sun and which ocean.)

Back reference and shared knowledge can combine. *He took **a picture**. **The click** of **the camera** woke **the man** up.* (We know that to take a picture you need a camera and that most cameras go click.)

Note: You don't usually use the definite article with plural or uncountable nouns. *Tigers are endangered. / Time is money.*

▶ **Now do Exercises 2 and 3.**

## Unit 8 *have / get something done*. Unreal conditional structures

### Part 1: *have / get something done*

You use *have something done* when someone does something for you. Compare the two sentences.

*Mandy cut her hair last week.* (= She cut it herself.)

*Mandy had her hair cut last week.* (= Someone cut it for her.)

Note: *get something done* is more informal.

▶ **Now do Exercise 1.**

### Part 2: Unreal conditional structures

You usually begin an unreal conditional clause with *if* when you are making questions. Here are some alternatives.

| Conditional clause | | | Main clause | | | |
|---|---|---|---|---|---|---|
| *If*<br>*Imagine (that)*<br>*Supposing (that)*<br>*Suppose (that)*<br>*Assuming (that)* | subject | simple past<br>past progressive<br>*were to* + infinitive<br>*might*<br>past perfect | *what*<br>*where*<br>*how*<br>etc. | *would*<br>*could*<br>*might* | subject | infinitive?<br>*be* + present participle?<br>*have* + past participle? |

***Imagine** you **were meeting** someone for the first time. How **would** you **introduce** yourself?*

***Assuming that** you **were to go** on another date, where **might** you **be planning** to meet?*

▶ **Now do Exercise 2.**

## Unit 7 Exercises

**1 Underline the correct past modals of obligation.**

**On my last vacation ...**

- **a** I **didn't have to** / **should have** get up early.
- **b** I **shouldn't have** / **didn't need to** speak a different language.
- **c** I **ought to have** / **had to** taken a good book to read.
- **d** I **wasn't allowed to** / **should have** use my cell phone on the plane.
- **e** I **couldn't** / **shouldn't have** eaten so much.
- **f** I **had to** / **ought to have** pay for my in-flight meals.
- **g** I **shouldn't have** / **couldn't** relax.
- **h** I realized I **needed to** / **should have** gone to a different place.

**Are any of the sentences true for you?**

**2 Complete the list below with *the* or put a dash (-) if no article is necessary.**

- **a** **Mountain ranges:** ___*the*___ Alps, ________ Himalayas
- **b** **Mountain summits:** ________ Mount Everest, ________ Mont Blanc
- **c** **Continents:** ________ Europe, ________ Asia
- **d** **Towns / cities:** ________ Prague, ________ Tokyo
- **e** **Parks:** ________ South Park, ________ Hyde Park
- **f** **Lakes:** ________ Lake Malawi, ________ Loch Ness
- **g** **Streets:** ________ Baker Street, ________ Hollywood Boulevard
- **h** **Months:** ________ January, ________ September
- **i** **Oceans:** ________ Pacific Ocean, ________ Indian Ocean
- **j** **Rivers:** ________ Nile, ________ Amazon
- **k** **"of" phrases:** ________ Statue of Liberty, ________ Houses of Parliament

**3 Complete the story with *a*, *an*, *the*, or put a dash (-) if no article is necessary.**

(1) ________ elderly couple from (2) ________ USA were driving through (3) ________ Mexico and were approaching (4) ________ city named Oaxaca. They saw (5) ________ sign with (6) ________ name of (7) ________ city printed in (8) ________ capital letters: OAXACA. (9) ________ couple tried to figure out how to pronounce (10) ________ name - Wacks-acka? Oaks-acar? They kept trying as they drove into (11) ________ city. Since they were hungry, they pulled into (12) ________ place to get something to eat. At (13) ________ counter, (14) ________ man said to (15) ________ waitress: "My wife and I can't figure out how to pronounce (16) ________ name of this place. Could you tell us and say it very slowly so that we can understand?" (17) ________ waitress looked at (18) ________ him and said: "(19) ________ Buuurrrgerrr Kiiiinnnng."

## Unit 8 Exercises

**1 Make questions from the prompts. Use *Would you ever + have/get* something done.**

- **a** shave head
  *Would you ever get your head shaved?*
- **b** whiten teeth
- **c** color hair
- **d** do a tattoo
- **e** wax legs
- **f** pierce ears
- **g** straighten teeth

**Work with a partner. Ask and answer the questions.**

**2 Put the words in the correct order to make unreal conditional questions.**

- **a** could take / what / do / Supposing / a year off work, / you / would you ?
  *Supposing you could take a year off work, what would you do?*
- **b** Who / Imagine / with anyone in the world. / could / choose / you / have dinner / would you ?
- **c** what / most of your money / you / would you / spend / Assuming / on / a millionaire, / were ?
- **d** was late / Supposing / for your first date, / how long / someone / you wait / would ?
- **e** went well, / your first date / before calling / how long / Assuming / would you wait / him/her again ?
- **f** do you think / a different job. / to do / Imagine that / you had / What / you'd have chosen ?
- **g** until 3:00 a.m., / you hadn't / be feeling now / Supposing that / gone to bed / you'd / do you think / how ?
- **h** Imagine that / of your character. / What / change one aspect / you / would / could / it be ?

**Work with a partner. Ask each other the questions and take turns answering them.**

## Unit 9 Past modals of deduction. *look, seem, appear*

### Part 1: Past modals of deduction

There are many ways of expressing degrees of certainty about something which happened in the past.

| Degree of certainty | Past modal auxiliaries | Other phrases |
|---|---|---|
| 99% certain it *WAS*. ✓ | *must* | I'm almost certain it was ... |
| | *may* | |
| | (*It*) *could* + *have* + past participle | I'm uncertain ... |
| | *might* | |
| 99% certain it *WASN'T*. ✗ | *couldn't* | I'm sure it wasn't ... |

*Stonehenge **might have been** a kind of temple. It **must** have taken a long time to move the huge stones.*

⚠ The opposite of *must have been* is *couldn't have been*: *It **couldn't have been** easy trying to move stones without wheels. They **must have been** really heavy.*

▶ **Now do Exercise 1.**

### Part 2: *look, seem, appear*

**_look / seem_ + adjective**

The verb ***look*** refers to the sense of sight and is followed by an adjective. *He **looks** great for his age*. The verbs for the other senses follow the same pattern (*She **sounds** nice*. *It **tastes** great. It **feels** cold. That **smells** good*.)

**_look like_ + noun**

This means *resemble* and is usually followed by a noun. *He **looks like** Brad Pitt*. (= He resembles Brad Pitt.)

**_look / seem as if / though_ + verb phrase**

You use this to describe what something seems like. The verb in the phrase can be in any tense. *It **looks as if** it fell over*. / *She always **seems as though** she's going to cry*.

**_seem / appear_ + to be**

These verbs help to describe your understanding of a situation. They can be followed by an adjective or noun phrase. *She **seems** sad*. / *He **appears to be** in trouble*.

▶ **Now do Exercise 2.**

## Unit 10 Relative clauses. Emphasis (cleft sentences)

### Part 1: Relative clauses

**Non-defining relative clauses**

You use non-defining relative clauses for two main reasons. You can either comment on the whole of the main clause or you can give some extra, non-essential information about the person or thing you are talking about. Compare the following:

*He's going out with Julie, **which I can't stand**.*
(= a comment on the whole of the main clause)

*He's going out with Julie, **who I can't stand**.*
(= a comment or "extra information" about Julie)

You always begin a non-defining relative clause with a relative pronoun, and you separate it from the main clause with commas.

You don't use *that* with non-defining relative clauses.

You always use *which* when introducing a comment on the whole of the main clause.

**Defining relative clauses**

You use defining relative clauses to identify exactly which person or thing you are talking about. When the relative pronoun (*who*, *that*, or *which*) is the subject of the relative clause you *can't* leave it out. *I like friends **who** never let me down.*

However, when the relative pronoun is the object of the relative clause you can leave it out. *He's got a job **that** he's really interested in.* or *He's got a job he's really interested in.*

Note: You don't need another object pronoun. ... *he's really interested in.* (NOT ... ~~*he's really interested in it.*~~)

⚠ You can never leave out *whose*. *That's the man **whose** dog bit my son.*

▶ **Now do Exercises 1 and 2.**

### Part 2: Emphasis (cleft sentences)

**_What_ structures (= The thing(s) that)**

You can use *What ... is/was ...* to emphasize either the subject or the object of a sentence. *I don't understand **why** it's so cold.* ➔ ***What** I don't understand **is why** it's so cold.*

You can replace *What* with *All* if you want to emphasize *the only thing that*. *I only want to play tennis.* ➔ ***All** I really want to do is play tennis.*

**_It is / was ..._ + relative clause**

You can use this structure to emphasize almost any part of a sentence. *Carla Bruni married Nicolas Sarkozy in Paris in 2008. **It was Carla Bruni** who married ... / **It was Paris** where Carla Bruni married ... / **It was in 2008** that Carla Bruni married ...*

You often use this structure when you are correcting what other people say. ***It wasn't Juliette Binoche** who married Nicolas Sarkozy, it was Carla Bruni.*

▶ **Now do Exercises 3 and 4.**

## Unit 9 Exercises

**1 Make sentences using *couldn't have, might / may / could have,* or *must have.***

- **a** It's possible that Albert Einstein was born in Austria.
  Albert Einstein may have been born in Austria.
- **b** US astronauts almost certainly didn't see the Great Wall of China from the Moon.
- **c** Picasso most probably produced more than 5,000 paintings in his lifetime.
- **d** There's a possibility Shakespeare didn't die on his birthday.
- **e** It is very likely that Mozart wasn't very well known when he died.
- **f** It is very likely that Walt Disney won more Oscars than any other entertainer.
- **g** There is a possibility that Leonardo da Vinci had an affair with Mona Lisa.

**Work with a partner. Four of these speculative sentences are true and four are false. Can you guess which is which?**

**2 Complete the sentences in a way that makes them true for you.**

- **a** Today I look ...
- **b** The weather looks as if ...
- **c** My mother always seems as though ...
- **d** Lately my teacher has seemed ...
- **e** My best friend looks like ...
- **f** My progress in English appears ...

**Compare your sentences with a partner.**

## Unit 10 Exercises

**1 Write the words in the correct order to make defining relative clauses. In each case there is one word too many.**

- **a** **a job** / in / that / it / interested / are / you
  a job that you are interested in it
- **b** **a bank account** it / out / never / that / runs
- **c** **a boss** get / him / with / who / you / on
- **d** **a car** it / that / down / never / breaks
- **e** **a government** voted / that / them / you / for
- **f** **a friend** who / you / she / down / lets / never
- **g** **a home** in / there / happy / you / that / are
- **h** **a partner** love / you / her / who / in / are / with

**In which of the defining clauses above can you omit the relative pronoun? Put items (a–h) in order of importance for you in your life. Compare with a partner.**

**2 In each case, make a single sentence containing a non-defining relative clause using the extra information in parentheses.**

- **a** He bought me an expensive dress. (I didn't really like him buying me the dress.)
  He bought me an expensive dress, which I didn't really like.
- **b** Adam turned up at 10:30 this morning. (Adam is almost never late.)
- **c** That woman works in our store. (She looks like my sister.)
- **d** Mike's father is in advertising. (Mike's father lives in San Francisco.)
- **e** There's an elevator in the building. (You can use the elevator to go to the top floor.)
- **f** Ellen got me a really nice jacket. (Ellen getting me the jacket was a complete surprise.)

**3 Write the words in the correct order to make cleft sentences.**

- **a** love / What / my country / weather / fantastic / is the / I / about
- **b** like most / is their / person / The / humor / thing / sense of / I / in a
- **c** enjoy / playing / What / is / I / most / tennis
- **d** most / is / thing / studying / The / the tests / hate / I / English / about
- **e** need / stress-free / What / is / in life / we all / a / most / job
- **f** never / understand / What / I / enough / don't / time / is why / I / have / free

**Which sentences do you agree with?**

**4 Change the emphasis in these sentences by starting *It is / was ...***

- **a** He met his wife in Mexico City.
  It was in Mexico City that he met his wife.
- **b** I only understood how serious it was when he called.
- **c** Ian didn't break that cup, you did.
- **d** Ben ate the cake, not Amy.
- **e** He wanted money, not love.
- **f** Stacey spends all her time on the computer, not the telephone.

## Unit 11 Future forms and future time clauses

#### *Will* (*'ll*), (*be*) *going to*, and the present progressive

These are the three most common future forms.

1 *Will* (*'ll*) is used for predictions or decisions reacting to circumstances such as offers, promises, and requests. *It'**ll** be worth a fortune in a few years. / I'**ll** give you my picture now.*

2 (*be*) *going to* is used for intentions or predictions based on present evidence. *I'**m going to** concentrate on my musical career. / Look at those clouds. It'**s going to** pour in a minute.*

3 The present progressive is used for arrangements. *I'**m moving** to Los Angeles next month.*

#### The simple present

You can use this tense to talk about fixed future events: timetables, routines, schedules. *My exams **start** next week.*

#### *might* and *may*

If you want to speculate about a future possibility you can use *might* or *may*. *He **might** have to get a part-time job.*

#### The future progressive

You use this tense to talk about something happening around a certain time in the future. *This time next week **I'll be trekking** in Patagonia.*

#### The future perfect

You use this tense to talk about something completed by a certain time in the future. *The builder **will have finished** the kitchen walls by the end of the week.*

#### Future time clauses (*if*, *when*, *as soon as* ...)

When it is clear from the main clause that the sentence is about the future, you don't use a future form in the subordinate clause. *When I **graduate**, I'm going to concentrate on my music career*. (NOT ~~*When I will graduate*~~, ...) / *It'll be a miracle if she **passes** the exam.* (NOT ... ~~*if she will pass the exam*~~.)

Other conjunctions which introduce subordinate clauses: *after, as soon as, before, once, the moment, the minute, unless, until.*

▶ **Now do Exercises 1 and 2.**

## Unit 12 Participle clauses. Nouns and quantity expressions

### Part 1: Participle clauses

When a present or past participle forms part of a relative clause, it is possible to leave out the relative pronoun (*who*, *which*, etc.) and auxiliary verb *be*. *We live in a house located downtown*. (= We live in a house which is located downtown.)

These are known as "participle clauses" or "reduced relative clauses." As with other relative clauses, there are both defining and non-defining participle clauses.

Defining participle clauses: *The man walking down the street is my neighbor*. (= The man who is walking down the street is my neighbor.)

Non-defining participle clauses contain extra, non-essential information which is separated from the main clause using commas. *His house, built in the 1930s, needs to be redecorated*. (= His house, which was built in the 1930s, needs to be redecorated.)

▶ **Now do Exercise 1.**

### Part 2: Nouns and quantity expressions

You use determiners (*every*, *most*, *no*) and quantifiers (*all of*, *most of*, *none of*) to express quantity.

1 Quantity expressions used with both **countable** and **uncountable** nouns: *none, not any, hardly any, some, a lot, plenty*.

2 Quantity expressions used only with **countable** nouns: *(very) few, a few, several, (too/not) many*.

3 Quantity expressions used only with **uncountable** nouns: *(very) little, a little, (too/not) much*.

4 When there is the definite article (*the*), a possessive pronoun (*my, your*, etc.) or a demonstrative pronoun (*that, these*, etc.) before the noun, you use a quantity expression with *of: Several **of my** friends live in small towns.* (NOT ~~*Several my friends*~~ ...)

5 When you want to talk about small numbers or amounts you can use *a few / a little* to emphasize the positive (*some*), or *few / little* to emphasize the negative (*not many/much*): *We did it because we wanted to have **a little** fun. Please hurry up! There's very **little** time.*

#### Verb forms

You use a singular verb form if the noun after *of* is uncountable (U) or singular. You use a plural if the noun is countable (C).

*There'**s** a lot of traffic* (U) *in the city.*

*There **are** lots of tourists* (C) *in the summer.*

▶ **Now do Exercises 2 and 3.**

## Unit 11 Exercises

**1 Complete the second sentence so that it has a similar meaning to the first sentence. Use between two and five words, including the word given in bold.**

**a** There's a possibility she won't pass the exam.
**might**
She *might not pass* the exam.

**b** I'm seeing the director at 3:00 p.m.
**arranged**
I ________ the director at 3:00 p.m.

**c** When I've finished this test, I'm leaving.
**soon**
________ I've finished this test, I'm leaving.

**d** I intend to concentrate on my acting career.
**going**
I ________ concentrate on my acting career.

**e** The builders are due to finish in a week.
**have**
By this time next week, the builders ________ .

**f** We won't go if you can't come with us.
**can**
________ come with us, we won't go.

**g** When he's finished, he'll come out.
**until**
He's ________ he's finished his homework.

**h** I predict a good result for the team today.
**to**
I think the team ________ win today.

**2 Write three sentences about the future: one about you, one about your country, and one about the planet. Compare with your partner.**

## Unit 12 Exercises

**1 Rewrite the sentences using a defining participle clause.**

**a** That man who is speaking very loudly is my cousin. That man ...
**b** The people who live on my street are very friendly. The people ...
**c** We keep the glasses in that cabinet. They are very expensive. The glasses ...
**d** The rooms that overlook the back of the house are the best. The rooms ...
**e** That place sells pizza. It is the best! The pizza ...

**2 Underline the correct alternative.**

My hometown is small but there (1) **'s** / **are** a lot of people out on a Saturday night. Sometimes there's so (2) **much** / **many** noise, you'd think it was daytime. If you want to go out, there are a (3) **few** / **little** really good nightclubs and (4) **plenty of** / **too much** bars. But the bars close early, so you often have very (5) **few** / **little** time to finish your drink. (6) **Some** / **Some of** my friends and I go bowling, but (7) **hardly any** / **hardly many** of us are any good. It might not sound like we have (8) **a lot of** / **many** fun, but we do – it's my home and I love it!

**3 Add an appropriate quantity expression from the box to make the sentences true for you.**

all of | most of | several of | not (very) many of | a few of | hardly any of | none of

**a** ________ my friends live in small towns.
**b** ________ the people I know go to work by car.
**c** ________ the stores near my home are open on Sunday.
**d** ________ the houses in my street have big backyards.
**e** ________ my neighbors have pets.
**f** ________ the buildings in my area are old.
**g** ________ the people I work with smoke.
**h** ________ these exercises are easy.

**Compare your answers with a partner.**

# Audioscript

## Unit 1

1.06

**(W = Woman; M = Man)**

**W:** Excuse me, is it OK if I sit here?
**M:** Sure, go ahead.
**W:** Thanks. ... Sorry, but you're American, aren't you?
**M:** Yes. How did you know?
**W:** Oh, I heard your accent. ... It isn't very busy here today, is it?
**M:** No, it isn't.
**W:** Are you on vacation?
**M:** No, I'm working here for a few months.
**W:** Oh, really? So am I. What do you do?
**M:** I work for the American Central Bank.
**W:** Oh. And do you like it here?
**M:** Yeah, I love it. But I can't stand the weather. It was so hot yesterday, wasn't it?
**W:** Oh yeah, you're right: the heat's terrible. But, you know, I love it here, too.
**M:** How long have you been here?
**W:** Oh, not long - a few weeks. How about you?
**M:** The same. What are you doing here?
**W:** I'm an artist, and I was asked to bring over some of my work to a small gallery just near here. I just had my first exhibition there.
**M:** Wow - that's impressive.
**W:** Thanks. So where are you from?
**M:** I'm from New York, Brooklyn actually.
**W:** Really? So am I! Don't tell me you went to Brooklyn High School?
**M:** Yes, I did, but I wasn't a very good student.
**W:** Me neither. What year did you graduate?
**M:** 2006.
**W:** That's weird - me, too. Do you remember Ms. Rivera?
**M:** The Math teacher? Yeah. She was really awful, wasn't she?
**W:** She's my mom.
**M:** Oh. ... Gee, I'm sorry. ... I didn't mean to ...

1.08

**(J = Journalist; R = Rick)**

1

**J:** Excuse me.
**R:** Me?
**J:** Yes, hi there! I'm working on a feature for *DUDES* magazine about men's personal style. Do you mind if I ask you some questions?
**R:** No, I guess not.
**J:** Could you tell me what image you're trying to achieve?
**R:** Image? I don't really have an image. I wear clothes I feel comfortable in - I guess you'd call it a casual look.
**J:** Do you think that you're aware of fashion?
**R:** Er, probably not, no. My style hasn't changed for years.

1.09

**(J = Journalist; M = Matt)**

2

**J:** Hello! I'm doing some research for an article about the way men dress. Can I ask you some questions?
**M:** Yeah, no problem.
**J:** Do you mind telling me what you wear to go out at night?
**M:** At night? You mean clubs and that kind of thing?
**J:** Yes, when you go clubbing.
**M:** I dress exactly like this.
**J:** You don't dress up then?
**M:** Well, put it this way - I never put a suit on. The clubs I go to don't let men in if they're wearing suits.
**J:** Really!? How strange. OK, one more question. I'd just like to know if there's an item of clothing you couldn't live without.
**M:** Sneakers. Definitely couldn't live without them. I've got about twenty-five pairs.

1.10

**(J = Journalist; C = Charles)**

3

**J:** Excuse me! Hello.
**C:** Hello.
**J:** I work for *DUDES* magazine and we're doing a survey about men's self-image. Do you mind if I ask you a couple of questions?
**C:** Oh. No, no, go ahead. What do you want to know?
**J:** Well, I'd like to know what your clothes say about you.
**C:** What do my clothes say about me!? Gee - I guess they say that I'm meeting a client this afternoon, and that means I have to make the right impression. So I have to wear a suit.
**J:** Would you say that you care about your image?
**C:** Oh, yes, I think I do. I like to look nice, even when I'm not working. Even when I wear jeans and a T-shirt, I like them to be neat and clean, and I think this says that I care about myself. It says that I have high self-esteem.

1.11

**(J = Journalist; A = Adam)**

4

**J:** Excuse me, sir. Is it OK if I ask you a couple of questions for an article I'm doing for *DUDES* magazine?

**A:** Yes, that's fine. Are you going to take pictures?

**J:** Yes, if you don't mind. But first I'd like to know whether your appearance affects your life in any way.

**A:** Oh, yes, totally. The way I dress is my life. It hasn't really affected my career so far, but I'm hoping it will. Basically I want to be noticed, and the reason I want to be noticed is that I want to get on TV.

**J:** Ah. And do you know what the last thing you bought was?

**A:** Oh, yes, I adore shopping. That would be a pink shirt I bought yesterday - oh, and a pink and black tie.

1.13

**(R = Rosa; I = Ian; M = Mike)**

**R:** Do you have the tickets?

**I:** No, I thought you had them.

**R:** Ian, honestly, I can't trust you to do anything.

**I:** Calm down - they're here.

**R:** Oh! You're so annoying.

**I:** You get worked up so easily.
Hey, look at that woman over there.

**R:** The one in the green dress?

**I:** Yeah.

**R:** What about her?

**I:** Don't you think she's the spitting image of Gwyneth Paltrow?

**R:** No, she doesn't look anything like Gwyneth Paltrow.

**I:** Yes, she does. She has the same hair.

**R:** What - long and blond?

**I:** Not just that - I'd recognize that smile anywhere.

**R:** How often has Gwyneth Paltrow smiled at you?

**I:** I've seen enough movies with her in them. She has a very distinctive smile.

**R:** It can't be her - she wouldn't come here to this club. And actually, that woman bears absolutely no resemblance to Gwyneth Paltrow.

**I:** Oh.

**R:** Hey, there's Mike. Hi Mike - how's it going?

**M:** Good - you'll never guess who I've been talking to.

**I:** Not Gwyneth Paltrow!

**M:** Gwyneth Paltrow?

**R:** Oh, ignore him - he's obsessed.

**I:** Sorry. You were saying?

**M:** Well, I was just at the bar, and I saw this amazing-looking woman walking towards me. I didn't recognize her until she was right in front of me. She's changed so much!

**R:** Who was it?

**M:** Sally - you know, my ex-girlfriend? Anyway, we ...

## Unit 2

1.16

**(HR = HR Manager; EM = Employing Manager)**

**HR:** Thanks for meeting with me about this next round of interviews.

**EM:** No problem. I'm really looking forward to meeting Andy again.

**HR:** Yes, he really stood out from the others. Of the three who passed to the next round, he is perhaps the most promising.

**EM:** Yes, I agree, but I am bit worried, because he has changed jobs quite a lot since he graduated from university.

**HR:** I see what you mean. It's difficult to know with the younger generation really, but it is quite common nowadays. Younger people rarely stay in a job for more than two or three years.

**EM:** Do you see that as a problem?

**HR:** No. In fact, it might even be a positive thing because it is essential for the company to find an employee with the right kind of experience for the job.

**EM:** That's a good point. And he will bring with him a lot of knowledge of the industry.

**HR:** Yes. It's important for us to find someone with the right balance of experience and qualifications.

**EM:** From what I saw on his résumé, he has the right qualifications. In fact, he went to one of the best universities in the country. I was impressed with that.

**HR:** Yes, but remember that if he passes this second interview stage, he will sit our internal exam, which will test his knowledge of the area.

**EM:** Will it provide us with enough information to make a decision?

**HR:** Almost. If he does well in the test, then we ask for three recommendations from former employers. These should tell us something about his personality and work ethic, which is more difficult to test.

**EM:** True. A strong work ethic is important. And he needs to be a strong character to deal with the kind of clients we have.

**HR:** If it works out and we offer him an attractive package, he is likely to stay with us for three to five years. Let's see how he performs in this new interview.

**EM:** (laughing) ... Yes, let's. Shall we call him in and get started?

1.17

**(I = Interviewer; A = Andy)**

**I:** And, how do you feel about this second interview?

**A:** I am a little nervous about being interviewed a second time, but I think it's normal in any hiring process to be a little nervous. I decided to apply for a job in a new company because I'm interested in facing new challenges. Besides, I have already been in my present job for two and a half years, which is good by today's standards - not so long that I become stuck in the same company, not too short that I seem unstable or unreliable to future employers. I think it is important to change companies occasionally as this is the best way to learn about my industry and to keep growing as a professional. On the other hand, some managers, especially more traditional ones, might see this as moving around too much and might think that I will not be reliable or stay long in their company so I'm afraid of being taken as irresponsible. Another thing that I worry about doing in this interview is freezing because of my shyness. I'm terrible at talking to people, and this can come across as unfriendly or stand-offish. However, I know that I have great industry experience and a suitable educational background, so I'm optimistic about meeting the requirements of the job.

1.21

**(J = Jennifer; M = Maria)**

**J:** Hello, Maria, come in. Did you have a pleasant flight?

**M:** Pleasant flight?

**J:** A good trip?

**M:** Oh, yes, thank you. Very good.

**J:** Well, welcome to our home. I hope you'll be happy here. It's not very big, but I think you'll have everything you need.

**M:** Yes, thank you. It's very nice.

**J:** Oh good, I'm glad you like it. Let me introduce you to the rest of the family, and then I'll show you around.

**M:** OK, thank you Mrs. Brown.

**J:** Oh, please, call me Jennifer. Now, this is Ben - he's thirteen.

**M:** Hello, Ben.

**J:** And this is Katy - she's eleven.

**M:** Hello, Katy.

**K:** Hello.

**J:** And this is Max - he's a baby so he can get a little excited. Down, Max. Sorry. I hope you don't mind dogs.

**M:** No, I love dogs.

**J:** Oh good. So, this is the kitchen - we usually eat breakfast in here. Help yourself to coffee. The refrigerator is here, look - and the cups and saucers are in this cabinet. I'm afraid the microwave is broken, but we seem to manage without it.

**M:** It's a nice kitchen.

**J:** Yes, it's my favorite room. Now, this is the living room - excuse the mess, but Ben and Katy have a lot of friends over. This is the dining room - Max isn't allowed in here, are you Max? Down boy! Now, if you'd like to leave your bags here for a minute, I'll show you the upstairs.

**M:** Thank you.

**J:** Here's the bathroom. Sorry about the pink walls - that was Katy's idea.

**M:** Oh, I like pink. My bedroom walls are pink.

**J:** Really? How funny. OK, this is Katy's room - we're not allowed to go into Ben's room, but it's probably just as well. And this is your room. It's quiet in here because the window looks out on the backyard.

**M:** Oh, it's great - thank you.

**J:** Now, you make yourself at home, and if there's anything you need, just holler, OK?

**M:** OK.

**J:** Oh, by the way, Ben's a vegetarian, so we don't usually eat meat because he gets upset. Is that OK with you?

**M:** Yes, I like vegetables.

## Unit 3

1.23

During the Gold Rush, Sam Brannan became one of the most successful businessmen in California. He arrived in California in 1846, when San Francisco (then called Yerba Buena) was just a small community of a few hundred people.

When gold was discovered on John Sutter's land in 1848, Sam Brannan was running the only store between San Francisco and the gold fields. Quickly recognizing a gap in the market, he bought up all the picks, shovels, and pans he could find, and then ran up and down the streets of San Francisco shouting, "Gold, gold on the American River!"

He had no intention of digging for gold! No, he was planning to sell shovels. And having cornered the market, he ended up with a lot more gold than the person who had to dig for it.

This was a man who really understood the laws of supply and demand. A metal pan that sold for twenty cents a few days earlier was now available from Brannan for fifteen dollars. In just nine weeks, he made $36,000. Within a few years, he had become the first gold rush millionaire.

In the end, though, Sam Brannan lost his fortune and his health, as did many of those who first benefited from the gold rush. Alcoholism finally led to his downfall, and California's first millionaire died an unnoticed death.

1.26

**(I = Interviewer; P = Patti; E = Eric; L = Lewis)**

**I:** It's impossible to have too much money - do you agree with that, Patti?

**P:** Yes. If you have dreams, money makes them possible. Personally, I can't imagine having too much money. I'm always broke. Anyway, if I ever felt I had too much money, I'd give it away to charity.

**I:** And Patti, would you prefer fame or fortune?

**P:** Being practical, I'd say fortune, but if I were single with no kids and no responsibilities, I'd go for fame.

**I:** Eric, were you given or did you earn an allowance as a child?

**E:** I was given a quarter a week by my father, but on the condition that I behaved myself. If I didn't behave well, I didn't receive it. Parents were much stricter in those days.

**I:** And Eric, what was the first thing you saved up for and bought yourself?

**E:** A set of toy soldiers. Not the plastic ones you get nowadays, but little metal ones, beautifully hand-painted. It took me almost a year to save up for them. If I'd known that they would become valuable antiques, I would've kept them. They'd probably be worth a fortune now.

**I:** Tell me, Lewis, if you could buy yourself a skill or a talent, what would it be?

**L:** Well, there are lots of things I'd like to be better at, but if I had to choose one, it would have to be soccer - I'd like to be a great soccer player!

**I:** And finally Lewis, what can't money buy?

**L:** Happiness. I tend to think that once I have enough money to buy some new clothes or get a better car, then I'll be happy. But it never works out like that.

1.28

**1 Chris**

I suppose you'd call it a vintage camera now. It's a Zeiss Contaflex, and I bought it in South Africa 50 years ago. It cost $50 which was a lot of money for me then, but it was still a lot less than I would have paid back home. So I was delighted - it was the best camera you could get at the time and it was a bargain. Unfortunately, I had to pay nearly $40 in tax at customs when I arrived back in the USA, so in the end it was less of a bargain. But I've certainly had my money's worth out of it. It's been everywhere with me, and all our family pictures were taken on this camera. Last year, for my 70th birthday, my children bought me a wonderful and very modern, digital camera. It takes much better pictures than my old Zeiss, but I can't use it. I'm afraid I'm too old-fashioned.

1.29

**2 Katie**

I know it sounds stupid, but this is the thing I would least like to lose. It's not because it's worth anything, although it is an expensive one because it's got GPS - you know, satellite navigation - on it, too. But the main thing is that if I lost this, I'd lose the addresses and numbers of practically everybody I know. It contains the details of about three hundred people.

1.30

**3 Heather**

This is my most precious possession because it saved my life when I got caught in an avalanche in Johnson Pass in Alaska's Chugach Mountain Range. It had been snowing for four days, and the temperature rose that morning - perfect avalanche conditions. When the first person in our group of snowboarders leaped off the cornice, the rest of us decided to follow his tracks - no traversing and no hard turns, so as not to disturb the snow. When it was my turn, I made it down the first pitch safely and thought I was out of danger. But the person behind me started before I was at a safe distance and nervously made a hard right turn. I heard a loud crack, and then WHOMPH! The snow hit me really fast in the back of the neck. I pushed my neck-warmer over my face, which kept the snow out of my mouth and nose, allowing me to breathe as the avalanche swept me up. I began frantically swimming and tried to stay aware of which way was up. When the snow finally settled, I had managed to get part of my glove up through the surface. It took the others a few minutes to find me, but I knew they would. Luckily, my neck-warmer allowed me the extra air to wait out those few minutes.

1.31

**(J = John; C = Cara; SC1 = Sales clerk 1; SC2 = Sales clerk 2)**

**J:** Thanks for doing this. I really don't know where to start.

**C:** OK, first you need to tell me what you're looking for. Do you have any ideas?

**J:** Well, diamonds are always good.

**C:** OK. And do you prefer gold or silver or platinum or white gold?

**J:** Whoa, hang on. Say that again.

**C:** Does Julia wear more gold or more silver?

**J:** Gold, I think.

**C:** And what's your budget?

**J:** My budget? I don't know. This is only the second time I've done this.

**C:** What? You were engaged before?

**J:** Yes, it was a mistake. We were too young.

**C:** And did she keep the ring?

**J:** Yeah, but it wasn't worth much - I was really hard up at the time, so I just got something cheap.

**C:** Well, you have to be prepared to splash out this time. It's a once-in-a-lifetime thing. Well, twice-in-a-lifetime for you, I suppose.

**J:** OK - my budget is ... three or four hundred dollars.

**C:** Hmm. OK, well, you may have to revise that figure.

J: What do you mean?

C: You'll see. Come on. Let's go.

SC1: Good morning. Are you looking for something special?

J: Yes, um, a diamond engagement ring, please.

SC1: I see - our diamond rings are over here, sir. If you'd like to take a look and then ask me to show you anything you particularly like ...

J: Thanks. Have you seen the prices?

C: I told you ...

SC1: Is there something you'd like to see?

J: Um, they're beautiful, but they're a little out of my price range.

SC1: Sorry we can't help you, sir. Goodbye.

J: Let's go somewhere less exclusive, OK?

C: OK, but you're going to have to pay a little bit more.

J: I'm not made of money!

C: No, I know, but this is a time when you have to push the boat out.

SC2: Can I help you with anything today?

J: Er, yes, I'm looking for a very simple engagement ring - perhaps one diamond?

SC2: And what are you looking to pay?

J: Well, around $600?

SC2: OK, this is $660 - it's a quarter carat diamond.

J: It's small, isn't it?

C: You get what you pay for.

J: OK, I was hoping for something a little more sparkly. How much is this one, for example?

SC2: That one's $1,400.

J: OK. I guess I was thinking of something a little less pricey.

SC2: What's your budget?

J: I suppose I could stretch to $1,000.

SC2: OK. This one costs $950.

J: What do you think?

C: I think it's beautiful, and I think Julia would love it.

J: I should certainly hope so. This is definitely the last time I'm doing this.

## Unit 4

1.35

**(I = Interviewer)**

I: Before I introduce my next guests, Julia and Anthony Giles, I thought it might be interesting for our listeners around the world who may not know much about Canada to have some background information on the country. This will bring the amazing adventure that Jules and Tony, as they are called by family and friends, into perspective.

As we said at the top of the program, Julia and Anthony are a brother and sister who traveled across Canada together this summer. This is no small feat, as Canada is the second largest country in the world, with ten provinces and three territories. It is a multi-cultural, multi-lingual country, with English and French as its official languages. Canada is famous for its very harsh winters in the east and milder winters in the west. Despite this weather, Canada is famous for its thriving agricultural industry. Crossing such a vast country with such varied cultures must not have been easy. Today we have a brother and sister duo to tell us about how they did it.

1.36

**(I = Interviewer; J = Julia; A = Anthony)**

I: It is a pleasure to have you here today. Julia and Anthony, welcome.

J: Thanks for having us.

A: It's a pleasure to be here.

I: So tell us how you came up with this idea.

A: Well, we had always planned to do a gap year traveling around. We had thought about different places like Europe, India and South Africa. Then we saw stories of other young people who had made trips across Canada and we thought it would be interesting to do the same once we graduated. It was a way to kick off our gap year. We are not the first to do this kind of trip. We were inspired by others who did the same.

I: And why on such a small budget?

J: Once we had decided to make this trip as our personal way of commemorating Canada's 150th anniversary, we thought it would be important to make the trip on a very low budget - for two reasons. One, we didn't want to ask our parents for the money. They have enough on their plate and pretty soon we would be going to university, which is expensive, especially when you are supporting two kids at the same time, so we didn't want to burden them even further. Secondly, we thought that doing it on a very low budget would force us to be more self-sufficient and resourceful. It certainly forced us to interact more with people than we would have if we had taken a more comfortable route.

A: Yes, for sure. Julia's point about being resourceful is very true. We each have unique skills, so we each were in charge of different tasks during the trip. I think that was one of the reasons we were able to get through such a challenging trip successfully. Julia was in charge of navigation and transportation and I was in charge of food and shelter. we make a great team.

J: (laughing) Maybe because as twins we have always had to work together.

A: (laughing) True ... Another thing to note is that although this was a cross country trip, we knew from the onset that it would be impossible to travel through all 10 provinces and three territories of Canada. It is probably impossible to travel across the second largest country in the world in two months with only

$200. So, if anyone wants to repeat our feat, and we do encourage people to get out there and get to know the country, they should keep that in mind.

**J:** And we did it in summer. It would have probably been impossible to do this kind of trip in our very cold Canadian winter.

**A:** As you showed in an earlier report, our parents, especially our mother, were very concerned for our safety.

**J:** Yes, she was. To help her feel better about our trip, we put some safety measures into place. We each had a cell phone with us at all times and we sent her two messages a day - one first thing in the morning and one before going to bed. She definitely felt more at ease knowing that we were a phone call away. Another thing we promised to do was to ask her to wire us money if we ever really needed it. Luckily, we never did, but it was good to have that as a back-up plan.

**I:** What was the highlight of your trip?

**A:** Hmmm (thinking) For me, I'd have to say it was the two days we spent with a family in Quebec and getting to know the French Canadian culture.

**J:** Really? For me the highlight was that day on the farm ... remember?

**A:** Oh, yes! That was quite exciting ... and scary!

**J:** Well, we had been working on the farm for a week, so we were quite familiar with the routine. On this day we wake up really early and head down to the fields to continue the harvest, which is done with a big machine called a combine. Anthony has been in training for a week, and this is the day he gets to drive the combine by himself. All is going well, when suddenly Anthony loses control, and the combine is racing off across the fields. It almost crashes into one of the barns, but luckily it stops just short of the barn and disaster is averted. Can you imagine what would have happened if he was not able to stop?

**I:** Wow! What a scare.

**A:** Umm hmm!

**I:** What advice would you give to other young people who might be thinking of doing a similar trip?

**A:** Well, it depends on a lot of things - what kind of trip the person wants to do, what time of the year they intend to travel, how much money they have to spend, and so on. So, all of these things need to be taken into account. Based on these factors, they can then decide on what kind of experience they want to have. The most important thing is to travel with at least one other person for safety and company and to have a plan. After that, everything else will fall into place.

**I:** Julia and Anthony, thank you.

**J, A:** Thank you.

1.37

**(P = Presenter; I = Interviewer; S = Steve)**

**P:** A recent survey revealed that only 38% of us would be motivated to do more exercise if our life depended on it. In other words, six out of ten of us would rather die than exercise!
We went out on the streets to find out how much exercise people are really doing, and if they're not doing it, what exactly is stopping them?

**I:** How much exercise do you do?

**S:** Oh, not as much as I should. I used to have an expensive gym membership, but I only went twice, so I canceled it. I'm not very sporty, so I don't do any team sports like baseball or anything. I do love baseball, but strictly as a spectator, not as a participant. I have noticed that it's harder to keep the weight off than when I was younger though, so I've started riding my bike into work. That's about forty minutes of exercise every day. Better than nothing.

**I:** What stops you?

**S:** I'm just so tired after work - I get home, sit on the couch, and do nothing.

1.38

**(I = Interviewer; M = Maria)**

**I:** How much exercise do you do?

**M:** I'm studying for exams right now, so I go running a lot, just to get some fresh air. There's nothing worse than being stuck inside all day. I think it helps if you have someone to go with - it's really hard to motivate yourself, but if you make plans to go running with a friend, you feel you can't let them down, and that forces you to go.

**I:** What stops you?

**M:** The weather! If it's raining, or really cold, I can usually talk myself out of it.

1.39

**(I = Interviewer; S = Sam)**

**I:** How much exercise do you do?

**S:** I run up the stairs, and that's it. Well, on weekends I do a few hours of housework - that must burn off a few calories. I hope so anyway, because when I've finished I sit down with a cup of coffee and a box of doughnuts. I certainly don't go to the gym if that's what you mean. Can you imagine me in Lycra? Ha, ha.

**I:** Is that what stops you from going to the gym?

**S:** Er, not really. It's finding time to fit it in around everything else I have to do. I have three kids under five, so there's no way I have time to go to the gym or anything like that. But I figure I run a marathon every day just running around after the children!

1.40

**(I = Interviewer; T = Tim)**

**I:** How much exercise do you do?

**T:** I go swimming and I work out at the gym. I try to do some kind of aerobic exercise for about thirty minutes three times a week, and I do weights a couple of times a week. On weekends, I often go for a walk in the park, and my girlfriend's trying to get me to go to salsa classes - she says it's a really good workout.

**I:** What stops you?

**T:** Nothing really - unless I've pulled a muscle or something, and it hurts. I love it. I sit at a desk all day long, and if I don't do some physical exercise at least three or four times a week, I feel really out of shape. But it isn't just about weight loss - exercise gives me a general feeling of well-being.

## Unit 5

1.43

My dad is the most ritualistic person I know, and many of his rituals involve his car.

We've never kept domestic animals in our house, but my father's car is as close as you'll get to the family pet. In fact, the car probably gets better treatment and more affection than a pet would.

Each night, the car is tucked up in its garage under a cozy blanket. Nobody - but nobody - is allowed in the garage in case they accidentally brush against "the precious one," causing who knows what damage.

When we were children, on the rare occasions when my dad would get the car out of the garage (for births, deaths, marriages, and national disasters - and then only if the buses weren't running), we would have to wear plastic bags on our feet in case we had a sudden urge to vandalize the seats with our shoes.

We would never be allowed to shut the car doors ourselves ... in case we slammed them too hard, I guess. I mean, three-, five-, and seven-year-old girls can do untold damage to a car by slamming the door shut.

Nowadays, we don't have to wear plastic bags on our feet, but the "Starting the car and setting off" ritual has never changed.

He'll start the engine and then sit there for at least five minutes with the engine on. As repulsive fumes pump out into the fresh country air, he'll try to tune in the radio unsuccessfully. Then he'll pick up the newspaper and read a couple of headlines. Next, he'll fold the newspaper perfectly. He always folds it like that. After these endeless minutes with a car full of choking passengers, he'll take the hand-brake off and reverse out of the driveway at breakneck speed.

It isn't pleasant being a passenger, but we've always let him get away with this strange behavior because he's the boss.

None of us would dare to complain.

My father used to be a pilot in the US Air Force, and I often wonder whether he would indulge in this kind of ritual before take-off and whether his crew would let him get away with it because he was the boss. Probably.

1.44

**(I = Interviewer; J = Jorge)**

**I:** Tell me about weddings in your country.

**J:** Well, in Spain, where I come from, there is this ritual that happens after the rings have been exchanged between the groom and the bride. It is called "*las arras*," and it consists of thirteen gold coins which the groom puts in the bride's hands. It symbolizes their intention of sharing everything: all the worldly goods they are going to receive together.

1.45

**(I = Interviewer; S = Sandra)**

**I:** Tell me about weddings in your country.

**S:** Well, in Taiwan we use a black umbrella to cover the bride's head, because we believe that it can protect the bride from the evil spirits. So normally an elderly person will hold the umbrella when the bride leaves her house to go to the groom's house.

**I:** And will this bring her good luck as well?

**S:** Yes, it will prevent bad luck.

1.46

**(I = Interviewer; I2 = Ilhan)**

**I:** Tell me about wedding traditions in Turkey.

**I2:** Weddings in Turkey are different from how they are in the US. There are a lot of people at the wedding. There are sometimes as many as four or five hundred guests, and one of the most interesting things, I think, about Turkish weddings is the fact that the guests at the wedding pin gold and money on the bride's and groom's costumes, on the bridegroom's suit, and on the bride's dress. I think, from what I can understand, that this money and gold is used by the bride and groom to set themselves up for their new life together, living in their new house, their new home, to buy things like a fridge, and other things they might need for their future life together.

1.47

**(I = Interviewer; L = Laila)**

**I:** Tell me about wedding traditions in Morocco.

**L:** Oh, Moroccan weddings are elaborate affairs. Preparations take weeks, and the whole community is involved! The bride gets lots of attention in the days leading up to the wedding - a group of women, usually older than the bride, but connected to her in some way, give her a sort of milk bath which is supposed to purify her. Then she has her hands and feet decorated in henna. This ritual symbolizes prosperity. It looks beautiful, and there's another custom which says that the bride isn't supposed to do any housework until the henna wears off.

1.49

**a**

"Well, I try to remember my wife's birthday every year, and on the way home yesterday I stopped to buy her some flowers – I think that's romantic, but she just thought I'd done something wrong."

**b**

"I'm very romantic, but I think most women are. I remember meeting my boyfriend for the first time. It was in a club and I remember seeing him across the room and thinking, 'He looks nice.' He was wearing a black T-shirt and really nice jeans. I even remember what he said to me – he said 'Do you want to dance?' When I asked him recently if he remembered meeting me for the first time, he had no idea."

**c**

"I don't know. I don't think my boyfriend would say I'm romantic because I always forget to buy him gifts or say nice things to him. But deep down I think I am romantic. Since I met my boyfriend, I've stopped looking at other men. Well, I haven't stopped looking, but I have stopped hitting on them."

**d**

"No, I don't think I'm romantic really. I don't like all that romantic nonsense. Women expect you to buy them gifts and remember their birthdays. And they try to make you give up sports and all those things I enjoy. I can't be bothered with all that. Maybe that's why I haven't managed to find a girlfriend!"

1.52

The purpose of the Three Good Things exercise is to focus our awareness on the positive, and cultivate an appreciation for all that is right in our lives. Here's how to do it:
First, at the end of the day, preferably at the same time every day so you don't forget, write down three good things that happened on the day.
For each of the good things, give a title, like, "Risotto came out perfectly."
Make sure that you describe in as much detail as possible what happened, what people said, etc.
As you are writing, include how it made you feel at the time, and how it makes you feel now.
Another important part of the exercise is to identify what caused the event to happen.
Finally, set a specific number of days for the practice, like a week or a month.
Voilà! Have fun with it and appreciate the good that is around you even in difficult times.

## Unit 6

1.54

**(I = Interviewer; JC = Jean Crowshaw)**

**I:** How did you become a restaurant critic?

**JC:** Well, I've been working for newspapers for more than twenty years. I started out as a journalist when I was twenty-three, and I've worked for several newspapers since then including this one. Then, when the last restaurant critic retired, I was asked to take his place. And I've been doing it for the last thirteen years.

**I:** How can you do this job and stay so slim?

**JC:** Yeah, that's a good question. I mean, I eat out two or three times a week. But as a matter of fact, to write about a restaurant and its cuisine, I need to taste the food, but I don't need to clean my plate. When I'm covering a restaurant, I always take three friends with me. Everyone has to order a different dish. So then I taste about two bites of everything on their plates, and then I eat the same amount of food on my plate. Then I stop eating. And that's not just so that I stay slim, it's so that I can remember all the different flavors.

**I:** Do you take notes?

**JC:** No, I don't write anything down because I don't want to draw attention to myself. So while I'm eating, I'm making mental notes about the restaurant. How does the room look? Is the lighting too dim, too bright? Is the service efficient or is it slow? How is the food presented? Are the waiters doing their job well? Do the customers look happy? Then, as soon as I get home, no matter how late it is or how tired I am, I write down my impressions – I write pages and pages of notes.

**I:** You must be pretty well-known on the restaurant circuit. Do you wear a disguise?

**JC:** What like a wig? Ha, ha, no, I couldn't do that. Like I said, I've been working around the Washington area for some thirteen years now, so inevitably, I do sometimes get recognized, but by that time it's too late for the management to call in another chef or change the serving staff.

**I:** Do people get upset if you give them a bad review?

**JC:** Oh, yes, but the bad reviews are the most fun to write! Once, a restaurant owner called my editor and threatened to come in with a gun – I don't think he did in the end.

**I:** Who pays for your food?

**JC:** The newspaper pays for the food. Nothing is accepted for free.

**I:** Have you had any particularly good or bad experiences that stand out in your memory?

**JC:** There was the waitress who tripped and poured my son's dessert and a glass of wine in my lap. I wasn't too happy at the time, but I managed to see the funny side of it later. But there's one thing I really hate and that's when the waiter keeps asking "Is everything all right?" Good, experienced waiters never ask that - they don't need to because they can tell if everything's all right just by looking at the customers' faces.

**I:** Have you met any rude waiters or waitresses?

**JC:** I've experienced every kind of waiter and waitress - rude and moody, chatty and enthusiastic, and over-familiar. The best waiters are those who are attentive but not intrusive. I can't stand those waiters who squat down beside you to take your order, and then proceed to tell you their favorite items on the menu, because they ate it on their vacation in Italy ... this kind of invasion of your privacy is totally unacceptable.

**I:** What's the best meal you've ever eaten?

**JC:** It was in Italy, in Umbria. I was traveling with my husband, and we stopped in a very rural place where we had the dinner I'll remember for the rest of my days. Olive oil pressed from the restaurant's own trees, lamb with so much flavor that it defines what the meat should taste like - wonderful bread, handmade pasta, local wines. It wasn't a formal restaurant, but I've never forgotten it and I've never enjoyed a meal more.

▶ 1.56

zero point two five
one million, two hundred and thirty-four thousand, five hundred and sixty-seven
seventy-fifth
three zero one, nine six two, seven eight seven seven
five sixths
July twenty-seventh, twenty twelve

▶ 1.57

**a** Rafael Nadal is winning two sets to love.
**b** My grandfather was born in 1908.
**c** It's really cold - ten degrees below zero.

▶ 1.58

**(W1 = Waiter; W2 = Waitress; M = Man; Wm = Woman)**

**W1:** Busy tonight, isn't it?
**W2:** Yeah. Who's the man at table four? He looks familiar.
**W1:** Oh, that's Burt Sinclair. He's a big cheese in the hotel industry, so if you butter him up, he'll give you a nice big tip.
**W2:** Oh right - I could do with some extra cash.
**M:** Excuse me! Excuse me!
**W2:** Yes, sir. Can I help you?
**M:** Yes, you can. The service in here is very slow this evening. We've been sitting here for ten minutes and we haven't even seen the menu yet.
**W2:** Oh, I'm terribly sorry, sir. We're very busy tonight. I'll get you the menus immediately.
**W1:** How are you doing with the big cheese at table four?
**W2:** Well, he obviously thinks he's the greatest thing since sliced bread, and so does the woman with him.
**W1:** That's his wife.
**W2:** His wife! Oh!
**M:** Excuse me!
**W2:** Yes, sir. Are you ready to order?
**M:** I'm afraid not. It's so dark in here that we can't read the menu.
**W2:** Oh, one moment, sir. I'll bring you a bigger candle. There, is that OK?
**M:** Yes, yes, that's fine.
**W2:** Would you like a few more minutes, sir?
**M:** No, no. I'll have the steak.
**W2:** OK, and how would you like it, sir?
**M:** Medium rare.
**Wm:** And I'll have seafood pasta and a salad.
**W2:** That's one steak, medium rare, and one seafood pasta.
**W1:** Everything OK with table four?
**W2:** They're tricky customers. I feel like I'm walking on eggshells.
**W1:** Just remember the tip.
**M:** Excuse me!
**W2:** Yes, sir?
**M:** I'm afraid this steak is overcooked. I asked for medium rare.
**W2:** I'm sorry, sir.
**M:** And there's another problem.
**Wm:** It's my seafood pasta - I think the scallops are bad.
**W2:** Oh, no. I'm very sorry. I'll talk to the chef.
**W1:** It's not looking very good for the tip, is it?
**W2:** That's not funny.
**M:** Excuse me!
**W2:** Grrr.
**W1:** Calm down. You have to take it all with a grain of salt. If you start taking it personally, you've had it.

## Unit 7

▶ 2.02

**1**

My favorite beach is in Cape Town. It's called Camps Beach, and I love it because the location is spectacular. But if you want to swim there, I'd advise you to wear a wetsuit because the water is freezing.

**2**

My favorite beach is in Florida, but nobody knows about it. It took a while to convince my friend that it was worth climbing down a very dangerous cliff to get there, but she had to admit that it was worth it.

**3**
My favorite beach is in Maui. I've traveled to hundreds of beaches in different countries, and I can now confirm that the best beach in the world is Kapalua Beach.

**4**
Travel brochures claim that the best beaches are in faraway places like the Caribbean or the Indian Ocean, but I can assure you that there are wonderful beaches closer to home. For example, my favorite beach is in Valparaiso, and I can drive there in a day.

**5**
My favorite beach is the man-made beach along the River Seine in Paris. In the summer, they import a load of sand and encourage people to go there to hang out and relax. I think it's great for families who can't afford to go away on vacation.

▶ 2.03

**Paul**
We decided to do something really special for Christmas. We both love skiing so we managed to book ten days in a small ski resort in Alberta, Canada. When we arrived there, though, we found out that the temperatures had been unseasonably warm. Basically, there was no snow. Well, there were a few centimeters of snow very high up on the black runs, but we weren't allowed to go there, because it was too high and too dangerous. So we had to find other ways to entertain ourselves, and in the end, this was really good because we were forced to relax. We didn't have to get up early to go skiing, so we could go out until late at night and sleep in the morning. We read books, had long lunches, went for walks, and drank lots of hot chocolate. At the end of the vacation, we felt completely relaxed.

▶ 2.04

**Amy**
When I was 18, I was desperate to go to Guatemala to see the volcanoes, but I wasn't allowed to go there alone - my parents thought I was too young. So my brother agreed to come with me, and we carefully planned a three-week tour. We set off from Chicago, and our destination was the Guatemalan city of Antigua, but we had a layover in Miami for a few hours. Anyway, we finally took off from Miami, and, during the flight, my brother asked a fellow passenger if he'd been to Antigua before. He replied that he had, and it was one of the most beautiful islands he'd ever come across. At that point, we realized we were on the wrong plane, going to the wrong place. Obviously we couldn't get off the plane there and then, so we had to go on and then figure it all out when we landed. There were no direct flights from the Caribbean island of Antigua to the Guatemalan city of Antigua, so we had to go back to Miami and start again. We lost a week of our vacation, but in the end it just made us appreciate Guatemala all the more.

▶ 2.05

**Rachel**
When I told my friends I was going on a cycling vacation in Spain, they thought I was kidding. But I thought it would be fine. OK, I don't actually own a bicycle, but I do go to the gym twice a week. In preparation, I went to a specialist bike store to get some gear. The helmet was compulsory, so I got one of those, but I didn't think I needed the padded cycling shorts. The guy in the store recommended them, but I thought they looked stupid, so I didn't get them. I should have listened to that guy. As soon as I met the other people I knew I was in trouble. One man had recently ridden from Paris to Madrid - for fun! Our Spanish tour leader looked as if she was about to set off on the Tour de France. I made a big effort to keep up on the first day, but by the evening my rear end was in agony, and I couldn't sit down. Fortunately we didn't have to carry anything - there was a car that took all our baggage from one place to the next. But I have to admit that I got a ride in the baggage car a couple of times. I never realized that that part of Spain was so mountainous.

▶ 2.07

**(F = Frank; A = Anna)**

**F:** Do you usually make friends while on vacation, Anna?
**A:** Not really but I made a good friend many years ago! When I was twenty I went to Brazil - I went to Rio de Janeiro - and while I was there I met Paulo.
**F:** What was he like?
**A:** Come to think of it, he was very funny, and we had a lot in common. We hit it off right away when we were introduced by a mutual friend at a party. From the very beginning he would always make me laugh. Just thinking about that time in my life puts a smile on my face. Anyway, it was the beginning of a great friendship.
**F:** Nice!
**A:** We got along so well together ... we would have conversations for hours about books we had read and movies we had seen. And he was always so insightful. I could really talk to him about fun things and more serious things as well, do you know what I mean? In fact, I thought we would be friends forever.
**F:** Yeah I know what you mean. So what happened next?
**A:** Well, eventually, my visa ran out and I returned to Texas. We then spent six months calling each other, writing letters, and sending packages. But long distance friendships were more difficult before we had so much technology to keep in touch.
**F:** What happened?
**A:** Basically, we just got busy with other things - university, work ... and we eventually lost touch.

**F:** Oh, that's sad.

**A:** Well, in the end I reconnected with him on social media, and we have been catching up. He is the same Paulo - funny and wise, just older, like me! He moved to São Paulo, where his wife is from. Now that it is easier than ever to stay in touch, we have rekindled our friendship. To tell you the truth, social media certainly has its upside!

2.11

**(T = Tim; S = Shannon)**

**T:** Where are you going on vacation this year?

**S:** I'm off to Paris.

**T:** Oh, great - I love Paris.

**S:** Oh, yes, you know it pretty well, don't you? Can you believe this is my first time there? Do you have any tips?

**T:** Well, there's so much to see. I'd definitely recommend the Eiffel Tower. Take the glass-sided elevator - when it comes out into the daylight, the views are spectacular.

**S:** That sounds like a must. What about museums?

**T:** Well, of course the most famous museum is the Louvre, but it's probably best to avoid it because of the long lines, but make sure you go to the Musée d'Orsay. It's one of the best museums in the world. You'll have to wait in line there too, but it's worth it. Where are you staying?

**S:** In a little hotel in the 3rd arrondissement.

**T:** Oh, that's a really nice area. While you're there, make sure you walk around the backstreets because there are some nice little stores - oh, and while you're there you should go to the Picasso museum. You won't be disappointed.

**S:** Oh, I love Picasso. And how should we get around? What are the taxis like?

**T:** Um, I think it's probably best to avoid taxis, because the traffic can be very slow. If I were you, I'd use the buses or the metro. They're very good.

**S:** Wow, that sounds great.

**T:** And whatever you do, don't leave Paris without tasting the oysters at Bofinger.

**S:** Bofinger?

**T:** Yes, it's a restaurant on Rue de la Bastille. It's the best place for seafood, and the décor is fantastic.

**S:** I think I need to write this down. How do you spell Bofinger?

2.13

**(NH = Neal Hurt; JJ = Julia John)**

**NH:** Welcome to today's show. I'm Neal Hurt, the host of *Health Watch*. In today's show we will be speaking to Dr. Julia John, a physician and wellness expert on relaxation techniques. Nowadays many people are under a lot of pressure, working long hours, facing long commutes and juggling numerous responsibilities. Dr. John will share some ideas on how we can alleviate the stress and anxiety that can result from such a hectic lifestyle. Dr. John, welcome to the show.

**JJ:** Thank you Neal. As you mentioned, our modern lifestyle can actually be a source of a lot of stress, which is detrimental to our health and well-being. Occasionally escaping from it all would be ideal to help us refocus our energies, but that's not always possible. The techniques I will present today are feasible and affordable ways to escape and will help us to find the serenity we need to carry on with our hectic schedules and many competing demands.

One of the most highly recommended relaxation techniques is meditation. For listeners who have never done meditation before, I recommend starting with five minutes and building up from there. Ideally, this should be done in a calm and quiet place. Sit on a chair or on the floor, with an upright posture and your eyes closed. Focus on one thought. Repeating a positive mantra or focusing on your heartbeat or breathing helps to focus and calm your thoughts. This can be done at two or three intervals during the day, according to your schedule. Research shows that meditation lowers the heart rate and boosts immunity, bringing benefits not just to the mind, but to the body well.

The second technique I'd like to talk about today, if we can call it a technique, is increasing one's social circle. And this is backed up by the research which shows that socially isolates people have more health problems and are twice as likely to die from heart disease. By joining a club or exercise group or volunteering we can meet other people and form strong social bonds which reduce stress levels and improves our immune functions.

Lastly, and related to the second suggestion somewhat, is to laugh! It might sound silly, but laughing actually has numerous health benefits such as reducing stress hormones and blood pressure and increasing T-cells and endorphins. It's easy to laugh with friends around, but you can watch a funny movie or TV show which can also do the trick.

**NH:** Those are some great suggestions. And we can do these things at no cost at all.

**JJ:** That's right!

**NH:** Thank you doctor John. We invite you to join us tomorrow for some more escape techniques by Dr. Julia John which can help us reduce stress and live a happier and healthier life. See you then.

## Unit 8

2.14

**(I = Interviewer; W = Woman; M = Man)**

**1**

**I:** What do you think makes a face attractive?

**W1:** For a woman, smooth skin and good bone structure.

**I:** And for a man?

**W1:** Um, nice white teeth, sparkling eyes, and a square jaw. That's what I like anyway.

**2**

**I:** What do you think makes a face attractive?

**M1:** Big eyes, full lips, and a big smile.

**I:** Like Beyoncé?

**M1:** Exactly.

**3**

**I:** What do you think makes a face attractive?

**W2:** It's probably easier to say what I don't like. On a man, I don't like a small nose - it doesn't have to be enormous, but a little turned-up nose on a man looks silly.

**I:** So you don't like Bruno Mars then?

**W2:** Well, I like everything about him except his nose!

**4**

**I:** What do you think makes a face attractive?

**M2:** High cheekbones, especially on a woman. Like Jennifer Lawrence. She's my ideal woman. I love her arched eyebrows.

**5**

**I:** What do you think makes a face attractive?

**W3:** I love dimples.

**I:** Do you mean a dimple in the chin?

**W3:** Yeah, I do like that, but I meant dimples in the cheeks when somebody smiles - it's so cute.

2.15

**(JO = Jean Oldham; RT = Rita Taylor; MH = Michael Hirst)**

**JO:** Personally, I'm dead set against cosmetic surgery of any kind. I work for a women's magazine, so you can imagine how many beautiful models I've met. But I'm also in daily contact with women who are not physically perfect, and I have to say that the most beautiful women I know are not models - they are the intelligent, interesting women whose life experience shows on their faces. I believe that true beauty comes from within, and no amount of cosmetic surgery can give you that.

**RT:** Yes, I agree with you, Jean, but not everybody has the confidence to let their inner beauty shine through. Cosmetic surgery can actually give people that confidence. I really don't think there's anything wrong with trying to improve on what nature has given us.

**MH:** Ah well, that's where I disagree with you, Rita. I think we should be grateful for what we have. The point is, it's selfish and indulgent of people to spend vast amounts of money on superficial improvements when there is so much poverty and sickness in the world.

**RT:** Actually, it's not that expensive, you know, Michael. I mean you could have your nose done for the price of a vacation, and quite frankly, cosmetic surgery can do more for you than a vacation, because the benefits last longer.

**MH:** Are you saying I need a nose job?

**RT:** No, of course not. I guess what I'm trying to say is that cosmetic surgery nowadays is almost as routine as going on vacation. Basically, it's here to stay, and I'm afraid you just have to accept it.

**JO:** Well, I don't go along with that at all. Growing old is a natural part of life and if you ask me, what we need to accept is that we can't look young for ever.

**RT:** Well, I would disagree with that, but let's leave it there.

2.18

**(P = Presenter; D.H = Dr. Hudson)**

**P:** Now, you may or may not have read the best-selling self-help book, *The Secret*, but almost two million people have, and the movie version has sold one and a half million copies to date. To tell us what all the fuss is about, we have with us in the studio today psychologist and expert in the "law of attraction," Dr. Rick Hudson. Welcome.

**D.H:** Thank you - I'm pleased to be here.

**P:** Dr. Hudson, *The Secret* is based on the "law of attraction," the idea that like attracts like. This isn't a new phenomenon, is it?

**D.H:** No, no, not at all. The theory behind the "law of attraction" has been around for ages. But it is the recent success of *The Secret* that has brought it to the attention of so many people around the world.

**P:** What exactly is the "law of attraction"?

**D.H:** Well, put simply, the "law of attraction" is all about positive thinking. We attract things we want and we also attract things we don't want. So, if you were the sort of person who was always cheerful and optimistic, you would give off good vibrations, and these good vibes would in turn attract positive energy, and good things would happen to you. Similarly, a stressed-out kind of person would put out stressed vibes, and they would attract more stress into their lives. Whatever you are thinking and feeling at any given time is basically your request to the universe for more of the same.

**P:** Hmm. So how can you apply this theory, this positive thinking, to your everyday life?

**D.H:** You can use it to make some very positive changes in your life. It depends what you want.

**P:** Where do I start?

**D.H:** Ha, ha. Well, let me give you a very simple example - OK, let's suppose you're on your way to the grocery store on a Saturday morning, so you're arriving pretty much at the same time as several hundred other shoppers! The one thing that would improve your life at that moment is a parking space. So you start focusing on that space. You visualize the ideal parking space, right near the entrance, and you imagine yourself swinging into the space as you arrive.

**P:** OK, I like that image.

**D.H:** And to make the positive vibrations really work for you, you need to imagine how you would feel if you already had that space.

**P:** I see.

**D.H:** Imagine that you already had that space - how would you be feeling?

**P:** Um, amazed?

**D.H:** Right, so you're still in your car on the way to the grocery store, but you're saying to yourself, "I'm so happy I found a space. I'm delighted and grateful that I found a parking space so close to the entrance." It works. Try it.

**P:** I must say, it sounds too good to be true. Suppose I really, really wanted a ten-million dollar house with a swimming pool - would I just think about it, and hey presto it would materialize?

**D.H:** Well, if you wanted to start living your life according to the "law of attraction," you'd have to learn a few simple techniques, and these are explained in *The Secret*. But basically, if that's what you really want, then yes, you can make it happen.

**P:** But don't you think it encourages people to be more materialistic? I mean, I don't need a house with a swimming pool. Isn't that just being plain greedy?

**D.H:** Listen, I'll give you another example. Imagine that a genie appeared in front of you and offered to grant your wishes. Would you ask for something small? Say a new bicycle? No. You'd be asking for bigger things. A business, a soulmate, a million dollars. The "law of attraction" is like a genie.

**P:** Hmm.

**D.H:** And here's why it's important to think big. There is so much that can be improved in the world. There is much more you can contribute. But you cannot do this by being mediocre. You owe it not just to yourself - but also to the world - to THINK BIG.

**P:** Well, thank you, Dr. Hudson.

2.20

**(S = Stacey; JO = John Orr)**

**S:** On today's podcast we have Corporate Communications expert John Orr talking to us about what we can do to improve the layout of documents such as reports to make them more attractive, more accessible, and easier to read.

**JO:** Thank you, Stacey. It is important to have well laid out documents, but this is much more than just aesthetics. When a document has a neat and organized layout, it helps to clarify the writer's logic and the structure of the ideas being presented. Additionally, people tend to pay more attention to attractive documents. If you want your document read and to get positive results, pay attention to content AND layout. Finally, a document is a reflection of its writer. A neat, well organized layout says that the writer is professional and cares about his or her work. It leaves positive impression on anyone who reads it. Here are ten tips to help you improve the layout of your document.

1. Use no more than two fonts in a document, although one font is usually enough.
2. Use neutral fonts. Word processing programs offer many options, but stick to the neutral ones for a more professional looking document.
3. Use size 12 font for the main document, font size 16 for headings and font size 14 for subheadings.
4. Use color to your advantage in headings, subheadings, tables, and charts. Do not overdo color. Be consistent throughout the document.
5. Paragraphs should be suitably spaced within the paragraph and between paragraphs. If lines are too close together, the document is more difficult to read.
6. Align the text to the left.
7. Number the pages of longer documents.
8. Add a table of contents for longer documents.
9. Use charts, tables, and images, but don't overdo it. Finally,
10. Use bullet points and numbered lists where appropriate.

I hope these tips are helpful. They have certainly come in useful in my own professional life, and I apply them to my everyday work.

**S:** Thank you, John. Join us next time for .... (fade out)

## Unit 9

2.21

**(OB = Oliver Bridge; RJ = Richard Jones)**

**OB:** It's a cold, gray morning. The sky is overcast and it's drizzling. For me, these are ideal conditions to visit the mysterious and ancient Stonehenge, my favorite place. As a child, when I first visited the stone circle, it was the sense of mystery that fascinated me - what are the stones for? How did they get here and what kinds of ceremonies and events went on here? As an adult, what I love about Stonehenge is that it's been standing there for 5,000 years - and it endures. I love the fact that after so many millennia, it remains such an enigmatic and enchanting place.
It's a little difficult to picture exactly how it was all that time ago, with only a few odd stones left and half of those fallen down. When it was complete, the stones would have been carefully laid out as a circle with a horseshoe in the center. Two types of stone were used

- sarsen and bluestone. The huge upright stones are sarsens weighing up to forty tons each. Then the inner circle is made up of bluestones, and they weigh a mere four tons each. The bluestones are so-called because they turn blue when they get wet.
Stonehenge is, without a doubt, one of the greatest engineering achievements of pre-historic times. The stones were huge, and not a single one can be found locally. One can only marvel at the phenomenal effort involved in bringing the stones here.
I'm joined by Richard Jones, an expert in Stonehenge history, to tell us about the latest theories about how the stones were brought here, and why.
Richard, these huge upright stones, the sarsens - I suppose they were dragged across the land?

**RJ:** They would have been dragged, yes, from the Marlborough Downs, about twenty miles away to the north of here.

**OB:** And the bluestones, they were, they came from Wales, is that right?

**RJ:** From South West Wales, from the sunny mountains of South West Wales. Yes, a good 250 miles away from here.

**OB:** So there must have been some really powerful reason for them to situate it here?

**RJ:** Yes, there must have been a very good reason to bring them all the way here. It couldn't have been easy to get these stones in place - they didn't have the wheel at that time. In fact, it must have taken them years.

**OB:** But the reason why it's located here remains a mystery.

**RJ:** Absolutely. Something drew them to bring all these materials here, to this place. Why they brought them here, no idea. And you know, if you put twelve archaeologists in one room, you'll have twelve different theories - but we will never know for sure because Stonehenge was built before written history began. So we don't have any written evidence of a motive, a reason for why Stonehenge is here.

**OB:** All we can do is speculate. No one really knows what went on here, and I've got a feeling that Stonehenge will always keep some of its secrets.

2.22

**a**

The big stones look like a doorway. The shape is very similar to those found in Japan at the entrance of some of our temples. I think it must have been a kind of temple, a religious place.

**b**

Well, apparently, the stones are aligned with the sun and the moon at certain times of the year - the solstices and the equinoxes. So I think it might have been a kind of prehistoric calendar. But it couldn't have only been a calendar. It was more important than that. I think Stonehenge must have been a place where people worshipped the Sun and the Moon.

**c**

I think it might have been a place where important ceremonies took place. It probably had a roof on it originally - if you think about it, it makes sense. It was obviously an important place, and it rains a lot around here.

**d**

We don't know, do we? It could have been a landing site for spacecraft from other planets for all we know. Some people believe it was. Personally, I think it's just a bunch of stones in a field.

**e**

Well, it's a mystery, isn't it? Even the archaeologists can't agree. There's one group who have dug up bones, and they think they can prove that it must have been a cemetery. Then there's another group of archaeologists who think that the bluestones may have had special properties, and that's why they brought them all the way from Wales. Personally, I think it may have been a kind of healing place.

2.23

This oil on canvas, *The Guitar Player* was painted by Almeida Júnior in 1899. This painter was known for depicting the rural life of Brazilians in the 1900s. His work portrays the people as they were and it shows the simple and somehow sad life they led, as you can see by their looks in this picture: the woman is wearing simple clothes and the man is wearing a rustic hat, a checked shirt and white pants. He is playing a folk instrument. The setting is the window of what seems to be an old house as you can see by the uncovered walls. It looks like the end of a day's work, when people just get together to relax. The pinkish color of the wall and of the clothes looks as if they are lit by the sunset. The woman seems to be singing to a sad or nostalgic tune, while the man just appears to be laid back.
This other oil on canvas was painted in 1899 too. It is called *Longing*. It also portrays life of simple people as you can see by the walls and floor as well as the country hat in this picture. The woman by the window is wearing simple clothes and flat shoes. She looks like a widow, as she is wearing dark, plain clothes. She looks as though she is reading a letter or document that may have sad news or memories. She looks sad as you can see tears in her eyes. Also, she seems to have suffocated feelings since she is covering her mouth with her shawl. Her hair seems to be a bit disheveled which gives the impression that she has forgotten about herself.

Almeida Júnior is famous for being a pioneer in regionalist paintings of naturalist style. He lived in the rural area for a long period of his life and seemed to know well the reality he portrayed. These two pieces were painted the year he was prematurely dead, stabbed by his cousin who had just found out he was having an affair with his cousin's wife.

2.24

**(I = Interviewer; TB = Trevor Baylis)**

**I:** Trevor, let me start by asking you what gave you the idea for the clockwork radio?

**TB:** Well, I was sitting where I am now looking at that television over there, and I was um actually watching a program about the spread of AIDS in Africa, and they said the only way they could stop this dreadful disease cutting its way through Africa was with the power of information and education. But there was a problem. Most of Africa doesn't have electricity. The only form of electricity available to them was in the form of batteries, which were horrendously expensive. And so I said to myself, hang on, hang on. Now, this is where dreams play an important part in everybody's life. Um, the beautiful thing about a dream is you can do anything you like in your dreams, right? Now why I am saying this to you is because I could see myself listening to some raunchy number by Dame Nellie Melba on my wind-up gramophone, mmm? And then I am thinking to myself, blimey, if you can get all that noise by dragging a rusty nail around a piece of old bakelite using a spring, surely there's enough power in that spring to drive a small dynamo which in turn will drive my radio, and so I was stirred enough to get off my backside and go to my, my shed and actually find enough parts to actually start doing those first primitive experiments ...

**I:** And, um, how long did it take you to design a prototype from the idea?

**TB:** Well, from the actual, from the concept to, er, having the first in-a-box model out there it would have taken me two to three months, I guess, so yes, it took about two or three months.

**I:** So you got, you got the prototype, how easy was it from that point on? How easy was it to find a backer and set up production?

**TB:** Well, first things first. I did know that there are these thieves about that will steal your idea. So I found a lady called Jackie Needle, a patent attorney, and I said to her "Jackie, I want to write up a patent, can you help me?" So we did a search and couldn't find any clockwork radios of the kind that I had done, and she filed for a patent to me, for me, and therefore then I had a starting date, as it were. Now I knew that nobody pays you for a good idea, but they could pay you for that piece of paper, so then I went round every British company I could think of with a confidentiality agreement, and they all talked down to me. "Oh, yes, I think we're, I think that we are working on something like this, aren't we Johnny?" You know all that old sausage. Um, I mean it was so humiliating ... and in the end, quite frankly after about three or four years of this, I thought, I have had enough of this. Why do I need this? I was fifty-six or something when this happened. So I was given a chance through the BBC World Service to meet up with the guys from the BBC *Tomorrow's World* program, and they said, "Come on, we'll do the story."

**I:** So the whole thing got off the ground. How long was it then before the production of them started?

**TB:** Well, the important thing was funding. The *Tomorrow's World* program was seen by a fellow in South Africa, a chap from a company called Liberty Life. He came to my house here, and we sat out there, and he said, "Look, um, we can help you make this happen, provided we can share in its success." I said of course, and so we formed a company called Baygen, Baylis Generators, and he wrote a cheque for three-quarters of a million pounds whilst I was in this room.

**I:** And how many radios are produced each month?

**TB:** Well, I'm sure they might tell me differently, but I'm sure they must be doing 200,000 a month.

**I:** And finally, what advice would you give to someone who had a good idea?

**TB:** Don't go down the pub and tell everybody about it. That's the first thing, right? Get on to the Patent Office. Get their literature, and read all about it, right? Nobody pays you for a good idea, but they might pay you for a piece of paper which says you own that idea. But remember, somebody might already own that idea, so you must do a search first. There's no excuse afterwards.

2.26

**(A = Alice; B = Brigit)**

**A:** Oh, I'm so glad you can stay here while we're away and keep an eye on the place.

**B:** No problem. It'll be nice to have a change of scenery for a couple of weeks.

**A:** Now, there are a few things I need to tell you. Did you get the keys in the mail?

**B:** Yes, I have them here.

**A:** OK, to open the front door, you need the small key.

**B:** OK.

**A:** You need to turn it twice counterclockwise.

**B:** OK. And I guess the big key is for the back door?

**A:** Exactly. Now, if you need the heating on, you just need to turn up the thermostat.

**B:** OK, and where do I do that?

**A:** There's a dial in the hallway, between the living room and the kitchen. Just turn it until it clicks.

**B:** OK.

**A:** And then make sure you turn it down again before you go to bed.

**B:** Of course.

**A:** OK – the TV's in the living room, and you use the silver remote control to turn it on and off, and the smaller black one for changing the channel. Do you think you'll watch a DVD?

**B:** Er, no, it's OK.

**A:** Now, what else? The smoke alarms are always going off in our house. The best thing to do is to have the fan on when you're cooking – just press the red button above the stove to turn it on. You can't miss it. And if the smoke alarm goes off, just stand under it and wave your arms.

**B:** OK. Is there anything else?

**A:** Oh, yes, I know what I haven't told you. Do you like coffee?

**B:** Yes, I love it.

**A:** Well, there's a coffee machine next to the stove. It's very easy to use. Basically, plug it in at the wall, and the on/off switch is on the back of the machine. Then you put a filter into the filter holder and put the coffee into the filter. Put water into the thing above it, and make sure the lid's on tight. Then put a cup under the place where the coffee comes out. The machine will warm the water up to the right temperature, so you just have to wait a few seconds. When the cup's full, take it out and your coffee's ready. Anyway, I'll leave you the instructions.

**B:** Oh good, thanks.

**A:** That's it then. Oh, and Molly needs a walk twice a day, and don't forget to let her out before you go to bed – we wouldn't want her to have an accident.

**B:** Molly? You didn't mention ...

**A:** Oh, didn't I? She's no trouble, are you? Yes ... oh, yes, you're good ... down girl, down.

▶ 2.27

In this unit we have seen examples of artists and inventors who can be considered geniuses. A genius is defined in the Macmillan online dictionary as "someone who is much more intelligent or skillful than other people." More than that, however, true geniuses are people who use their gifts to present solutions to problems or enhance people's lives in some way. Listen to the profile of Uzo and find out how she found solutions to everyday problems and enhanced people's lives.

▶ 2.28

Uzo from Lagos, Nigeria has always loved sewing and making things with her hands. She grew up in her father's tailor shop, where she would use the scraps first to make clothes for her dolls, then bags and other accessories for herself and her friends. By the time she was a teenager, she had a whole list of things she was making from scraps. Back in her home town after graduating from university, she saw many young women out of work and with dim prospects for the future. She decided to gather scraps from all over town and started teaching the women the techniques she had developed over the years. Soon they were making bags, clothes, and hats for sale locally and regionally. Uzo took a simple idea and used her skills to create jobs and bring hope to dozens of women in her home town.

## Unit 10

▶ 2.30

**Joe Smedley**

Children are much easier to reach with advertising than adults are – they like it, and they pick up on it really fast. So, it's the advertiser's job to capitalize on this.

We have a term "pester-power," which means the marketing potential of children nagging their parents to spend money. And I'm not just talking about toys here – our aim is getting children to pester parents to buy something for the whole family, like a vacation or a car. What we try to do is to produce advertisements that appeal to both children and adults.

Another key concept for advertisers is peer pressure. Children want what their friends have – playground credibility is very important. In other words, brands give children a sense of identity and help them fit in with a peer group.

So you can see children are a very important market for us, and in return, we like to promote education. This is something that's already happening across America. Companies donate free computers and in exchange they can advertise their brands on book covers and posters. I think it's fantastic – the kids benefit and the companies get brand loyalty from a very early age.

I'd love to be a child today. They really know what they want and they have so many more choices. Advertisers respect children's opinions.

▶ 2.31

**Sally McIlveen**

Basically, children are being brainwashed by all the advertising that goes on around them. Quite honestly, if the children in my school remembered any of their schoolwork as well as they remember the advertising jingles they hear on TV, my job would be a pleasure.

Usually the students at our school wear uniforms, but Friday is a non-uniform day, and that's when you really see the power of advertising. The kids are dressed from head to toe in labels, mainly sports gear like Adidas®, Nike, that kind of thing. And they all look the same!

There's a great deal of pressure on parents to buy children all these labels and gadgets, and I feel so sorry for the families who don't have much money because the pressure is just the same.

I really believe it's time the government put a stop to all this aggressive TV advertising.

Some schools are actually being subsidized by companies like McDonalds™ and Pepsi. OK, the school gets free equipment

from these big companies, but then the children have to add up burgers or multiply cans of Pepsi in their math class. It's terrible to think that the schools end up promoting a product that's not even good for the children.
What I think is really sad is that children are being forced to be consumers from such an early age. I don't think all this choice is liberating for children - it just means that they're encouraged to be materialistic instead of focusing on more important basic values, such as kindness and respect for others.

2.32

**(P = Presenter; S = Shelley Russell; J = Jim Falmer)**

**P:** Good evening and welcome to *Talkback*. Recently, the popular press has been under fire yet again, this time for their apparent disregard for truth and accuracy.
In the studio tonight we would like to welcome Shelley Russell, Oscar-winning actress, and Jim Falmer, editor of *Celebrity Lives* magazine. Shelley, let's start with you. Do you think there should be greater restrictions placed on the press and the stories they print?

**S:** Yes, absolutely. I can't open a magazine without reading stories full of false information about myself or people I know. It's getting ...

**J:** Sorry, but I can't believe that you're actually complaining about free publicity. I mean, I remember, Shelley, before you were famous, you were begging us to write features about you ... anything ...

**S:** If you would just let me finish - of course the press have been important. I'm an actress and I understand the power of the press. But the thing is, I rarely seem to read anything true about myself these days. Take last week - your magazine wrote this story about me and my co-star, who, incidentally, happens to be married to a very good friend of mine - having breakfast together.

**J:** Oh, that. That was ... well, that was just some fun. I don't think you should take that too seriously.

**S:** Oh, really! You don't think that it's at all serious that my co-star's children woke up to the headline: SHELLEY AND SHAUN'S EARLY MORNING ROMANCE or that his wife is now filing for a divorce ...

**J:** Look, I don't know whether ...

**S:** Anyway, to get back to what I was saying ... The point I'm trying to make here is that famous people have families with feelings. I am sick of the popular press making up stories just so that they can splash sensational headlines across the front page and sell more magazines - it's irresponsible and it messes up people's lives.

**J:** Look, Shelley you're just angry about that particular article because the pictures we printed of you weren't very flattering. Anyway, we made a public apology and said that there'd been some inaccuracies in the article.

**S:** Yes, but what you didn't say was what the inaccuracies were, so ...

**P:** If I could just come in here. I think we need to address the root of the problem. Jim, why do certain magazines continue to print these stories when it's obvious that they are not true?

**S:** To increase circulation and make more money.

**J:** If you would let me answer the question - I think we have to look at the relationship between fame, the public, and the press. The public is fascinated by fame and scandal, and they love to read about their favorite stars. The problem is, it's not always clear what's true and what isn't. I mean, if a magazine prints something scandalous or embarrassing about a famous person, they're bound to deny it, but that doesn't mean it's not true.

**S:** Are you trying to say ...?

**J:** No smoke without fire, if you ask me.

**P:** Well, I'm sorry to interrupt you, but we'll carry on after this short break for some travel news ...

2.34

**(I = Interviewer; G1 = Girl 1; B1 = Boy 1; B2 = Boy 2; G2 = Girl 2; G3 = Girl 3; B3 = Boy 3)**

**1**

**I:** Excuse me. Do you mind if I ask you how you feel about seeing this movie?

**G1:** Pretty nervous, actually. I don't really know what to expect, but I think I'm going to be scared.

**2**

**I:** Excuse me - are you feeling nervous about seeing this movie?

**B1:** Yeah, a little uneasy, I must admit ... but I brought my girlfriend, so I can hold her hand if I get scared.

**3**

**I:** How do you feel about seeing this movie?

**B2:** I'm looking forward to being scared to death.

**4**

**I:** What are you expecting from this movie?

**G2:** To be scared stiff - hopefully.

**5**

**I:** Do you think you're going to enjoy seeing this movie?

**G3:** Er, no - I don't think enjoy is the right word. But I've heard so much about it that I can't wait to find out what it's all about. In fact, I feel pretty apprehensive, but I love horror movies, and this one sounds like it's going to be really scary.

**6**

**I:** Any expectations?

**B3:** Well, I've been visiting the website for a while now and I'm really looking forward to finding out what happens. I expect it to be absolutely terrifying!

2.35

**(I = Interviewer; G1 = Girl 1; B1 = Boy 1; B2 = Boy 2; G2 = Girl 2; G3 = Girl 3; B3 = Boy 3)**

**1**

**I:** So, how was it for you?

**G1:** Extremely disappointing. I wasn't the least bit scared, and you know from the start that everybody dies, so there's no suspense. Anyway, the characters are so annoying that I felt like killing them myself. It does not live up to the hype.

**2**

**I:** What did you think of it then?

**B1:** Absolute garbage. My girlfriend fell asleep, and I spent the last half of the movie with my eyes shut - not because it was scary - but because the camera angles made me feel sick. Don't see it if you suffer from motion sickness. In fact, just don't see it.

**3**

**I:** So were you scared to death?

**B2:** No way. After all the hype, it was a massive letdown.

**4**

**I:** What did you think?

**G2:** Over-hyped nonsense. I spent most of the time waiting for something to happen. I feel completely disillusioned.

**5**

**I:** Did the movie live up to your expectations?

**G3:** No, it didn't. I don't think I've ever been so bored in my entire life, and I still don't have a clue what it's about. In fact, there's no story to speak of. This movie is a perfect example of hype over substance.

**6**

**I:** Your verdict?

**B3:** A total waste of time. I was bored out of my mind. The website was much more entertaining than the movie.

2.36

**Eric:** ... now that you've seen our sales figures and all that we offer, let me ask you - do you want to be a part of the footwear revolution? With our innovative business model, 10% of all the profits will go to charity to help provide shoes to children in need. In the past year alone, we've provided over 10,000 pairs of sneakers to children who would otherwise have none. Just imagine the real effect that your contribution could have to increasing this number. If you know that you can make a profit and improve the lives of others, then what's stopping you? And with our locally-produced materials and manufacturing, you will also be supporting the local economy.
I truly believe that with our passion and your investment, we can join forces to build a new kind of shoe company, one that is on the cutting edge of style, while maintaining our core company beliefs. Now, don't you think that is a goal worth pursuing?
I'm sure that you want to know more, so let's open up this meeting for questions ...

## Unit 11

2.38

1 Acquired Immune Deficiency Syndrome
2 Bachelor of Science
3 Frequently Asked Questions
4 Master of Business Administration
5 North Atlantic Treaty Organization
6 Organization of Petroleum Exporting Countries
7 Doctor of Philosophy
8 Personal Identification Number
9 United Nations International Children's Emergency Fund
10 Internal Revenue Service

2.39

**(I = Interviewer; Mrs. B = Mrs. Benitez; Mr. B = Mr. Benitez)**

**I:** What is Serena going to do when she graduates from school?

**Mr. B:** Until a few months ago, she was going to go to college, but she's changed her mind. Now she figures she's going to make it in the music world.

**I:** And how do you feel about that?

**Mr. B:** We think she's making an enormous mistake.

**I:** But surely she can go back to her studies if her music career fails?

**Mr. B:** That's true, but once she gets a taste of freedom, she'll find it harder to go back to college. I just think it's such a waste - four years from now, she'll have graduated and she'll still be young enough to try out the music business. At least if it doesn't work out, she'll have a qualification behind her.

**I:** Have you discussed this with her?

**Mr. B:** Of course, but she's made up her mind. We're just hoping that she'll get it out of her system and then come to her senses and go back to her studies. When I graduated from high school I didn't go to college, and I've regretted it ever since. I just don't want her to make the same mistake I did.

**I:** Will you support her while she's trying to be a rock star?

**Mr. B:** You mean financially? No. She won't be living at home, and we can't afford to pay for her to live in Los Angeles, so it's up to her to make it work.

2.41

"Last year I almost died when I contracted a nasty parasite. I made a huge newbie mistake of drinking water without treating it. Almost instantly, with miles and miles to go in my hike, I started to feel like I was going to die. My stomach was bubbling and boiling, and I vomited incessantly. I barely crawled into town, and they raced me to the hospital, where they pumped me full of meds. It took almost a year to recover."

2.42

**(I = Interviewer; S = Sam)**

**I:** Ah, come in. Sam, isn't it?

**S:** Yes.

**I:** Well, Sam, tell us a little about yourself.

**S:** I'm 24, and I was born in Twin Falls, Idaho. I like baseball. In the winter I go skiing and in the summer, I like sailing and windsurfing. Oh, and I'm a black belt in karate. Well, I say I'm a black belt. In fact, I'm a brown belt but I'm taking my black belt in a few days, so ... um, anyway, I graduated last year, and now I'm looking forward to getting a job.

**I:** OK. And why do you think you'd be right for a position in this company?

**S:** Oh, well, er, I'm interested in what your company does. Um, I haven't really thought about it.

**I:** In your opinion, what are your greatest strengths?

**S:** I'm outgoing and friendly, so I get along well with people.

**I:** What would you say your weaknesses are?

**S:** My weaknesses? I can't think of any. Ha, ha. Oh, I know - I tend to be at my best in the afternoon. Mornings are tricky.

**I:** OK. And what are your long-term objectives?

**S:** To be the best I can - and to make a lot of money.

**I:** What would you like to be doing five years from now?

**S:** Lying on a beach in the Caribbean! Ha, ha.

**I:** Do you have any questions you'd like to ask us?

**S:** Er, no. I'm fine.

**I:** OK, well, we'll be in touch.

2.43

**(I = Interviewer; L = Layla)**

**I:** Ah, come in. Layla, isn't it?

**L:** Yes, that's right.

**I:** Well, Layla, tell us a little about yourself.

**L:** OK. I graduated from college last year, and then spent four months traveling in South America. That was a great experience, but now I'm ready to embark on my career, and I'm very interested in working for a company like yours.

**I:** OK. And why do you think you'd be right for a position in this company?

**L:** Well, I've always been interested in working in the media. I think I'm well-suited to this kind of work because I work well under pressure. I don't have much experience yet, but anything I don't know, I'm willing to learn.

**I:** In your opinion, what are your greatest strengths?

**L:** I'm highly motivated and conscientious. I'm a team player, but equally I can work on my own.

**I:** What would you say your weaknesses are?

**L:** I would say my greatest weakness has been my lack of proper planning in the past. However, since I've come to recognize that weakness, I've taken steps to correct it.

**I:** OK. And what are your long-term objectives?

**L:** I'd like to gain some experience in this field for a few years, and then decide which area I want to specialize in.

**I:** What would you like to be doing five years from now?

**L:** Ideally, I'd like to be managing my own team.

**I:** Do you have any questions you'd like to ask us?

**L:** Yes, I'd like to know a little about the training opportunities in this job.

**I:** Yes, that's a good question. We believe in on-going training here, and we provide regular opportunities for our staff to attend relevant courses.

**L:** Oh, that sounds great.

**I:** OK, well, thank you for coming in, Layla. We'll be in touch.

## Unit 12

2.44

**Room 1**

This is obviously a family room. The couch is big and comfortable, but the use of colors suggests that both comfort and style are important. I imagine a small family with a young child sitting on the couch to watch a movie or listen to a story. There are several cushions which may look attractive, but nine times out of ten, they don't make seats more comfortable. I'd say that this apartment belongs to a family with a sense of style, who want a beautiful living space. So with that in mind I imagine they would have chosen the brightly colored furniture and the rest of the matching decor together.

The room has a neutral palette with some splashes of yellow around the room on the cushions, the lamp stand, and the picture on the wall. The big glass door adds to the brightness of the room.

The room is very tidy and I imagine that, like many families nowadays, both partners pitch in with housework in the evenings and on weekends.

I think the people who live here are sociable young professionals who enjoy entertaining, but like to keep a tidy home and would get upset if someone spilled wine on the rug.

2.45

**Room 2**

This one's more difficult to guess because there are very few clues here about the type of person who lives in it. I think it's a man because there are hardly any personal objects on display - for instance there aren't any family pictures around the place. There's plenty of evidence to suggest that a successful career person lives here. There is a stylish leather and chrome armchair which is probably Italian design and worth a lot of money - whoever lives here certainly has good taste which may indicate that this person works in a creative field such as advertising or the media.

There isn't really enough furniture to make this look like a home, which suggests someone who spends most of his

time traveling might live here. I think this is somebody who doesn't actually spend much time at home and when he does, he's obsessively neat. You only have to look at how his books are organized on the shelves to see that he likes things to be in order. The minimalism suggests that he wants to be ready to pack his bags and leave at short notice.
He has little time to socialize, except in a working context, and probably never entertains at home.

2.46

**(I = Interviewer; L = Lizanne)**

**I:** Lizanne, you're from the USA. What do you have for breakfast?

**L:** Er, eggs, bacon, pancakes, and some toast on the side.

**I:** And what to drink?

**L:** Usually we start with orange juice and have a lot of coffee.

**I:** And your eggs - how do you like to have them done?

**L:** Sunny side up.

**I:** What does that mean?

**L:** That means that the yolk is facing upward - it hasn't been turned over.

**I:** Thank you.

2.47

**(I = Interviewer; N = Nicola)**

**I:** Nicola, you're from Germany. Tell me about breakfast. What do you have for breakfast?

**N:** Well, in Germany it's different. Some people like jelly or cereals, but the typical breakfast is, of course, with cold meat like salami, bacon, or ham, and cheese. And we always have hot bread rolls and coffee. But I don't like coffee very much. And, of course, boiled eggs - they are very important in Germany and very typical, with salt or pepper.

**I:** You don't drink coffee for breakfast. What do you like?

**N:** I like to drink tea.

2.48

**(I = Interviewer; M = Michiko)**

**I:** Michiko. What do you have for breakfast? What do you have to drink for breakfast?

**M:** We drink green tea for breakfast.

**I:** OK, and what about, what do you eat?

**M:** We eat rice, miso soup, pickled vegetables, er, grilled fish - like salmon, and a Japanese omelet, and seaweed.

**I:** What, what do you have in the Japanese omelet? What does that ...?

**M:** A Japanese omelet is sweet, and it's different from the Western omelet.

**I:** And miso soup. What is in that?

**M:** Miso soup is a salty soup, which often has seaweed, vegetables, and tofu.

2.51

**(I = Interviewer; P = Psychologist)**

**I:** What are some of your suggestions for dealing with differences?

**P:** When we are faced with differences in opinions or ideas, it is important to have the right attitude. I have five simple suggestions. Firstly, be respectful. Never shame or put someone down for their point of view. We should always listen and respond respectfully. Secondly, if there is disagreement, try to communicate face to face. Non-verbal communication like body language and tone of voice can help to make a message clearer and avoid misunderstandings. Thirdly, if you are going to have a difficult conversation, a change of scene is advisable. Taking the conversation to a neutral space can help to diffuse a tense discussion. Next, find common ground. Sometimes a disagreement may be on only one or two points. Find points you agree on and build up from there. Finally, sometimes we need to agree to disagree when we cannot find common ground. In these cases, we can disagree respectfully.

**I:** Can you also suggest some useful expressions to be used in such situations?

**P:** Yes. In these situations it is important to know how to express your opinion, agree and disagree effectively. To express your opinion, you can start by saying "My opinion is that ..." or "To my mind ...", then complete according to the situation. If you want to agree with someone, you can say "I share your view" or "Fair enough". Pay attention to the intonation I used here. Depending on how you say it, your interlocutor could get a different message, so you must sound positive. When disagreeing you can use "I take a different view" or "I see what you are saying, but that argument does not hold water", and complete your argument. Sometimes, when you don't agree, you could simply make an alternative suggestion or present an alternative point of view by saying "How about ...". These are just some suggestions, there're many other phrases which can be used in these situations, some of which you probably already know. If used with the correct intonation, these phrases can be very effective.

# Glossary

main verb | adjective | conjunction | modal auxiliary verb | adverb | article | pronoun | main verb

**Learn these useful words and you can understand more about the language you are studying.**

determiner | noun | pronoun | main verb | preposition | noun | auxiliary verb

**Agents** are people or things that perform an action in a passive sentence.
*He was brought up by* ***his aunt and uncle****.*

**Antonyms** are words that mean the opposite of other words.
*rich ≠ poor   dead ≠ alive   tall ≠ short*

**Back-shift** is when a verb moves "one tense back" in a conditional clause or reported statement.
*If you* ***were*** *a woman, you'd understand.*
*"I can't come."* → *He said he* ***couldn't*** *come.*

**Clauses** are groups of words containing a subject and a verb.
main clause   subordinate clause   main clause   time (subordinate) clause

*I waited   but she didn't come.   I'll call   when I get there.*
Note: Subordinate clauses are introduced by conjunctions.

**Complements** refer to adjective or noun phrases which give more information about the subject of a clause.
*She was* ***very happy****.   It's* ***my fault****.   I feel like* ***a complete idiot****.*
Note: Complements usually follow verbs like *be, seem, feel*.

**Conjunctions** show a connection between one clause and another.
***Just as*** *we were leaving the hotel, I spotted a friend.*

**Consonants** are all the letters of the English alphabet except for the five vowels *a, e, i, o,* and *u*.
*b, c, d, f, g, h, j, k, l, m, n, p, q, r, s, t, v, w, x, y, z*

**Expressions** are groups of words that belong together where the words and word order never or rarely change.
*black and white   That reminds me.   How do you do?*

**Idioms** are groups of words with a meaning which cannot be understood by taking the meaning of each individual word.
*My father* ***footed the bill****.   Let's* ***play it by ear****, OK?*

**Intransitive verbs** do not take an object.
*He* ***arrived****.   **Is** Marta still* ***sleeping****?   Stop* ***shouting****!*
Note: Many verbs can be either intransitive or transitive. It depends on the meaning or context.
*He* ***opened*** *the door.* (Transitive)   *The door* ***opened****.* (Intransitive)

**Linkers** show a connection between one sentence and another.
*Many motorists drive too fast.* ***As a result****, there are more and more accidents.*

**Numbers** can be cardinal (*1, 2, 3, ...*) or ordinal (*1st, 2nd, 3rd, ...*).

**Objects** usually come after the verb and show who or what is affected by the verb.
*She closed* ***the door****.* *My dog hates* ***me****.* *I made* ***a cup of coffee****.*
Note: Some verbs take both a direct object (DO) and an indirect object (IO).
*She gave* ***him*** (IO) ***a kiss*** (DO). *He sent* ***her*** (IO) ***some flowers*** (DO).
*I teach* ***students*** (IO) ***English*** (DO).

**Participles** are the forms of verbs used in compound tenses and as adjectives.
*What are you* ***doing****?* *I've* ***finished****.* *It's* ***freezing****!* *He's* ***injured****.*

**Particles** are the adverbs or prepositions that form part of a phrasal verb.
*turn it* ***on*** *take* ***off*** *get* ***along with*** *her*

**Partitives** are words or expressions that show that only part of something is being referred to rather than all of it.
***a piece of*** *cake* ***a bag of*** *potato chips* ***a bunch of*** *flowers*

The **phonetic alphabet** is a set of special symbols which shows speech sounds in writing.
mother = /ˈmʌðər/ television = /ˈteləˌvɪʒn/

**Phrasal verbs** are combinations of a verb and one or two particles.
*turn on* *come up with*

**Pronouns** are words used in place of nouns or noun phrases. There are many classes of pronoun.
Subject pronouns: *I*, *you*, *she*, etc.
Object pronouns: *me*, *you*, *her*, etc.
Possessive pronouns: *mine*, *yours*, *hers*, etc.
Demonstrative pronouns: *this*, *that*, *these*, *those*

**Proper nouns** are words that refer to a particular person, place, or institution.
*Janet, San Diego, the United Nations*

**Proverbs** or **sayings** are short, well-known statements that give practical advice about life.
*When the cat's away, the mice will play.*

**Register** describes a level and style of a piece of language which is appropriate for the circumstances in which it is used.
*I am very grateful for your help.* (More formal)
*Thanks.* (More informal)

**Relative clauses** are clauses that modify a noun or a noun phrase. They give additional information about the noun and are joined to a previous clause by words such as *who*, *that*, or *which*.
*That's the man* ***who helped me****.* *This the pen* ***(that) I lost****.*
*Everyone is well,* ***which is really great****.*

**Synonyms** are words or expressions which mean the same as another word or expression.
*tolerate sb = put up with sb* *I'm off now. = I'm going now.*

**Transitive verbs** take an object.
*You're wasting* ***your money****.* *He cut* ***his finger****.*
*I can't pronounce "****comfortable****."*

**Vowels** are the letters *a*, *e*, *i*, *o*, and *u*.

# Phonetic symbols

## Single vowels

| | | | |
|---|---|---|---|
| /ɪ/ | ship | /ʃɪp/ | (build, business, gym, spinach, women) |
| /i/ | need | /nid/ | (bean, he, key, niece, people, sardine) |
| /ʊ/ | put | /pʊt/ | (could, foot, woman) |
| /u/ | pool | /pul/ | (flew, fruit, lose, rule, shoe, through, two) |
| /e/ | egg | /eg/ | (breakfast, friend, many, said) |
| /ə/ | about | /əˈbaʊt/ | (arrive, husband, lemon, nervous, police) |
| /ɔ/ | saw | /sɔ/ | (abroad, caught, talk, thought, water) |
| /æ/ | back | /bæk/ | (bag, fast, laugh) |
| /ʌ/ | bus | /bʌs/ | (blood, does, enough, onion) |
| /ɑ/ | father | /ˈfɑðər/ | (car, heart, pasta) |

## Diphthongs

| | | | |
|---|---|---|---|
| /ɜr/ | verb | /vɜrb/ | (learn, curly, skirt, word) |
| /eɪ/ | face | /feɪs/ | (break, eight, fail, say, they) |
| /ɔɪ/ | boy | /bɔɪ/ | (noise) |
| /oʊ/ | nose | /noʊz/ | (although, coat, know, shoulder) |
| /aɪ/ | white | /waɪt/ | (buy, die, eye, height, high, my) |
| /aʊ/ | mouth | /maʊθ/ | (town) |
| /ɪr/ | hear | /hɪr/ | (near) |

## Consonants

| | | | |
|---|---|---|---|
| /p/ | pen | /pen/ | (happy) |
| /b/ | bag | /bæg/ | (rabbit) |
| /t/ | tea | /ti/ | (ate, fatter, worked) |
| /d/ | dog | /dɔg/ | (address, played) |
| /ʧ/ | chip | /ʧɪp/ | (natural, watch) |
| /ʤ/ | jazz | /ʤæz/ | (age, bridge, generous) |
| /k/ | cake | /keɪk/ | (chemistry, kitchen, knock, toothache) |
| /g/ | girl | /gɜrl/ | (foggy) |
| /f/ | fat | /fæt/ | (different, laugh, photographer) |
| /v/ | very | /ˈveri/ | (of) |
| /θ/ | thin | /θɪn/ | (think) |
| /ð/ | these | /ðiz/ | (they) |
| /s/ | snake | /sneɪk/ | (city, message, race) |
| /z/ | zoo | /zu/ | (has) |
| /ʃ/ | sugar | /ˈʃʊgər/ | (description, machine) |
| /ʒ/ | measure | /ˈmeʒər/ | (garage, usual) |
| /m/ | map | /mæp/ | (summer) |
| /n/ | name | /neɪm/ | (sunny, knife) |
| /ŋ/ | ring | /rɪŋ/ | (thanks, tongue) |
| /h/ | house | /haʊs/ | (who) |
| /l/ | leg | /leg/ | (hill, possible) |
| /r/ | road | /roʊd/ | (carry, write) |
| /w/ | wine | /waɪn/ | (one, why) |
| /j/ | yes | /jes/ | (used, usual) |

## Stress

Word stress is shown by underlining the stressed syllable: *water, amazing, Japanese*.

## Letters of the alphabet

| /eɪ/ | /i/ | /e/ | /aɪ/ | /oʊ/ | /u/ | /ɑr/ |
|---|---|---|---|---|---|---|
| Aa | Bb | Ff | Ii | Oo | Qq | Rr |
| Hh | Cc | Ll | Yy | | Uu | |
| Jj | Dd | Mm | | | Ww | |
| Kk | Ee | Nn | | | | |
| | Gg | Ss | | | | |
| | Pp | Xx | | | | |
| | Tt | | | | | |
| | Vv | | | | | |
| | Zz | | | | | |

# Irregular verbs

| Infinitive | Simple past | Past participle |
| --- | --- | --- |
| be | was/were | been |
| beat | beat | beaten |
| become | became | become |
| begin | began | begun |
| bend | bent | bent |
| bet | bet | bet |
| bite | bit | bitten |
| blow | blew | blown |
| break | broke | broken |
| bring | brought /brɔt/ | brought /brɔt/ |
| build /bɪld/ | built /bɪlt/ | built /bɪlt/ |
| burst | burst | burst |
| buy /baɪ/ | bought /bɔt/ | bought /bɔt/ |
| can | could /kʊd/ | (been able) |
| catch | caught /kɔt/ | caught /kɔt/ |
| choose | chose | chosen |
| come | came | come |
| cost | cost | cost |
| cut | cut | cut |
| deal /dil/ | dealt /delt/ | dealt /delt/ |
| dig | dug | dug |
| do | did | done |
| draw | drew | drawn |
| drink | drank | drunk |
| drive | drove | driven |
| eat | ate | eaten |
| fall | fell | fallen |
| feed | fed | fed |
| feel | felt | felt |
| fight | fought /fɔt/ | fought /fɔt/ |
| find | found | found |
| fly | flew | flown |
| forget | forgot | forgotten |
| forgive | forgave | forgiven |
| freeze | froze | frozen |
| get | got | gotten |
| give | gave | given |
| go | went | gone/been |
| grow | grew | grown |
| hang | hung/hanged | hung/hanged |
| have | had | had |
| hear | heard /hɜrd/ | heard /hɜrd/ |
| hide | hid | hidden |
| hit | hit | hit |
| hold | held | held |
| hurt /hɜrt/ | hurt /hɜrt/ | hurt /hɜrt/ |
| keep | kept | kept |
| kneel | kneeled/knelt | kneeled/knelt |
| know | knew /nju/ | known |
| lay | laid | laid |
| lead | led | led |
| leave | left | left |
| lend | lent | lent |
| let | let | let |
| lie | lay/lied | lied/lain |
| light | lit | lit |
| lose | lost | lost |
| make | made | made |
| mean | meant /ment/ | meant /ment/ |
| meet | met | met |
| must | had to | (had to) |
| pay | paid | paid |
| put | put | put |
| read | read /red/ | read /red/ |
| ride | rode | ridden |
| ring | rang | rung |
| rise | rose | risen |
| run | ran | run |
| say | said /sed/ | said /sed/ |
| see | saw /sɔ/ | seen |
| sell | sold | sold |
| send | sent | sent |
| set | set | set |
| shake | shook | shaken |
| shine | shone | shone |
| shoot | shot | shot |
| show | showed | shown |
| shrink | shrank | shrunk |
| shut | shut | shut |
| sing | sang | sung |
| sink | sank | sunk |
| sit | sat | sat |
| sleep | slept | slept |
| slide | slid | slid |
| speak | spoke | spoken |
| spend | spent | spent |
| split | split | split |
| spread | spread | spread |
| stand | stood | stood |
| steal | stole | stolen |
| stick | stuck | stuck |
| swear | swore | sworn |
| swim | swam | swum |
| take | took /tʊk/ | taken |
| teach | taught /tɔt/ | taught /tɔt/ |
| tear | tore | torn |
| tell | told | told |
| think | thought /θɔt/ | thought /θɔt/ |
| throw | threw | thrown |
| understand | understood | understood |
| wake | woke | woken |
| wear | wore /wɔr/ | worn |
| win | won /wʌn/ | won /wʌn/ |
| write | wrote | written |

Macmillan Education

Companies and representatives throughout the world

American Inside Out Evolution. Student's Book Upper Intermediate


Adapted by Peter Maggs and Catherine Smith
Content Writers: Ben Naismith, James Michael Ubriaco and Lavaughn John
Macmillan is a registered trademark.
First edition published 2018

ISBN: 978-607-473-641-0

Based on New American Inside Out Student's Book Upper Intermediate


Director of Languages Brazil: Patrícia Souza
Editorial Manager: Patricia Muradas
Art Editor: Jean Aranha
Content Editors: Cintia Zaitune and Larissa Vannucci
Digital Editor: Ana Paula Girardi
Concept design: Martha Tadaieski
Page make-up: Figurattiva Editorial
Illustrations: Gustavo Gialuca
Graphic Production: Kelly Gobbo and Tatiane Romano
Proofreaders: Edward Willson and Larissa Vazquez
Photographic research: Cintia Zaitune, Denis Araujo, Jean Aranha and Marcia Sato
Image Processing: Denis Araujo and Jean Aranha
Cover concept and design: Jean Aranha
Cover photo: Songquan Deng | Dreamstime.com

The authors and publishers would like to thank the following for permission to reproduce the photographic material: Fotoarena/Reuters p8; iStock/Jeremy_Hogan p8; iStock/kapulya p8; Reuters/Fotoarena p8; iStock/PeopleImages p9; iStock/JohnnyGreig p9; iStock/Bartosz Hadyniak p9; iStock/DMEPhotography p9; iStock/vchal p10; iStock/Antonio_Diaz p10; iStock/MilosStankovic p11; Alamy/Fotoarena p12; Fotoarena/NBC/Everett Collection p13; Reuters/Fotoarena p13; Getty Images/Axelle/Bauer-Griffin/FilmMagic p13; iStock/monkeybusinessimages p14; iStock/freemixer p14; iStock/m-imagephotography p14; iStock/Ales_Utovko p14; iStock/BigWest1 p15; iStock/alexis84 p15; iStock/SafakOguz p15; iStock/Paday p15; iStock/AntonioGuillem p16; iStock/Tassii p17; iStock/knape p18; iStock/vadimguzhva p18; iStock/PeopleImages p19; iStock/Geber86 p19; iStock/mapodile p20; iStock/laflor p20; iStock/izusek p21; iStock/DMEPhotography p21; iStock/DjelicS p22; iStock/hedgehog94 p23; iStock/AzmanL p23; iStock/DjelicS p24; iStock/kupicoo p24; iStock/rbv p25; iStock/nicolamargaret p25; iStock/TonyBaggett p28; iStock/studiocasper p28; Biblioteca de Birkbeck, Universidade de Londres, Inglaterra p29; Getty Images/Minnesota Historical Society/Corbis p29; iStock/monkeybusinessimages p30; iStock/Sezeryadigar p31; iStock/pixelfit p31; iStock/YinYang p32; iStock/Juanmonino p32; iStock/adamkaz p32; iStock/RodrigoBlanco p32; iStock/AleksandarNakic p33; iStock/zefart p34; iStock/Petar Chernaev p34; iStock/eclipse_images p35; iStock/skyNext p35; iStock/MelissaAnneGalleries p35; iStock/dja65 p35; iStock/gavran333 p35; iStock/EXTREME-PHOTOGRAPHER p37; iStock/Pgiam p39; iStock/tostphoto p39; iStock/iprogressman p39; iStock/iprogressman p39; iStock/ossHelen p39; iStock/PeopleImages p39; iStock/PeopleImages p39; iStock/Neydtstock p39; iStock/marcoventuriniautieri p39; iStock/fstop123 p40; iStock/chaofann p41; iStock/fizkes p41; iStock/artoleshko p41; iStock/rabbit75_ist p41; iStock/Marco_Piunti p42; iStock/innovatedcaptures p43; iStock/deimagine p43; iStock/microgen p44; iStock/monkeybusinessimages p45; iStock/ANessiR p45; iStock/monkeybusinessimages p45; iStock/AzmanJaka p45; iStock/okwragg p46; iStock/anilakkus p46; iStock/sezer66 p47; Fotoarena/Alamy p51; Getty Images/David Cannon p51; iStock/GeorgiosArt p51; Fotoarena/Kristin Callahan/Everett Collection p51; Fotoarena/Alamy p51; iStock/Daisy-Daisy p52; iStock/SasaJo p53; iStock/Wavebreakmedia p53; iStock/eli_asenova p54; iStock/SensorSpot p55; iStock/imtmphoto p55; iStock/NicolasMcComber p55; iStock/SrdjanPav p55; iStock/Neustockimages p55; iStock/colorcocktail p56; iStock/Nata_Slavetskaya p56; iStock/monkeybusinessimages p56; iStock/izusek p56; iStock/shapecharge p57; iStock/shapecharge p57; iStock/Poike p57; iStock/joyfnp p57; iStock/MilosStankovic p59; iStock/Minerva Studio p60; iStock/Kemter p61; iStock/chaofann p61; iStock/Wavebreakmedia p62; iStock/fiphoto p62; iStock/SOMATUSCANI p63; iStock/Chesky_W p64; iStock/demaerre p65; iStock/Devonyu p66; iStock/valentinrussanov p66; iStock/MachineHeadz p66; iStock/RichVintage p68; iStock/Ridofranz p71; iStock/Anna_Jedynak p72; iStock/valio84sl p73; iStock/Nadezhda1906 p74; iStock/jmatkins p75; iStock/Martinan p75; iStock/SL_Photography p75; iStock/Izabela Habur p75; iStock/Image Source p75; iStock/PeopleImages p75; iStock/themacx p76; iStock/4FR p76; iStock/Goryu p76; iStock/Mlenny p76; iStock/AmyLaughinghouse p76; iStock/mariusz_prusaczyk p76; iStock/Poike p77; iStock/Wavebreakmedia p77; iStock/monkeybusinessimages p77; iStock/coopermoisse p81; iStock/Anna Pietrzykowska p81; iStock/Sami Sert p81; iStock/simonbradfield p81; iStock/Farbregas_Hareluya p81; iStock/iconogenic p83; iStock/Juanmonino p84; iStock/vgajic p84; iStock/Neustockimages p84; iStock/sturti p85; iStock/Georgijevic p86; iStock/filadendron p86; iStock/AH86 p87; iStock/Sidekick p87; iStock/bowie15 p83; iStock/ajr_images p87; iStock/sergio_kumer p87; iStock/miss_j p87; iStock/deimagine p87; iStock/damircudic p87; iStock/jacoblund p87; iStock/ajr_images p87; iStock/m-imagephotography p87; iStock/Baimai23 88; iStock/selensergen p88; iStock/bowie15 p89; iStock/Ranta Images p89; iStock/Milkos p90; Getty Images/Pablo Blazquez Dominguez p92; iStock/clodio p92; iStock/jslsvg p93; iStock/kravcs p94; iStock/volschenkh p94; iStock/PobladuraFCG p95; Pinacoteca do Estado de São Paulo; Fotoarena/Alamy p97; iStock/lolostock p98; iStock/georgeclerk p98; iStock/prmustafa p98; iStock/stocksnapper p98; iStock/trait2lumiere p98; iStock/akinshin p98; Getty Images/WPA Pool p98; iStock/Bogdanhoda p99; iStock/GeorgeRudy p99; iStock/NaiveAngel p99; iStock/Andrew Rich p100; iStock/BrianAJackson p101; iStock/Grassetto p101; iStock/FLDphotos p101; Fotoarena/Album p103; iStock/garett_mosher p104; iStock/code6d p104; iStock/Ekaterina79 p104; iStock/winhorse p104; iStock/AlessandroColle p104; iStock/YvanDube p104; iStock/UberImages p105; iStock/Ridofranz p105; iStock/drbimages p105; iStock/BackyardProduction p107; iStock/g-stockstudio p107; iStock/mattjeacock p108; iStock/GSPictures p108; iStock/mediaphotos p108; Fotoarena/Dee Cercone/Everett

The team of publishers of the series is especially thankful to Cristina Neville and her team for all the support throughout all the stages of the editing process of this publication.

CANIEM No. 2275

Macmillan Publishers S.A. de C.V.
Insurgentes Sur 1886
Col. Florida, CP 01030
Álvaro Obregón
Ciudad de México
Tel: +52 (55) 5482 2200
elt@grupomacmillan.com

www.grupomacmillan.com
www.macmillan.com.mx
www.macmillanenglish.com



Printed in Brazil

This book was printed in January, 2025 by: Eskenazi Indústria Gráfica Ltda, Avenida Miguel Frias Vasconcelos, 1023 - Jaguaré - São Paulo - SP.